The
South & West
Yorkshire
Village Book

THE VILLAGES OF BRITAIN SERIES

Other counties in this series include

Avon

Bedfordshire

Berkshire

Buckinghamshire

Cambridgeshire

Cheshire

Cleveland

Cornwall

Cumbria

Derbyshire

Devon

Dorset

Essex

Gloucestershire

Hampshire

Herefordshire

Hertfordshire

Kent

Lancashire

Leicestershire
& Rutland

Lincolnshire

Middlesex

Norfolk

Northamptonshire

Nottinghamshire

Oxfordshire

Powys Montgomeryshire

Shropshire

Somerset

Staffordshire

Suffolk

Surrey

East Sussex

West Sussex

Warwickshire

West Midlands

Wiltshire

Worcestershire

East Yorkshire

North Yorkshire

Most are published in conjunction with
County Federations of Women's Institutes

The South & West Yorkshire Village Book

Compiled by the South and West Yorkshire
Federations of Women's Institutes from notes
and illustrations sent by Institutes in the Counties

Published jointly by
Countryside Books, Newbury
and
the SYFWI, Doncaster
the WYFWI, Leeds

First Published 1991
© South and West Yorkshire Federations of Women's Institutes 1991

Countryside Books
3 Catherine Road
Newbury, Berkshire

ISBN 1 85306 136 0

Cover photograph of Oxenhope
taken by Mrs Sheila E. Nash

Produced through MRM Associates Ltd., Reading
Typeset by Acorn Bookwork, Salisbury
Printed in England by J. W. Arrowsmith Ltd., Bristol

Foreword – South Yorkshire

A picture many people conjure up of South Yorkshire is of industry, especially coal mining and steel works. We are very fortunate in the diversity that makes up our county from the urban landscapes of our main towns Barnsley, Doncaster, Rotherham and the city of Sheffield famous for its renowned cutlery to the beautiful woodlands, green pastures and agricultural areas.

There is a general lack of knowledge of the great antiquity of our ancient villages, rich in legend and history with their Yorkshire warmth, character and tranquillity.

I hope you are encouraged by this book to come and spend some time in our county and discover for yourselves the treasures, charm and rich varied heritage which are a small part of England's green and pleasant land here in South Yorkshire.

Jean Greaves
County Chairman

Foreword – West Yorkshire

West Yorkshire, to people who live outside Yorkshire, conjures up a picture of industrial grime, along with mills, mines and moors. A visit to West Yorkshire will quickly change your mind.

We are steeped in history. Famous men and women from all walks of life were born here, inventors, pioneers, composers, sculptors, authors, painters and philanthropists (visit Saltaire, the purpose built village for Sir Titus Salts' mill-workers). We have beautiful stately homes, such as Harewood House and Nostell Priory. Explore Holmfirth, *Last of the Summer Wine* country and Haworth with its Parsonage and moor which vividly bring to life *Wuthering Heights* and the Brontes.

We boast three cities, Leeds, Bradford and Wakefield, all full of interesting places. And around, between and beyond these, our villages offer a range of architecture that has stood the test of time along with the warmth and humour of their inhabitants.

As an 'incomer' myself, when visiting our Institutes throughout the Federation I never fail to be surprised and delighted by the beauty and majesty I see all around. So, do turn off the Motorway and discover for yourselves another part of our rich heritage.

Rosemary Coverdale
County Chairman

River Aire

LEEDS

BRADFORD

HALIFAX

River Calden

WAKEFIELD

HUDDERSFIELD

River Don

South Yorkshire

West Yorkshire

BARNSLEY

River Don

DONCASTER

ROTHERHAM

SHEFFIELD

River Rother

N

Acknowledgements

The SYFWI and the WYFWI wish to express their appreciation to all those Institutes in both County Federations who have supported this project with their entries and line drawings. Thanks are also due to the many friends and local historians who provided additional information.

Special thanks are given to the Co-ordinators of the project: June Stevenson and Christine Stanley for South Yorkshire Federation, and Susan Fell for West Yorkshire Federation.

F. BEAUMONT 90

Addingham 🌿

Because of its situation on one of the routes across the Pennines, Addingham must always have been concerned with traffic. It is true that the Romans built their road from Olicana to the west on high ground skirting the site of the present village, but that was their custom everywhere. For safety's sake they liked to be able to see what was lurking in the countryside around them. Later roadmakers kept to the river valley for as long as possible before they took to the hills and Addingham stands at the point where westbound traffic begins its ascent and eastbound finishes its descent.

It takes just eight shortish strides to cross Addingham Main Street and when its width was determined by the building of houses, inns and mills along both sides of it, this must have been considered quite wide enough for the horse-drawn vehicles which used it then. Around 1850, Elizabeth Gaskell and her husband drove through Addingham and she relates what happened here in her *Life of Charlotte Bronte*. Shortly before they passed, a boy had jumped into the beck and cut himself badly on broken glass that had been thrown there. He staggered, bleeding, into a cottage and the Gaskells did what they could for him. She tells the story to illustrate the roughness and callousness of the inhabitants of 'these out of-the-way villages' but at the same time gives the impression that there was nobody but themselves travelling on the road at the time, the only other persons present being village yokels.

How amazed, even terrified, these people would have been if they could have had a prophetic glimpse of this same road a century and a half later! Better surfaced, but no wider, it would be carrying a fast-moving mass of gigantic, noisy vehicles in both directions, sometimes hardly able to pass each other. Even before conditions became as bad as this, the people of Addingham had asked that traffic should be taken away from their street and sent round the village on a bypass. Septuagenarians today remember that when they were children a bypass was being talked about but nothing came of it.

At last, on the morning of Wednesday 17th October 1990, the bypass was ceremoniously opened. At mid-day, the parish council invited all residents of Addingham to a soup-and-sandwich lunch in the Memorial Hall and, early in the afternoon, through traffic turned onto the new road from both ends, leaving the village in comparative peace. People who were in Main Street at the time said that it was an uncanny experience and they wondered for a second or two what was wrong. At first the old road looked somewhat forlorn, rather like the bed of a river that has changed its course.

Perhaps it is no coincidence that the latest of Addingham's roads almost follows the route of its earliest recorded one, the Roman road along which the Legions marched and drove their chariots. Since then, many have travelled on the roads around and through the village – a pre-Conquest Archbishop of York, when fleeing from the Danes, took refuge here. Later, soldiers of the Civil War passed along them, packhorse traders, drovers, cripples and the flotsam and jetsam of the poor who were bandied about from one village to another. In the 19th century when the textile industry was flourishing and there were six mills operating in Addingham, the clatter of millworkers' clogs on cobbled pavements was heard. Cloth was carried along the roads and even a steam engine, which had been brought from Birmingham by canal, finished its journey by road to one of Addingham's mills.

Now, all these have passed away. Through commercial traffic, for which Addingham meant no more than a troublesome stretch of the A65, has been removed to the bypass. Today, many who travel through the village are on their way to Wharfedale, one of the most beautiful of the Yorkshire Dales. Others use the roads leading to Addingham because they have chosen to live here for its friendliness and very attractive surrounding countryside.

Adel 🌿

Adel village lies five miles north-west of Leeds. The church of St John the Baptist dates back to 1160 and in 1960 the parish held a pageant to mark the octocentenary. The rectory garden was the setting for this wonderful production. In 1970 Mystery plays were held in the church and church-yard and many hundreds came to see a very moving performance on three evenings. The old stables still acts as the church hall for social events, but the duck pond was filled in a few years ago and the rectory was sold in 1975, the building now housing four families.

An original school building was on the main Otley Road, a new one being built in 1875. The 'old' school became two cottages and in the 1930s an old couple, Mr and Mrs Coates, lived there and their kitchen acted as a 'shop' where they sold tea, sweets, eggs etc. 1962 saw that bit of old Adel come down to make way for a petrol station. The 'new' school was in existence until 1977 when this was sold and made into two houses. The smithy was next to the school and is now a joiner's and undertaker's.

What used to be quiet country lanes, such as Holt Lane, Church Lane and St Helen's Lane, are now very busy roads to and from new housing estates. A far cry from the days when Long Causeway had a raised path, and that flagstone path still remains. Adel Crags and Adel Woods have long been a favourite walk through to the Seven Arches and there used to be a small cafe in the woods.

A wonderful development has just been completed by Arncliffe at Adel Mill, just beyond the church. The mill dates back to the 12th century but the oldest of the existing buildings is the 17th century barn. The corn mill was built about 1740, but in the mid 1800s, it was a full working farm. Archaeologists believe that there may have been a monastery on the site before the mill and that long before that it was part of a Roman encampment. The buildings are Grade II listed and there are now 14 luxury houses set around courtyards. The name of each house has been chosen to reflect the character of the house or to depict a use in the past or a historical detail. Features such as the original mill wheel and spindle have been preserved. A 19th century box mangle used for ironing clothes was found in the attic of The Tudors and has been presented to the Social History Museum at the Abbey House, Kirkstall.

Back to the church, and opposite the gate is a footpath over two fields to the main Otley Road which can be traced right to Kirkstall Abbey, a journey which the monks used to take. A slimline font installed in Adel church in 1801 was replaced and is now on permanent loan to Leeds General Infirmary where it is always adorned with flowers.

Farmland and the farm having been sold, the large Holt Park estate was started in 1971 and the subsequent shopping centre which necessitated Holt Lane being widened and made into a bus route. In 1921 the Cookridge Gardens estate was developed on moorland to the west of the Otley Road and plots of approximately half an acre were laid out with a restriction of no more than two houses per plot.

The War Memorial Hall in Church Lane was opened in 1928, the hall and grounds being paid for by public subscription as a memorial to the dead of the First World War and now to both World Wars. A large boulder from Adel Moors once bore an inscription which included 'For the use of the people of Adel for all time'. Also in Church Lane was Church Lane House, which became Sadler Hall in 1949, a Hall of Residence for Leeds University students.

The Headingley Golf Club moved to Adel in 1905 and is just beyond the church, so giving a large open space. The Methodist chapel in Holt Lane was built in 1938, but was a combined church and meeting room. In 1964 a church was built. The burial ground site for the Society of Friends had been in their possession since 1868 and a meeting house and cottage came into being in 1938. In the grounds in the 1940s, a community centre was built and this has been well used for many societies and activities.

Adwick-le-Street ⚜

Adwick is near to the line of a Roman road which ran from Doncaster to Castleford. The addition of 'le street' to its name was added to avoid confusion with the nearby village of Adwick upon Dearne.

At the time of Edward the Confessor Swein Glunier and Archil owned land here, which eventually passed to Roger de Busli, who also held land in Cadeby. In more modern times the area was developed as an important part of the South Yorkshire coalfield.

The church, dedicated to St Lawrence, dates back to Norman times and has connections with the Washington family, who lived here in the 16th century. Inside there is an alabaster tomb of 1579, with a portrait of James Washington, his wife and twelve children. He is dressed in Elizabethan armour, with the family crest on his breastplate. His coat of arms bears the heraldic design of three stars and stripes, which have encouraged legends of the relationship with George Washington, founder of the USA and the origins of the American flag. (Over the years the church has had many American visitors). The Washingtons lived in the village for nearly two centuries, but their old home, Adwick Hall, no longer exists.

In the lady chapel is a tomb said to have contained from 1470 one of the Fitzwilliams, whose earliest relative in England had been an important officer in William I's army. Floor stones commemorate other descendants of this family, who inherited large estates given by William the Conqueror to their ancestors.

There are remains of an old cross in the churchyard, and whilst crosses were once a common feature of the medieval landscape, most were destroyed or broken at the time of the Reformation.

At Castle Hills is an ancient monument, the site of a former castle, and nearby is a moated manor house site – Radcliffe Moat. Twenty years ago children would fish in the stream for sticklebacks, but because of pollution there are no longer any fish there.

Pear Tree House, a 17th century farmhouse, and at one time a petrol station, is now a private dwelling, as is the 18th century Mill. Another very old dwelling is Glebe Cottage, which stands close to the Rectory. The old school was demolished and bungalows built in its place, but the school house is still there. It was built of stone from the demolished Adwick Hall, as were some extensions to nearby Brodsworth Hall, both of which have weathered badly. There was a very old stone barn in Clarke's Yard, but sadly this, too, has gone. A railway station was opened in 1861, but this was closed in 1967.

There are two active farms in Adwick-le-Street, mainly arable, but Manor Farm is now a private house and Central Farm has gone and the land developed for private houses. There is a Post Office/Newsagent's shop, and the bowling green is on the site of the former Adwick Hall. Near the church is a very pleasant park, with fine chestnut and elm trees.

Almondbury 🐝

The village of Almondbury in West Yorkshire is situated approximately two and a half miles south-east of Huddersfield, and is mainly a residential area with properties ranging from traditional small terraced cottages to large detached houses originally lived in by wealthy land and mill owners.

Almondbury is a thriving village with a varied selection of food shops, clothing retailers, hairdressers, building societies, a bank and a post office. Also in the village are doctors, dentists and opticians, serving a population which has increased within the last 50 years, due to an estate which was built just after the Second World War and also a collection of new houses now occupying land which was once a large market garden.

Almondbury still retains a great deal of its village character. The name appears in the Domesday Book (1086) as Alemanberie. In the Concise Oxford Dictionary the pronunciation is given as 'ambri'. In the oldest part, centred around the church, are folds and yards dating back many hundreds of years.

The village contains both church and chapel, which are prominently situated at the heart of the village. The parish church of All Hallows is a monument of many centuries and has a chancel dating from the 13th century. The tower and chapels were added later, but the whole church was substantially altered in the mid 1800s. The church is well worth a visit to view the roof bosses on the nave ceiling and to read the poem around the perimeter of the ceiling. The chapel was built in 1969, although Methodist occupation of the site goes back to 1812. Zion United Methodist church was founded in 1853 and was combined with the older and larger church in 1960.

The annual Sing in Molly Carr Woods on Whit Sunday mornings – a custom started by Zion – has been continued. About 200 people walk through the bluebells and sing at traditional halts.

Opposite the church is found one of Almondbury's most famous buildings – Wormall Hall. This is a half-timbered house with the initials 'IWM' and the date '1631' carved on the lintel. The inscription commemorates Isaac Wormall and his wife, who were responsible for partly encasing the old house in stone. It is now the Conservative Club.

The road leading from Westgate round the vicarage to the church is now called Stocks Walk – the stocks can be seen just inside the small gate near the tower, but it was formerly more picturesquely named 'Heckfold', and then contained the clerk's house, two or three cottages, a timber yard, and the old hearse house. 'Heck' was the local word for a small gate or wicket.

A well known landmark near Almondbury is Castle Hill. The mere 900 ft height marked on the Ordnance Survey map gives little indication of the prominence and dominance of Castle Hill over the local scene, and no suggestion at all of the historic past of this best known local land-mark. From its summit are superlative views and on a clear day York Minster can be seen. Castle Hill has been the scene of archaeological digs, and bonfires to celebrate Royal and other occasions. In 1588 beacon fires were lit there on the defeat of the Spanish Armada, and in 1988 a beacon was fired on Castle Hill as part of the national network to commemorate the fourth centenary of Sir Francis Drake's victory. The Victoria Tower on top of Castle Hill was built in 1898–9 to celebrate the Diamond Jubilee of Queen Victoria. The first public house was built on Castle Hill between 1811–12, while on 1st April 1820 the beacon was set alight at the time of the Huddersfield Riots. Many Roman coins were found at Castle Hill in 1829.

King James's grammar school has a Royal Charter and this, together with the statutes of the school, may now be seen in the library of King James's College. For many years the charter and statutes had been considered lost, and the events leading to their handing over to the school on 6th April 1954, make a remarkable story. In May 1952 the School Surveying Society visited an exhibition of historical documents in the library of the Yorkshire Archaeological Society in Leeds. There, by chance, the charter was 'discovered' by boys from the school and it was also learned that the statutes were in the Yorkshire Archaeological Society's archives.

The 17th century building of Fenay Hall is a splendid example of work in half-timber and plaster. Alongside the curving private drive leading from Fenay Lane to the Hall is the base of the ancient Fenay Cross, whose purpose can only be surmised. Was it an early preaching post, or a boundary mark?

The last remaining piece of Almondbury Common is an enclosed triangle of land with a notice recalling that it was here that the villagers used to assemble for the dubious sport of bull-baiting; the last perform-ance took place at the Rushbearing (the first Monday in August) in 1824.

Altofts ✖

Altofts is situated on the south side of the river Calder and is part of the parish of Normanton. It is four miles from Wakefield and nine miles from Pontefract. The village is pleasantly situated and its residents enjoy the local beauty spots.

Altofts could be said to comprise one long meandering main street, with all its development springing up on either side. At its centre is the parish church of St Mary Magdelene.

The village has a long and proud history. It was in existence at the time of the Domesday Book, which stated that the name 'Altofts' is Scandina-vian. Originally it was referred to as 'Tofts' which means homestead.

Martin Frobisher, the great navigator and seaman who won his knighthood against the Armada in 1588, was born in 1535 at Frobisher Hall. The Hall stood in the centre of the village at the angle of Whitwood and Normanton roads until 1859 when it was pulled down.

Altofts was almost entirely a farming village until the Industrial Revolution, when it was awakened by the advent of the railways and the mining industry. At the lower end of the village the Pope and Pearson Colliery became established. The colliery owners then created a 'settlement', making a community within a community. This settlement comprised several streets collectively known locally as 'The Buildings'. One row of houses, Silkstone Row, named after a coal seam, was at the time of its building the longest row of colliery houses in the country.

Among the buildings themselves were three types of houses, provided variously for pit officials, deputies and colliers. Also there was an infants school with its master's house. A junior school was built almost opposite the main colliery gates. A Co-operative store and a Wesleyan chapel were also built as an integral part of the community. Further provision by the colliery company for its workers included allotment gardens and a recreation ground.

The colliery itself had much pioneer work to its credit. In a souvenir brochure of Altofts, published in 1911, it records that the 'Ambulance First Aid' class established at the Altofts collieries in 1884 was the first of its kind ever held in Yorkshire.

In 1886 tragedy struck the Silkstone pit when 22 men were killed in an explosion. As a direct consequence a series of exhaustive experiments were performed between 1908 and 1911 into the dangers of coal dust. This experimental work was undertaken by (later Sir) William E. Garforth, manager of the colliery. As a result of his work, a station for training men in the use of his portable breathing apparatus was established at the collieries in 1901, again the first of its kind.

Many of Altofts' older residents remember those days with affection. The school children had occasion to be grateful to Garforth for his experimental work. The schools often had to be closed as a result of the explosions, so the students obtained many an extra half day's holiday! Sir William also used to buy the residents of 'The Buildings' a bird for their Christmas dinners. This was to compensate them for their many broken windows.

With regards to The Buildings, life continued in this way until the last coal was drawn from the colliery on the 7th October 1966 and an issue of a closure order on The Buildings was given in 1976. Despite pleas from local historians the majority of The Buildings has now been demolished.

As a result of the closure of the collieries, and the railway station at Altofts, village life has changed yet again. The majority of residents now work in the nearby towns, and one could say that the village has reverted to a sleepy agricultural area, but this would be far from the truth. A plethora of new housing has sprung up throughout the village and subsequently its population has increased dramatically.

The new terminal to bring freight from the continent, via the Channel tunnel, has been proposed to be built in Normanton and Altofts. This will result in many changes in village life. However, some things never change, and Altofts will always be able to pride itself on being a close-knit, caring community.

Alverthorpe 🌿

Many present residents of this village, on the main road from Batley to Wakefield, will probably not realise that it was once a bustling township with its own identity, having a town hall on Green Lane, slaughterhouse, refuse vehicles and workhouse off Light Lane and sewage farm off Rufford Street. Its boundaries extended to include the whole length of Westgate beck and the highway alongside, with the west side of Balne beck from Beckbottom to Wakefield gaol. It was part of the ancient manor of Wakefield until incorporated within the city of Wakefield.

The most prominent feature 100 years ago, providing employment for hundreds, was Colbeck's Mill and dam upon the upper reaches of the beck, known at its source as Heybeck, but lower as Bushy beck, then Alverthorpe beck. Sadly, the mill has recently been closed, after having provided high quality worsted cloth and, later, green baize for snooker tables, for almost 150 years. The huge square chimney, built in 1874, is almost certain soon to be destroyed.

Alverthorpe had a magnificent 17th century Hall and grounds, still in excellent condition after its use by troops in the Second World War, but it was irrationally destroyed to provide a primary school, to which was appended the name of the adjoining village of Flanshaw, perhaps in order to seal Alverthorpe's incorporation within the Borough.

Recently there has been a resurgence of new building after old cottages and farms have been swept away. Coach, and motor body, building has disappeared; but new industries using structural steel, garage repairs and computext signs now provide limited employment. Most residents however commute to nearby towns.

The magnificent church of St Paul, funded initially by the money made available for new churches after Waterloo, is a landmark for miles around though it still retains its blackened exterior from the soot of belching chimneys, now happily discontinued.

The Wellington Hotel disappeared with slum clearance around 1935, but the Albion, Cock inn, Green Light (Malt Shovel) and the more recently erected Crown Hotel are frequented by patrons. The board school is now a youth club and the old church school is now Happiways Dancing School.

16

Alverthorpe also holds the unfortunate site commemorating the death of seven miners trapped underground in 1973. There was an inrush of water into the Flockton S9B face of Lofthouse colliery as they, at midnight, removed coal three miles from the pit bottom whilst under Alverthorpe, some 400 yds from the church. Their memorial pillar with seven trees stands off the main road at the junction with Wrenthorpe Lane.

The new local junior and infants school, alongside the church on the hill, is likely to provide the central attraction for local families in the future as, in addition to students' requirements, they also successfully promote the annual procession and carnival. Local shops and post office have a struggle to compete against more distant supermarkets, but they retain loyal supporters and those unable to travel.

One character who is still remembered by the older folk was the local joiner and undertaker, who it is said made his own coffin and lined it with lead, but sold the lead before he died to pay for drink. He always wore a blue rosette throughout the year and constantly lambasted the likes of Atlee, Morrison, Bevan and Wilson.

Armthorpe 🌿

The Domesday Book of 1086 refers to Ulchel, local Lord of the Manor, and Ernuin, as Priest. William the Conqueror dispossessed Ulchel in favour of his son-in-law, the Earl of Warenne, who ruled his northern estates from Conisbrough Castle. In 1154, Armthorpe was called Her-woldsthorpe, and the church was a mere chapel attached to the Parish of Kirk Sandall, which probably accounts for both buildings having similar porches.

The church of St Mary and St Leonard includes a late Saxon or early Norman chancel arch, where the carving on one of the two capitals is a quaint feature. It has an octagonal bell turret and traces of a mass dial, from the days before clocks. There is a complete list of clergy displayed and framed in the nave. The lancet windows are an early feature, (there would be no glazing). Only with the increasing use of glass would bigger 'lights' be required, hence the 14th century masonry of the large windows on the south side of the church. The door is thought to be 15th century, and in the south wall and east window the stained glass shows examples of Kempe's work, which was much in demand, with its jewelled elaboration, towards the end of the last century. In the north aisle is a memorial to the late Lord Auckland of Edenthorpe, who in 1885 completed the restoration of the church.

An Armthorpe resident recalls: 'My village of Armthorpe was both very old and very pretty. I came with my parents and older brother to live here when I was about two months old – 79 years ago. The coal mine was under construction, and, as we grew older, we used to walk up to what is now called Mansfield Crescent, to watch the railway trucks running across the main road, carrying building materials for the start of the new village. There was only a Church school with two teachers. There was a butcher's shop, two grocery shops (one a beer-off licence). Aspidistras filled the window of one of the shops. There was also a village reading room. There were no cars, but plenty of horses. A pub opposite the house where I lived acted like a magnet to the drivers at mid-day, when there was always a line of horses outside, with their feed-bags on. I used to run across the road to these horses, which were mostly large Clydesdales, and, sitting down between their large front hooves, clasped their hairy forelegs and talked to them without fear.

'There used to be a feast each autumn, in a field opposite the school, and, one year, there was great excitement when a model of a pit was brought, and it was explained to us what ours would look like. We had two choices when making a journey to town. When Mr Belk from Glebe Farm or Mr Pearson from Brook House Farm were going to Doncaster market, they could carry four or five people on their drays, among their produce. If there was not enough room, we had to walk to Doncaster – a distance of four miles. Trams did travel just a short distance from the town, and a ride in to market cost one penny. I remember one lad who wore leg irons walking a distance of two miles to school every day. When a doctor was needed, someone had to cycle into town to inform him, and the doctor would then get his bicycle out and they would ride back together.

'We lived in a row of four cottages, called Woodleigh Cottages, with a pump for drinking water halfway down the front gardens. Water from rainwater butts was used for cleaning and washing purposes. In the event of a drought we loaded our 'peggy tub' in the barrow, and pushed it up the main road to the village pump, which was opposite Beech Road. Our first 'official' transport to town was a mobile butcher's van, running twice a week, belonging to Arthur Brain. There was no such refinement as a timetable – he merely stopped and waited for regular customers. This carried on until Messrs Wilson moved into Woodleigh House, when they started to race each other round the village in an effort to pick up the most passengers.

'I remember well the blacksmith's shop, an extremely busy place in those days, the small chapel, and the village church, with a 'lepers' peep' for those inhabitants of the village stricken with the dreaded disease. Although they were not allowed inside the building, they could still take part in the service. Needless to say, a great many things have changed since those days.'

Armthorpe used to be a farming village, which consisted of a single straggling street, with a church at its highest point, and, in 1743, there were 29 families in the parish. At one time Roche Abbey owned a farm in the village.

Today it has good shopping facilities and easy access to Doncaster. It was an agricultural settlement until Markham Main Colliery was sunk in 1914 by German engineers, but work was suspended during the Great War, the first coal production being made in 1924. At the present time, the colliery is still working. Due to expansion, the village now has an industrial estate. The amenities include a sports' centre, park, numerous play areas, and youth clubs. In addition to the parish church, there is a Methodist church, and a Roman Catholic church. Close by is Sandall Beat Woods, which was reset in the spring of 1810, with nearly 107,000 assorted trees.

Aston 🌿

The village of Aston, situated close to the M1, is one of considerable antiquity. There has been a church here since about the year AD 700 and in the Domesday survey of 1086 the village, then known as Estone, was recorded as being an area of arable, pasture and woodland with a value of eight shillings.

The manor house, known as Aston Hall, had been built by Archbishop Melton but was destroyed by fire on Christmas Day 1771. The present house, now an hotel, was designed by John Carr of York about 1772. Carr also built the former rectory opposite the church which is now known as High Trees. The rector at that time was the poet William Mason, whose friends included Horace Walpole, the actress Sarah Siddons and the poet Thomas Gray, all of whom visited the house. Gray's *Elegy in a Country Churchyard* is reputed to have been written in the summerhouse in the grounds of the rectory. High Trees is said to be haunted by the ghost of a rector's wife who, having been found having an affair with her butler, was murdered by her husband. There is said to be a bloodstain on the floor which cannot be removed.

Aston school was founded by the rector in 1743, when £4 was paid to a schoolmaster to teach ten poor children. The school building, known as the reading room, is situated on Aughton lane and is currently in use as a hardware shop.

Prior to the 1800s the villagers had mostly been agricultural workers. In the 19th century coal mining brought many new people into the area. Aston Main colliery opened in the 1840s; local mines employed 52 people in 1851 but 20 years later the number had swelled to almost 400, of whom just over 100 were local. The mining companies provided housing for their workers but most of the properties were demolished in the 1960s and only four houses now survive on Brookhouse Road. Mineworking under the village has now ceased.

When the Hall and village were sold by auction at the Blue Bell in 1928, 1,500 acres were put up for sale, together with eleven farms and numerous cottages. The Hall itself, comprising a hall, a suite of entertaining rooms, 16 bedrooms and four bathrooms was purchased by Sir Ronald Matthew. Some years later it was converted into a mental hospital by the Health Authority, then, having been empty for some time, was renovated and is currently in use as the Aston Hall Hotel.

At the time the estate was sold the area was described as a 'rapidly developing neighbourhood.' The village's population grew considerably when the glebe land was sold in the late 1960s and a large private housing estate built. The inhabitants of Aston now follow a wide range of occupations. There are still three farmers, two publicans and nine shopkeepers but with the village being within 20 minutes travelling distance of Sheffield and Rotherham, the majority work outside the village. The parish church has recently benefited from an extension to its north side which provides a meeting room and kitchen. Apart from the several different groups organised by the church, the village has an active social life, with a WI, a Music Society and the Ladies Circle amongst others. The parish hall is the venue for a variety of activities and there are plenty of opportunities for those who wish to become involved in village life.

Auckley

'Alkeley is an agricultural village bounded on the north by the river Torne'; so was the village of Auckley described in 1598, but its origins can be traced much further back. The spelling has altered from Alkeley to Awkely and then Auckley, and it is said that the name derives from a colony of 'little auks' which once made their home there. There are still a number of farms, mainly arable, and it still has the typical layout of a Yorkshire village, with a main road running through, mainly north to south, and lanes running off or running parallel to the main road.

There is now a population of about 1,280 people, with a much fewer number working on the land. Since there is a large Royal Air Force station nearby, there is also quite a large moving population. There are still a number of old houses and lanes, but many new houses have been built, and many older people who have lived here all their lives say that the village is hardly recognisable from the place they knew in their childhood.

In the 19th century Rector Harvey (a relative of Squire Harvey), who was also a man with a great interest in the education and welfare of the people of the area, was given £100 by a rich friend to buy a clock for the church, but spent it instead on education. Using local labour, a schoolroom was built on the site of the present church, proceeds from a Harvest Supper providing money for floorboards, thus completing the first village school. Squire Harvey gave the bell and supported the school, and by

1870 girls and infants had been included. When the Education Act came into force in 1870, the school had 50 pupils, and the village of Auckley had separated from the adjoining villages of Blaxton and Finningley and was in a position to manage its own church and education affairs.

The village has grown quickly in the last 30 years and now has a junior school, built in 1974, adjoining the little infants school of 1874, which in turn replaced the school on the site of the present St Saviour's church.

At the north end of the village there is the village green, Methodist chapel and the 'Little Manor', and a short distance away on the site of a very old inn, the present Eagle and Child. This was originally called the Bird and Bastard and has an interesting history. In the 14th century an ancestor of the Stanley family, a Sir Thomas Latham, who owned the land, had one daughter, Isabel, but no son to carry on the name. A serving wench is said to have borne him an illegitimate son and, to enable him to present the baby boy to his wife for adoption, he arranged for the child to be left at the base of a tree, in which there was a bird's nest which Sir Thomas had been observing. The baby boy was duly adopted, but in spite of the success of his plan, when Sir Thomas died he left all his estate and wealth to his daughter, Isabel. The daughter eventually married Sir John Stanley and, in memory of her half-brother, she persuaded her husband to include him in the family coat of arms – hence 'The Bird and Bastard'. This name persisted until propriety required it to be refined as the Eagle and Child, as so it remains. The first inn dates back to 1492 and the present property to 1830. The mounting block is still to be seen dating from the days of horses and horse-drawn vehicles. The old smithy close by was closed soon after the war.

In spite of many and ever speedier changes, Auckley remains a pleasant place to live, with easy access to Doncaster, Sheffield, Lincoln and York, and with open and very pleasant, if flat, countryside all around.

Austerfield ✍

Austerfield, a linear village lies on the A614, one mile north of Bawtry.

In AD 702 a synod was held on the plains of Austerfield (then called Esterfield or Oustfeld), when certain church disputes were settled, in particular an attempt to decide whether Easter Day should be calculated in the Continental or Celtic manner. Wilfred (later St Wilfred) won the day for the Continental manner.

St Helena's (in the diocese of Southwell), built in 1080 by John de Builli, is situated on the main road, and is one of the best existing examples of a Norman church. It is crowned by a bellcote, and has a Norman font which is used to this day. In the porch is a leaning Norman doorway, its arch carved with zig-zags and beak-heads. The tympanum over the door is carved with a strange dragon creature with an arrow-like

Austerfield Manor

tail end – a rarity in the area. In the *Southwell Review*, 1954, Rev Edward Dunnicliffe placed the date of this as probably 8th century, about the time of the synod.

Austerfield is the birthplace of one of the Pilgrim Fathers, William Bradford, son of a yeoman farmer, whose baptism is recorded in the church register on the 19th March, 1589. He lived at the manor house, which is still in good repair and occupied today. He sailed to America in 1620 aboard the *Mayflower* and, at the early age of 32, he was elected Governor of Plymouth Colony, a position he held with few interruptions until he died in 1657, when he was mourned by Red Indians and Englishmen alike. A brass inscription in the church states that the aisle was rebuilt by the Society of Mayflower Descendants and other citizens of the United States, in memory of William Bradford. 'First American citizen of the English race who bore rule by the free choice of his brethren'. In 1970 celebrations were held in the village to commemorate the 350th anniversary of the sailing of the *Mayflower*. The 400th anniversary of William Bradford's birth was celebrated on 19th March 1989 when many of his descendants were invited from America and elsewhere to participate in the event. Austerfield is very much aware of its connections with the New World and welcomes many American visitors who travel the Pilgrim Way.

Employment in the early years was mostly on the land, there being as many as ten farms in the parish. However, since the Second World War, there has been a gradual decline in farming and today only one farm remains. In the 1920s, a Mr R. Edwards of Scunthorpe began to make silica bricks in a sand quarry, which had many kilns (still there but not in use), and this provided alternative employment for local men and women. Expansion in 1954 resulted in a factory making refractory bricks for furnaces, and in 1969 this became a carbon works. Villagers today are employed in all walks of life. 1991 saw the retirement of the 'Post Lady' after 40 years of delivering mail to the village on foot or by bicycle. Until the 1960s there were three provisions shops, but since that time improved transport and modern supermarkets have brought a decline in local business, and two shops were closed. However, the post office and hairdressing salon remains.

At the centre of the village stood the White Hart inn, a cottage-type building with a very long frontage, built in 1822. This was replaced in 1938 with a modern inn on land behind the original building, which was demolished to construct a pavement. It was decided in 1989 to change the name to the Mayflower, to coincide with the William Bradford 400th Anniversary. At the north end of the village a restaurant called Auster-field Manor was built in 1983/4, on the former site of a petrol station.

From 1981 to 1984, two new housing developments were built, namely William Bradford Close and Pilgrim Rise. In 1990 there were only 206 dwellings, and a population of 394 adults on the electoral roll, and Austerfield remains a very small but thriving community.

Badsworth ॐ৶ৄ

Kelly's Directory for 1927 describes Badsworth as a 'pretty village' with a church (St Mary's) in the late Perpendicular style with Norman remains, its four bells dating from 1580. Perhaps this last detail is mentioned in order to refute the rumour that Badsworth bells were removed from All Saints' church in Pontefract after it surrendered to a Parliamentarian siege in 1644.

Badsworth is listed in the Domesday Book as Badeswurde, which means Bade's or Baedi's enclosure. The township has had a population of about 200 inhabitants throughout most of its history – presumably what the water in the village wells could support. Until this century most of the inhabitants were concerned with farming and were seldom caught up in any but local affairs. But one period when the whole area was in turmoil made Badsworth notable.

During the Civil War most of the inhabitants were Royalists and when Parliamentary forces were approaching, legend has it that the beautiful stained glass windows were removed from the church and buried. Unfortunately the person responsible was killed in the subsequent battle and the windows have never been recovered. After the war the Parlia-mentary leader, Sir John Bright, who handled the formalities for the surrender of Pontefract Castle, bought Badsworth Hall and its estate from one Robert Dolman.

From the Civil War until 1926 almost the whole of the village was part of the Badsworth Hall estate. The owners at the end of the 19th century were landed gentry rather than aristocrats. 1926 represents a watershed in the development of the village since that was the date of the sale and break-up of the estate. Many of the tenant farmers at that time were able to buy their farms and their sons and grandsons still own the land, perhaps farming rather differently from the original owners.

Only one of the farmsteads, High Farm, in the original rectangle of Badsworth survives as a working farm building; Manor Farm and Rockingham Farm buildings have both been redeveloped. Stables and barns have become 'mews cottages' and the farm houses are grand executive homes. One farmer said that he had got more money from the sale of the farm house than he had earned in a lifetime of farming.

The old Hall itself has disappeared, demolished in 1940, but the arched gateway and stabling block is still in existence, transformed into a pleasant private home by filling in the gateway with semi-circular foundation stones from the cellar of the old Hall. Also still in existence is Badsworth Grange, built in the 1890s for two maiden sisters of the owner of the Hall, Col Heywood-Jones.

The availability of public services has meant that a greater population can be housed here – in 1981 the census shows a population of 393 and this has probably increased by another 50. Most of the newcomers have arrived since 1964 with the building of four cul-de-sac estates and some 'ribbon' development along the access roads.

Bardsey-cum-Rigton 🍃

'Bardsey twinned with Kisdorf' is the modern sign which greets travellers along the A58 between Leeds and Wetherby. This busy road now effectively separates Bardsey from East Rigton and causes difficulties for pedestrians and delivery men. The association is several centuries old between Bardsey, nestling in the valley of the Gill beck, and East Rigton up on the hill with village green and mounting steps. There are picturesque stone cottages near All Hallows' church, interspersed by large modern detached houses. More modern developments are strung out along the lanes, and an attempt has been made to provide low cost housing. Many properties have spectacular views across farmland and woodland. To add to the delivery men's difficulties there are five farms, two hills and one moor, all called Rigton!

Bardsey-cum-Rigton is a busy and lively community of about 3,000 people. Many commute to Leeds or Harrogate, but some still work on the farms and grow grain, rapeseed or root crops, or rear sheep and cattle. There are riding stables, caravan sites, plant nurseries and a nursing home. The primary school thrives with 202 pupils, and altogether there is a diverse community of young and old.

There are attractive walks to the duck pond, through bluebell woods, or to the Hetchell nature reserve, where the millstone grit outcrops with the magnesian limestone. The reserve is one of only three sites in Britain where thistle broomrape grows. A small area of woodland was donated to the village in 1985 by Mr Tom Willans. He lived to be over 100 years old and was known as 'Mr Bardsey', for he tried to visit all newcomers and interest them in village affairs.

Socially Bardsey is very much alive and village societies cater for a multiplicity of interests. Meetings are held in the village hall, founded in 1927 and the Callister Hall, which was the original school, founded in 1726 by the bequest of Lord Bingley. There are tennis courts, a bowling green and a new sports club with training floodlights and facilities for football and hockey. The village cannot support a post office and the bus service is infrequent. There is a garage, a shop and a hairdresser's on the A58, but the doctor's surgery is two miles away. Once there was an inn and a smithy in East Rigton. The Bingley Arms claims to be the oldest inn in England.

The village's greatest claim to national significance was the birth of William Congreve at Bardsey Grange in 1669. He was baptized in Bardsey church, which has very old parish registers. His mother just happened to be travelling through the village and her son, who became a famous dramatist, never revisited his birthplace.

Bardsey Grange and the 18th century corn mill, associated with the Midgley and Mawson families, are reminders of the fact that in medieval times Bardsey was a grange or sheepfarm of Kirkstall Abbey. The land was given to the Abbey about 1160. After 1539 the estate had various owners until Nicholas, Earl of Scarsdale sold it in 1720 to Robert Benson, first Lord Bingley. His descendants are the Lane Fox family at Bramham. Their sales of land from 1920 onwards contributed largely to the present structure of the village.

The most prominent landmark in Bardsey is Castle Hill. This could be the site of a castle built in the troubled 12th century and demolished as a result of Roger de Mowbray's part in the rebellion of 1173 against Henry II. There is no documentary reference to any part played by the castle in national affairs and there has been no thorough scientific excavation. However, people today still find sling shot in their gardens and aerial photography suggests to some that there may have been an older Celtic fortification.

The church is the oldest building in the village and in spite of restoration at the beginning of the 20th century, is of considerable architectural interest. There are traces of Saxon work in the tower and masonry from the Norman and Early English periods survives. Zigzag and beakhead carvings embellish the south door.

A straggling village with a long history! In 1816 described as 'retired and silent', Bardsey-cum-Rigton is now outward-looking and full of life.

Barnby Dun ꧁

There has been a church in Barnby Dun since the 11th century, recorded in the Domesday Book. The present church of St Peter and St Paul dates mainly from the 14th century, but the chancel was largely rebuilt in the middle of the 19th century. A major refit was done in 1990, to completely modernise the building and make it appropriate for the worship of God in this modern era.

Although Barnby Dun did not have what one calls 'important people', it certainly had its share of interesting ones, one being Roger Portington, who had an allegiance to the Royalist cause in the 17th century. There is a memorial in Barnby Dun church to him with an inscription which reads as follows:-

'Approach boldly reader whosoever thou art if a follower of the king; if not away immediately lest unknowingly thy wicked foot should touch those pious ashes, for Roger Portington's ashes can ill bear a rebel's foot – a man who was of an ancient and honourable stock and who suffered imprisonment, rapine, etc – broken down by old age only, not in spirit – here he lies, with Jane, his wife, waiting for the last trumpet's call.'

Along with his brother, Robert, he gained a reputation for his fierce opposition to the Roundheads. He maintained a troop of soldiers at his own expense and was imprisoned at Hull for eleven years, finally dying an impoverished man. An ancestor of the Portingtons, called Thomas, fought in the War of the Roses on the Yorkist side. After the battle of Bosworth, when all seemed lost, he resisted armed arrest in his own home, the manor house, and was killed by a trooper.

Moving on a few hundred years to 1923, it is remembered that Barnby Dun was a very pretty village with leafy lanes, and orchards which always seemed full of fruit – Keswick apples and Hazel pears. There was no water laid on, but most homes had a pump outside the house, and a communal pump was placed in a suitable spot in the village. Houses were lit by paraffin lamps and candles for bedtime, the well-off having oil lamps.

A Feast was held the nearest weekend to St Peter's Day. This was a special occasion to invite relatives and friends for the day, and was held in a field opposite the existing parish hall. There were coconut shies, cocks and horses, pony rides and 'the cake walk' (this was a moving platform). On the Sunday, an open air service was held to raise money for the hospital, when a guest speaker was invited.

Work in Barnby Dun was mainly farming, the large houses renting out land and cottages. Because church was part of life and everyone wore hats, the village even had its own milliner. The malt kilns were another source of work, brewing for outside the village. The blacksmith's cottage is still here, but the blacksmith's shop is a modern bungalow.

There do not seem to be many legends or myths in Barnby Dun, just a superstition about a passage leading from Barnby Dun church to Kirk Bramwith. This seems strange, because the area is noted for its flooding. Also it is said that the road bridge between Barnby Dun and Kirk Bramwith has, at intervals, ghostly shapes passing over 'like little pigs with curly tails'.

The Star and the White Hart were the local pubs even then, and are not far from Kirk Bramwith.

Barnby Dun is a very pleasant village, with plenty of walks. Although it lies in the shadow of Thorpe Marsh power station, this can be forgotten as one wanders round the nature reserve, much time having been spent to create this very attractive spot.

Barwick-in-Elmet ☙

Barwick-in-Elmet is a village of about 3,000 inhabitants set in rural surroundings about seven miles from the centre of Leeds. Once an agricultural settlement, with coal mining an important source of employment during the 19th and early 20th centuries, Barwick is now a residential village whose inhabitants work in Leeds and elsewhere.

It is an ancient settlement. The defensive possibilities of its elevated site overlooking valleys to the north and east were appreciated by Iron Age men who 2,000 years or more ago constructed a large hill fort of banks and ditches on a site now called Wendel Hill at the northern end of the village.

Main Street runs through the village on level ground in a north-south direction. Even as late as the 20th century, some of the stone houses were farms, which have since been converted into modern dwellings. However, many of the old house plots or 'tofts' remain, running back from the street to the old 'Back Lane' or Elmwood Lane as it is now called. At the northern end of the village, Main Street begins at a T-junction where one finds perhaps Barwick's most celebrated feature, its maypole. Standing almost 90 ft high and made of two fir sections spliced together, it is probably the tallest in the country.

For so long a time that 'the memory of man runneth not to the contrary', every three years on Easter Monday under the direction of a pole-master, a large number of inhabitants of the village have taken down the pole by a time-honoured method using ropes and ladders. The pole is taken apart, repaired if necessary or from time to time replaced, then painted in red, white and blue hoops, decorated with floral garlands made by women's groups in the village and finally re-erected by similar means on Spring Bank Holiday Tuesday. A climber, after detaching the ropes, shins up to the top of the pole and gives the fox weathervane a spin. The ceremony attracts thousands of people to the village, as does the preceding procession and gala, with the crowning of the Maypole

Queen and the 'plaiting' of small maypoles by the schoolchildren of the village.

The view from the pole to the west shows a large artificial mound called Hall Tower Hill which, with its surrounding ditches and banks, formed the motte of a Norman fortification. An ancient way called 'The Boyle' winds its way round the hill to the Rake beck valley below. It may have derived its name from the bailey, the outer enclosure of the castle.

Looking east from the maypole one sees the Barwick parish church, dedicated to All Saints, with its Perpendicular Gothic architecture, square tower and red clock face. A church at Barwick is likely to have been one of the three mentioned in the Domesday Book entry, but the existing building was begun later in the 12th century. The old rectory dates back in part to the 15th century and now, with its outbuildings, has been converted into four separate dwellings. A new rectory has been built at the end of what was the old rectory garden.

At the foot of Hall Tower Hill stands the Wesleyan Methodist chapel opened in 1900 and dedicated to William Dawson, a well-known 19th century local preacher, who lived in the hamlet of Barnbow nearby. The chapel replaced an earlier building opened in 1804, which still exists as the Welfare Institute, a village amenity used for many purposes including Roman Catholic services.

About a mile out of the village in Rake Hill Road stands the old workhouse, now renovated to form three dwellings. During the 19th century it housed paupers from the 40 or so townships and parishes which formed the Barwick Gilbert Incorporation. Another well known Barwick landmark, the windmill on Leeds Road, was finally demolished in the 1950s, but the miller's house remains and some of the mill cottages.

In the last three decades, many new houses have been built in Barwick, mainly in two large developments at the south end of the village, but leaving the central part virtually untouched. Barwick is well supplied with a good selection of shops at the maypole end of Main Street; new buildings mostly, but some created by extending the old manor house. Three well-appointed and popular public houses serve the needs of villagers and visitors alike.

Batley 🌿

Batley today houses many varied industries which have developed due to the decline of the textile industries which produced cloth, blankets, carpets and other heavy woollen goods, which had been made in Batley for centuries.

Until the end of the 18th century, Batley was largely an agricultural area, consisting of small hamlets whose inhabitants depended on the land for food and clothing. The land was cultivated to provide food, and sheep and cattle were reared to provide meat. The wool from the sheep was spun and woven into cloth for clothing. Cottage industries developed and the cloth not required was sold to furnish other families with an added source of income.

All this was changed however, with the coming of the powered machine mills, the first manifestation of the Industrial Revolution which was to sweep the North of England. Large mills were built to accommodate the looms and other heavy machinery for the processing of wool, from the spinning of the raw wool to the weaving of the cloth. One of the largest mills was set up by Theodore Taylor, who employed a few thousand people from the hamlets around Batley – Carlinghow, Brownhill, Healey and Batley Carr, to name but a few. Workers also came from further afield and had to be accommodated. Long terraces of houses were built for this purpose and some of them are still occupied to this day. Theodore Taylor introduced the first 'Worker's Share Holding Scheme'. Its purpose was mainly to keep his workers; the workers, however, were very glad to have a little bonus of income when the dividend days came round.

The manufacture of shoddy cloth became the main industry as it was cheaper to produce than woollen cloth, being made from rags and old clothes which were recycled and made into a yarn which could be woven.

Around 1847 the railways provided much needed transport and raw materials could be brought to the mills much more quickly and the finished cloth delivered more speedily. Batley station was rather a grand building in those days and the approach road was lined with stately Victorian buildings to impress visiting buyers.

Batley grammar school was founded in 1612 and many famous people received their education there, including Joseph Priestley, discoverer of oxygen, and Sir Titus Salt the industrialist.

Batley became a borough in 1868 when it was granted its charter, but it had no town hall and council meetings were held in the upper rooms of the Wilton Arms Hotel. The town hall was eventually built in the prime position it occupies today, on the corner of the Market Place and Commercial Street.

The parish church of All Saints dates back, in part, to the 15th century and is mentioned in the Domesday Book. It has a fine carved screen and, in addition to its being the sole place of worship for many years, it was a place of security in times of emergency. The battlements on the square tower are a reminder of this.

Around 1780 followers of John Wesley introduced Methodism and it became an alternative religion. Chapels were built both in the town and in the surrounding districts. Today, many have been closed and used for other purposes, but the central Methodist chapel, formerly known as the Zion or 'shoddy chapel' survives. It is a beautiful building occupying a prominent position opposite the town hall. The term 'shoddy chapel' was used because it was said that more trading was done on the steps of the chapel after morning service on Sundays, than was done during the rest of the week.

Bagshaw Museum in Wilton Park was the former home of George Sheard, a millowner. Charles Robinson, also a millowner, bought the surrounding land and gardens for £5 and presented it to the Corporation to be merged with land offered by the Earl of Wilton, to become the town's park. Today, it is an area of natural beauty with a lake, bowling greens and tennis courts for the enjoyment of the people of Batley.

Oakwell Hall in Birstall was first recorded as a manor house in 1310 and was rebuilt during the Wars of the Roses. In the mid 1800s Charlotte Bronte was a regular visitor to the Hall with her friend Ellen Nussey. The Hall is precisely described in Charlotte Bronte's novel *Shirley* and the details are easily recognisable by the present day visitor. The Hall is now furnished with period furniture, and is surrounded by its own country park – 87 acres of the original estate with its period garden, herb garden and arboretum.

To this day, Commercial Street is the main shopping area of the town. It has modern shops which can supply most of the things needed by a modern society, usually a busy area, but on market days, Fridays and Saturdays, it positively bustles with shoppers who come in from the surrounding districts. There is an excellent bus service to nearby towns and on the whole it is quite a pleasant place to live. Estates of modern houses have been built in the surrounding districts, which were originally the hamlets of the 'old Batley'.

Ben Rhydding 🌿

Ben Rhydding is a village one mile from Ilkley, nestling beneath the Cow and Calf Rocks on the famous Ilkley Moor in Wharfedale, once in the West Riding of Yorkshire, now in West Yorkshire.

It has a most interesting history; some of the old cottages and Wheatley Hall (still lived in) dating back to 1670. It was originally called Wheatley.

In 1844, impressed by a cold water cure devised by a Silesian peasant and taken at Grafenberg in Germany, Hamer Stansfield (later Mayor of Leeds) and four friends built in the fields above the village a grand hydropathic establishment (the first in England). It was built in the Scottish baronial style and named the Ben Rhydding Hydropathic Hotel. The name, rather than being reminiscent of the Scottish Highlands, may have been derived from nearby Bean Rhydding or bean clearing. In the early days men came from as far afield as London and were mostly gentlemen of the professional classes – ladies also attended.

When, in 1865, the railway came to the district, Ben Rhydding station was especially built for the visitors to the 'Hydro'. It was a small wooden station with a booking office, waiting room and retiring room for ladies. (There is still a station at Ben Rhydding but of a rather different character!) Horse-drawn carriages would be sent, usually by prior arrangement, to collect the visitors and the hotel had its own stables where accommodation was provided for gentlemen's own carriages and 20 horses.

In 1891 the village was known either as Wheatley or Ben Rhydding but by 1908 it had become Ben Rhydding. When hydropathy declined the Hydropathic Hotel became the Ben Rhydding Golf Hotel, meeting the changing needs of the leisured classes. Later it was turned into flats. During the Second World War it was used by the Wool Control and after being empty for many years was unfortunately demolished in 1955, the land being used for a large housing development.

The railway divides Ben Rhydding and below the railway bridge at the bottom of Wheatley Lane is the river Wharfe, crossed originally by stepping stones (still there today) to the Middleton side of Ilkley. Within the last 40 years the river has risen twice to flood over the roadway of the bridge – still referred to as the Toll Bridge.

Expansion was (and is) taking place all the time – hostelries were being built in Ilkley and in Wheatley the Cow and Calf Hotel (now the Wheatley Hotel) was erected in 1863. (The present day Cow and Calf Hotel stands opposite the Rocks in Hangingstone Road and was itself originally the Highfield Hotel, lit by gas lamps well into the 1940s). In the 1880s houses were erected in Bolling Road, where at the east end a long row of large terraced houses and twelve shops were built. Whilst several shops have seen many changes in use others have retained their original trades – newsagent, baker, butcher, grocer and greengrocer.

In the 1890s, because of the growth of the village, parishioners felt the need for their own church as it was difficult to get to Ilkley church a mile away. In 1901 services had been conducted in the Hydro but in response to an appeal sufficient money was raised to start building the church of St John the Evangelist (now just called St John's) in 1904 and it was completed in 1910. Whilst a chapel was opened in Ilkley in 1834, Methodism only came to Wheatley about 1852 when services were held in the farm buildings of Wheatley Hall.

Billingley ✨

Just off the busy A635, seven miles from Barnsley and eleven miles from Doncaster, is the small, quiet village of Billingley.

Adam fitz Swein was the last Saxon Lord of Billingley, and the Chartulary of Monk Bretton contained early records showing that he was the same person who gave the Church of Silkstone to Pontefract.

According to Charters relating to the village, the great Saxon House of Swein kept herds of brood mares here which fed on the rich pastures.

Approaching the village from the main road, there is a grassed area known as Billingley Green (near Flatt Lane), which used to be the village pond. This dried up about 25 years ago and, when rubbish began to be dumped there, it was filled in and grassed over by a local farmer, and daffodils were set. A seat was provided by the local Council, and almond trees were planted by the Parish Council.

The village stocks were situated where the War Memorial now stands, and is known locally as 'Stocks Hill'. The forge, too, has long since gone, and the old slaughterhouse is now a private dwelling. Although there used to be two small general stores and a butcher's shop, there are now no shopping facilities. For a few years, in the late 1920s, the village even had a fish and chip shop (fish 2p, chips 1p), but that closed when the owner moved away, and the pub, too, has gone. Billingley has never had a school, the children being educated in nearby Great Houghton. There was a cricket team in the 1920s, who played on a field near the main road. The point-to-point used to meet there too.

The Methodist chapel, built in 1818, still has a small weekly congregation. In 1986 it was licensed for weddings, and in 1986/7/8, weddings took place there. However, these were recorded in the Barnsley Register, as the chapel had no safe where the records could be securely kept. In 1990 a safe was installed, and the wedding solemnised that year was the first to be entered in the Billingley Register.

Beech House was at one time a farm and, together with Billingley Hall, were the two principal farms. There were also 12 smaller farms, but these have now gone. In recent years, Beech House has suffered from considerable subsidence. It has been demolished stone by stone to be rebuilt on a nearby site, very close to the beech tree from whence the original house took its name.

Billingley Hall, a three storeyed dwelling, was built in 1744, and over the years has had many owners. It ceased to be a farm about ten years ago, when the Wentworth Estate built a new farm – Hall Farm – a short distance away. A previous owner tells of the gravestones kept in the cellar, but where they came from is not known, though it is thought there used to be a graveyard nearby. One of these grave stones is now inserted in the wall along Back Lane, and states that 'Here lieth the body of John Shemeld died 1752 aged 37 also the body of Elizabeth 1758 aged 40 years.'

At one time there were four wells in the gardens of cottages north of the village, but the only one remaining is in the garden of a private residence along a footpath known as Well Lane. This used to be a communal well, and was used by the villagers for their supply of water. One older resident can remember her grandmother charging 1p for the use of her mangle – very popular on washday!

Many years ago villagers would keep a pig, and a few kept a cow.

Butter was made from the milk, and taken to Wath-upon-Dearne to sell. A threshing machine was housed in the village, and, until the combine harvesters took over, did one day's work on each farm – the farmers providing meals for the workers. In addition to the farm workers living in Billingley, miners also lived there, working at Hickleton, Houghton Main and Dearne Valley Mines. Now only one farm worker actually lives in the village, in a tied cottage.

Billingley is now very much a commuter village. Many of the barns have been tastefully converted into private dwellings, and six former council houses are now privately owned. Unlike some small villages, it does have a frequent daily bus service.

Birdsedge 🐦

Birdsedge is a small rural village, often coupled with its neighbouring hamlet of High Flatts. It is situated on the edge of the Pennines, on the A629 about nine miles south of Huddersfield and only a couple of miles north of the West Yorkshire/South Yorkshire border. It is about 1,000 ft above sea level with its highest point, Castle Hill (reputed to be an Iron Age settlement site), standing at 1,025 ft above sea level. The height and open aspect gives it a fair share of weather, most of it seeming to be horizontal in winter!

There is no Anglican church, the village being split down the middle into two parishes by the young river Dearne which rises in the fields immediately above Park Head at the north end of the village. That half falls into the parish of Cumberworth, while the southern end of the village officially comes under Denby. In the village itself is a Wesleyan Methodist chapel which serves the community under the guidance of villagers Tom and Pat Wood.

The Quakers had a great influence on the surrounding area and many of the properties in Birdsedge were originally under their control. Birdsedge itself grew up later. Although a couple of farms date back to the 17th century (Birdsedge Farm has a date stone of 1638), most of the houses were built to house workers at the mill which was originally built by Elihu Dickenson, the clothier, possibly around 1800. After his death in the 1830s it passed into the Firth estate through his daughter Mary's marriage to John Firth in 1817. The mill grew to prominence around 1850.

Around this time most of the solid stone cottages were built to house the influx of workers. Access to the village was made easier when the turnpike roads were built. The particular section of turnpike through Birdsedge and High Flatts was built by the famous 'Blind Jack of Knaresborough' in 1825 at a cost of £340. The mill used water from the Dearne, and two dams were built which control the water flowing down

'Ten Row', Birdsedge

the valley to Denby Dale. The mill, a listed building, was sold by the trustees of the Firth estate in 1921 to Z. Hinchcliffe and Sons of Denby Dale. It closed during the slump of 1929 but is now used for blending wool, the main processes being carried on at Hartcliffe Mills in Denby Dale.

The main function of the village now is as a dormitory for the surrounding towns, Huddersfield, Barnsley and Wakefield. Within easy reach of the village by car are also Leeds, Sheffield and Manchester. There is a small school which was opened in 1911 to replace the small Quaker-founded school which ran in the building which is now the village hall.

Around the turn of the century the village was well off for shops and had two general dealers (one with a corn merchant and a haberdashery department), a milliner and a cobbler. There were also two pubs, the Cross Pipes (which closed in the 1920s) and the Crown (which became a private house in the 1960s). Today there is only one shop remaining, which is a post office and grocery shop at Park Head.

Despite the small population Birdsedge has a thriving community, with several small groups meeting on a regular basis in the village hall, school or Wesleyan chapel Sunday school rooms. The village hall itself was purchased by public subscription and literally belongs to the people of the village. It is administered by a committee of volunteers under the guidance of elected trustees.

Bolsterstone 🦜

The village, 984 ft above sea level, is a delightful place, situated on the hill above Stocksbridge and the beautiful Ewden valley. It is surrounded by superb scenery, and is an excellent starting point for moorland walks leading to Derwent, Midhope and many other remote and rural areas.

The village square is surrounded by stone houses, cottages, the church, school and the Castle inn. At one time this was owned by Sam Costa, a popular performer in radio programmes, including *ITMA*, broadcast during the 1940s. There is also a shop-cum-post office.

There have been a succession of churches since the 12th century, but the present St Mary's was built in 1879. In the vestry are the Bland Dole Boards, formerly displayed on the whitewashed walls of the previous Bland church. They gave information as to who was eligible to receive funds, but not if they were receiving parish relief, nor if they were Methodists. This money was paid on Christmas Eve. The Dole Boards were found in the roof of the chancel, and there is a list of incumbents from 1412 to the present day. In 1871, the village had its own parish hearse, which was kept in the former bier house.

To the east of the church is a porter's lodge doorway and part of an archway, which were probably part of the castle built about 1250 by the Sheffields, who were in the area until the 14th century. By the lychgate are the village stocks, which are still in good condition – what a pity they are no longer used! In the south-east corner of the churchyard are two gigantic stones, perhaps lintel stones of a stone circle.

Two fields away from the village in Walder's Low is the burial ground of Walder, a Saxon chief. This is a hilltop, 1,009 ft above sea level, and the mound has a heap of stones surmounted by one large upright stone, and has yet to be explored. It was dismantled during the Second World War, as it was thought to be a landmark for enemy bombers, but when hostilities ceased it was re-erected.

There are good walks by the Ewden reservoir. The nearby village of Ewden was flooded during the construction of the dams and the village now consists of just a few modern houses. In the Second World War, the Dambusters practised over the Ewden dams, which resulted in many complaints being sent in about the low level flying.

St Mary's is a typical village church, where the bells are rung prior to the services, with bell ringers coming from far afield to visit the church.

Annually a village fair is held to raise money for church funds and charities. Across the road from the church is the Church of England village school, built 300 years ago.

The Bolsterstone Male Voice Choir enjoys the reputation of being one of the top choirs in the British Isles. It was formed in 1934 by a group of village lads, fed up with nothing to do. The choir, which still has one original member, has grown in size and stature, and now has nearly a hundred singers. Their reputation is world wide, a fact proven by several Continental tours.

Bradfield 🐾

High Bradfield and Low Bradfield are the two villages which, with Bradfield Dale, comprise Bradfield. It lies seven miles from the city of Sheffield, and since the new boundaries were formed is now part of the city. Bradfield is on one of the seven hills which form the 'frame' of Sheffield, and since the building of the four dams to serve the city, it has become known as the 'Sheffield Lake District'.

High Bradfield was once known as Kirkton and Low Bradfield as Netherton. Neither village is mentioned in the Domesday Book, but in 1141 the area is referred to in Papal Bulls as 'Bradefeld'. The surrounding land is mostly moorland, which can be very bleak and barren. According to Addy, a former rector and historian, 'the hamlet contains 24 houses and a church, a place which God began but never finished' – an unfair description.

The beautiful old church of St Nicholas in High Bradfield has stood guard many years over the surrounding countryside. Built in the 12th century, it was a chapel dependent on Ecclesfield church, with visiting priests walking across the moors to take services, and sometimes staying overnight in the sunken vestry, a most cold, inhospitable stone room. Bradfield, however, has had its own rector for many years now. In 1745 a watch house was built at the church gates to combat the body snatchers, who were very active.

There is a curious story about the church papers. It was discovered that a large number of these had been stored in a room of an adjoining cottage, the doorway of which had been covered over. The two elderly sisters whose home it was, did not wish to be disturbed, but upon the death of the last sister the house was entered and the hidden room found. It was filled with documents of all types, which, after being sorted, were put on display at the council offices in Low Bradfield, where they are stored for safe keeping.

The church has a fine peal of six bells, recently rehung. During this restoration a stone was found which read 'Jonathan Gillott – Churchwarden 1597', revealing the long service the Gillott family had given to the church, the last Jonathan Gillott, also a churchwarden, dying in 1935. This is just an example of the continuation of family commitment in village life, the old names occurring again and again. In Low Bradfield there is a Methodist chapel which was built in 1899, the village being a staunch Methodist stronghold.

Because the land is hilly, with steeply sloping fields – 'uneasy land' as the old folks say – farming was hard, but it was the main source of work. The Land Enclosures Act and the Industrial Revolution brought changes. Farming remained the main industry, but a number of farmers had small workshops and did outwork such as knife blade grinding, nail making, etc, for the works in Sheffield. These were transported by horse and cart, and the finished goods collected at the same time. Now agriculture provides little work, mostly it is the dams, clay mines, stone quarries,or commuting to Sheffield.

The terrible Bradfield Flood, the worst disaster of the century, occurred on the night of 11th/12th March 1864, and devastated the valley. The Dale Dyke dam was not yet in use, but was filling up, and the heavy rain caused the bank to burst. Millions of gallons of water cut a path of destruction down the valley, nearly into the centre of Sheffield. Farms, homes, grinding wheels, small workshops, all disappeared and 240 people lost their lives. A memorial is to be placed on the site of the old dam bank to commemorate the dead.

Many old traditions are dying out, like the 'Bradfield Stattes' which was really 'The Statute Hirings' where farmhands came to be hired. They had in their buttonholes a symbol in plaited straw, which denoted their job, and were hired for twelve months on the shake of a hand or on receiving a fastening penny.

The Knights Hospitallers of Jerusalem left their mark upon Bradfield. In the reign of Henry I they were granted lands and manors by Willim-de-Lovetot, lord of the manor of Hallam. Upon their dissolution, property in the chapelry of Bradfield went to the Talbots, Earls of Shrewsbury. Many old farmhouses still have the Knights' cross on the roof corbel stones.

Cricket is still enjoyed in Low Bradfield, with a very fine cricket team. Summer weekends find the village filled with visitors watching the matches and picnicking. How evocative of England, men in their whites playing cricket on the green.

Braithwaite ✒

Braithwaite, seven miles from Doncaster, is a small cluster of farms and cottages, with a Methodist church. The former Hermitage and early Victorian school have been extensively altered, and are now private residences. The following shows the evolution of the New Junction Canal during the last 100 years.

'Early this century a young girl watched from the window of the farmhouse as the fields in front of her home were being cut in two as part of the New Junction Canal. Even today it is often referred to as 'The Cut'. Large gangs of navvies would toil all day, with pickaxe, shovel and wheelbarrow, digging out the canal.

'In 1919, the little girl had now grown up and married her soldier sweetheart, remaining at the farmhouse. Eventually they had two daughters and a son. This little family would watch from the window as the barges passed slowly by. If there was a slight breeze, a sail would be hoisted, otherwise the boats would be towed by horses. The bargee would lead the horse, while his wife steered the boat. The coming of engines to drive these barges made life much easier, but, unfortunately, pollution from the oil spilling into the water killed the fish. During the Second World War, the village Youth Club were allowed to use it for a few hours each week for swimming lessons.

'The family had now grown up, and the two daughters left home, but the son, like his mother, married and remained at the farmhouse. The two little boys from this marriage possibly saw the canal at its busiest. Barges would be passing by the window from early morning to late at night. These little boys would watch for certain boats, as the boatmen would wave to them. They would wait eagerly each day to see the 'tom pudding'. This would pass by mid-morning and return in the late afternoon. A tom pudding was a tug, pulling tubs of coal. In the bitter winter of 1963, ice was a problem. Each day the ice-breaker from Goole would crash its way through the ice, to keep the canal open, but despite all its efforts, one day three barges were brought to a standstill by the thickness of the ice. As the boys grew up, there were fewer boats, and even the tom pudding ceased to run.

'Times have changed, and the two little great-grandchildren of the original little girl now see the canal in a completely different way. They stand at the window and watch the numerous pleasure boats pass by. Pretty painted narrow boats, houseboats in all sizes, even ocean-going craft. Once again the water is much cleaner, the fish have returned and herons have become a familiar sight. Fishermen too have returned, and many a weekend the banks are lined with them, trying to lure the biggest fish on to their line.'

Nearly a century later, looking at the canal built all those years ago, and reflecting on the hard work that went into its construction, the residents are indeed fortunate to live by its calm, quiet peacefulness, in the little village of Braithwaite.

Bramhope 🦢

The pretty village of Bramhope stands in an elevated position overlooking Wharfedale.

The history of the village goes back many years, but the oldest part of the present village dates from the 18th century when the population was about 300. There are two weavers' cottages in Eastgate dated 1709, which are now modernised and occupied. The village was centred round the Cross, which stands at the crossroads at the top of Church Hill. It is near this site that the village public house, the Fox and Hounds, is to be found, which is dated 1758.

Bramhope Hall first came into existence in the 16th century. The Hall was the home of the Dyneley family; their coat of arms is carved on the stone above the gate of Old Manor Farm, which is situated at the bottom of Church Hill. The Hall was demolished in the early 1960s and a large hotel, known as the Post House, was built and opened in September 1971.

Robert Dyneley, a devout Puritan, built the Puritan chapel in the grounds of the Hall in 1649. The chapel is still in existence, being open to the public in the summer. The original box pews and pulpit are still in evidence. A village carol service, attended by members of the parish council, is held in the chapel each year.

The Town mill, where the corn was ground, was at the bottom of Hall Drive down in the valley. Water was drawn from the Old Town Well, which is across the main road from the church near the bridle path, but is now covered in undergrowth. The villagers were mostly employed on the surrounding farms. The cottage which was the village smithy stands near the Cross in the centre of the village, and is occupied at the present day as a private dwelling.

With the coming of the Leeds to Thirsk railway it was necessary to build the Bramhope Tunnel, which runs under Bramhope. This took place between 1846–1849 and was the cause of a considerable increase in population, as the workers and their families were brought into the area. The workers were housed in temporary wooden huts. Many workmen, and horses, lost their lives when the tunnel was being constructed, and there is a memorial in Otley churchyard erected to the men who died. It is built in the form of a replica of the entrance to the tunnel, which is castellated.

St Giles' church, which stands at the bottom of Church Hill, was built and consecrated in 1881. The Methodist chapel in Eastgate was built in 1895, replacing an earlier one which stood on the site now occupied by the house known as St Ronan's. The chapel is known as 'The Cathedral of the Dales', perhaps because of its tall spire and stained glass window.

The development of private house building began before the Second

World War with the building of the Crowther estate and was continued in the 1950s and 1960s, when the Wimpey estate was constructed. The population of Bramhope today is between 4,000 and 5,000.

Brampton Bierlow 🐝

Brampton Bierlow lies towards the southern end of the river Dearne, about halfway between Barnsley and Rotherham. It is almost on the dividing line between the coal-producing and heavy industrial areas, and that part of the county which was occupied formerly by large estates, Wentworth Woodhouse being the nearest. The farming area, which lies to the west of the village, is still as sparsely populated as it has been for centuries, and stretches to the eastern slopes of the Pennines. To the east, the Dearne valley was, until 1984, the scene of very many coal mines, including Corton Wood Mine where the miners' strike of 1984 began, but in the years since then all the mines in the area have been closed, with a very high rate of unemployment and its resultant distress.

Many of these mines were opened up from 1830 onwards, and were the source of economic wealth of the area. Furthermore, they provided the basis for the whole structure of the area, so that each village is almost an enclosed community, where many families appear to be inter-related and can trace their ancestry back for about four generations to the mining families imported from Wales, South West Scotland and the North-Eastern counties of Durham and Northumberland.

Within the boundaries of the village are many small, but interesting, signs of the past life of the area. There is, for instance, a gateway, now backed by scrubland, which is part of the 'warren' granted to a member of the Ellis family in 1290 by King Edward I. Behind is a huge spoil tip, a relic of Corton Wood colliery. This gateway was an entrance to Wentworth Woodhouse estate, and from there a road was built to provide easy access for carriages from the mansion to the Pontefract-York road, which runs from west to east through the northern end of the village. Also worth noting are the many 'old pits' dotted about the area from which coal has been dug by the 'Adits' system (drift mines), long before deep mines were sunk.

A most interesting feature of the village is that, since 1680, there have been schools. The oldest of these is the Brampton Ellis School, so called because the original was founded by George Ellis 'for the education of 14 boys and six girls of poor parents living in the village'. The original house that George Ellis lived in is now an hotel known as Brampton Hall, and at one time he also owned the Bull's Head.

In 1853–1855 the parish church of Christ Church was built on a corner site, and is dominated by a 70 ft high tower which forms a landmark in the district. The interior of the church is remarkably bright and airy, in contrast to the pollution-begrimed exterior, so that it seems to glow with light. This in part is due to the colourful east window, a memorial to the first vicar, Rev Charles Hayes, and his wife, Sarah.

Maps around the year 1700 show that Brampton and the adjoining hamlet of West Melton had three inns, but there was no Independent chapel until 1840. At present the combined villages have five active churches and six public houses, a few shops, post office, fire station, and miners' welfare club. Functions are held in the parish hall, and there is also a hall attached to the church.

Branton 🐾

Branton, originally called Brampton, is a self contained village boasting a post office, newsagent, grocer, butcher, hairdresser and, most of all, a regular bus service to Doncaster. A far cry indeed from the past, when the only shop in the village was in someone's front room, and the odd housewife selling tobacco and 'pop' as a sideline from her cottage door.

There were no cars as there are today, with people commuting to industrial towns miles away, but men riding on bicycles, or going on foot, to work on the neighbouring farms or the local woodyard. This was owned by Earl Fitzwilliam, who also owned the nearby stately Cantley Hall and estate. When he died the estate had to be sold to pay the death duties and all the tenants were offered their dwellings at a very low price, and many were quick to take up the offer. The villagers were very proud of their cottages and were keen gardeners. It certainly helped the low wages when they could grow their own produce. It was quite usual to find a few hens scratching around and a pig at the bottom of the garden. The local pig killer went to whoever had a pig that needed killing. When the pork pies and sausages etc were made, some of them were distributed among family and friends, who, when they killed their own pig, duly returned the favour.

The children of the village attended the church school at Cantley, the only way of getting there being to walk, and some had quite a trek from the outlying farms. On Sundays they were expected to attend Sunday school at either St Wilfrid's church at Cantley or the Methodist chapel at Branton. Sadly this has been knocked down, as has the little church in Chapel Lane. This was the venue for the annual crowning of the May Queen and the start of the procession round the village.

One of the prominent features of the area is the old mill which used to grind the corn, though it no longer has its sails.

The local hostelry is the Three Horse Shoes. Believed to have been rebuilt in 1907, the earliest reference to it was in 1861. Mr Sid Dugher, the landlord, was quite a character. The beer used to be brought up from the cellar in a jug, and if the hand was not steady much of it did not reach the glass! If anyone complained of the beer being flat, he was always known to ask 'what's tha'ed for thi tea?' To eke out a living the landlord used to farm land which was tenanted from the brewery along with the pub. Part of this establishment housed the local blacksmith. Horses were a very common sight, being used on the farms, and also to pull public transport on market days.

The pub housed the laying-out board. This was a strong piece of wood about the size of a door, used for laying-out those who had died. When this happened Granny Tyas was always sent for. This was a job she specialised at, and when she could no longer carry on her daughter-in-law took on the task. The cobbler in the village was Bill Tyas. Not only did he repair boots, but he also made them at his cottage at the corner of Brockholes Lane, his wife making sure they were well polished before being collected. On a site near the Three Horse Shoes stood the old bake house, the baker's name being Mr Marshall. Nurse Harding, the district nurse, used to tour the villages in her starched apron on her big 'sit up and beg' bicycle.

Branton Feast was always held on the nearest weekend to the 20th October, and caused much excitement in the village. It was all the fun of the fair – coconut shies, side stalls and wonderful roundabouts. These were powered by the big steam engines, belching out clouds of black smoke, and adding to the atmosphere. Best of all, the youngsters were always pleased to see Donkey Dick arrive with his string of donkeys – he was a firm favourite.

How the pace of life has changed in Branton. Today people commute to industrial towns miles away.

Briestfield ✒

Briestfield, near Dewsbury in what was formerly the West Riding, is a pretty village situated on high ground, commanding a panoramic view of the surrounding countryside. When you take the road to the village it is almost like entering another world and it is not always an easy place for strangers to find.

In 1954 pygmy flints were found in the ridge of hills bordering Briestfield known as 'The Tops' at Thornhill Edge, and local legend has it that sometime around 1924 'little brown men' or 'fairies' were seen in the caves at dusk. The cause of some mirth nowadays.

We do not know how Briestfield fared at the time of the Domesday survey, but records show that in 1150 it was known as Brerethuisel. In 1680 Whitley, a near neighbour, and Briestwell contributed five shillings and one penny towards the building of St Paul's in London. Furthermore a map of 1772 shows Briestfield as Briestwistle, meaning 'common land or waste overgrown with briars in the confluence of two rivers'.

In the year that Briestfield chapel was built the Stockton & Darlington Railway was opened, and the first practical application of steam locomotive power was tried. It was an age of religious and economic upheaval and Briestfield felt the effects of the great Methodist movement and was one of the first villages to provide its own chapel. Money was hard to come by. The site of the chapel cost £50 but these were the times when farm labourers received wages of £10 per year and worked very long hours.

Over 150 years ago, before the chapel was built, Briestfield was very different from the village it is today. Then it was a comparatively busy industrial centre, noted for its hand-loom weaving. The weavers, mostly men, had their own hand-looms and took their pieces to Leeds, or other large business centres, to sell. Briestfield was the home of some of the most earnest and spirited Luddites.

A cottage previously known as Croft Cottage, since renamed, has a 'Wedding Stone' over the fireplace on which is carved 'Thomas and Mary Green 1729'. Their marriage and subsequent family is recorded in Thornhill parish church. A grindstone and small cannon ball have been found here, and a tiny silver thimble which was buried in the walls. An old custom was to bury a silver thimble in the structure of a house to scare away witches. The cannon ball and another much larger one found in the adjoining garden had probably lain here since the Civil War, when Lady Anne Savile, a Royalist, defended Thornhill Hall against the Roundheads.

Nowadays the village has changed a lot, people have moved away and new ones arrived. More houses have been built, but the atmosphere is friendly. Sometimes people have a little difficulty in finding us, but all agree that it is a lovely village, especially in the summer.

Brighouse

Many people who have heard of Brighouse associate it with the Brighouse and Rastrick Band. For over a hundred years this brass band has been an excellent ambassador for the area. Perhaps it has become most widely known because of its sale of a million records of the *Floral Dance*. Today it is the only 'first division' brass band not to be commercially sponsored.

Brighouse, in Calderdale, stands on the north bank of the river Calder, approximately equidistant from Huddersfield, Halifax and Bradford. The name itself derives from 'the house by the bridge'. The early bridges were made of timber and were frequently damaged or washed away in times of flood. It is said that some of the wooden piles of the last timber bridge can still be seen from the more modern stone bridge at Bridge End when the water level is very low.

The Industrial Revolution was responsible for the growth of Brig-house. In about 1760 the broad canal – or more accurately the Calder and Hebble Navigation – arrived. The canal basin still survives, and one company occupies old converted warehouse premises to build prestigious narrow boats and even floating restaurants. The basin is full of pleasure craft and creates a relaxing holiday atmosphere. This contrasts with the commercial barges which used to ply the waterway, but which have been absent locally for many years. One original feature of interest which still remains is a roving or 'turn over' bridge. This allowed the horse drawing the barge to cross the water from one towing path to the other without the need to unhitch the tow rope. In addition, the current-day visitor who is alert, quiet and patient may well be rewarded with a sighting of a kingfisher.

An important industry was textiles – mostly wool, but some cotton and silk – and there still remain a few mills and even fewer mill chimneys. Invariably they were built of local stone, for quarrying was also very important in the area. High quality stone was abundant and the streets of many cities in Britain and abroad were paved with local flagstone. The industry which today dominates the area appears to be flour milling because of the huge silos which are visible from a great distance; the site was mentioned in the Domesday Book (1086) as a flour mill. Today, each grain of wheat travels nearly two kilometres through various machines, extractors and rollers before it becomes flour.

The shopping centre is currently experiencing some regeneration by restoring shop fronts to their original Victorian style. One public house of particular visual interest is the Prince of Wales inn; although it looks very old it was only built in 1926, using timber and panelling from a wooden battleship, HMS *Donegal*, built in 1858. The fine carving on the external beam ends is by a local craftsman.

Within easy walking are attractive open spaces. Wellholme Park was formerly the private grounds of the house (now demolished) of a local mill owner. On the last Saturday in June each year it is the venue for the Brighouse Charity Gala; this is preceded by a long procession of floats and bands which attracts huge crowds of supporters. Rydings Park is an acre or so of attractive gardens and trees adjacent to the Rydings, built in 1841 and originally the home of a corn mill owner, but now a public library. A purpose built art gallery – the only one in Calderdale – was added in 1907.

The parish church, dedicated to St Martin, was built in 1831 as a result of the 'Million Pound Act' of 1818 which made money available to build new churches in industrial areas. It has a full peal of bells and an enthusiastic team of ringers practise on Friday evenings.

Despite the claims of Nottingham and other places to have Robin Hood's grave, there is strong feeling in Brighouse that he is buried locally. Although there is not too much concrete evidence,one can rely on legends and probabilities to connect him with Kirklees. At present

Kirklees Hall, Kirklees Priory and Robin Hood's Grave are all in private ownership and not accessible to the public. However, a local society exists to promulgate the claims that it was here that Robin Hood fired his last arrow in 1247 and was buried where it fell.

Brinsworth 🏹

Brinsworth, formerly 'Brinsford' meaning ford over the river, is a bustling residential area, acting to some extent as a dormitory village for Sheffield and Rotherham. At the turn of the century it was a very different story. In Roman times Ryknild Street, running northward, passed through Brinsworth on its way to Templeborough. During the 17th and 18th centuries, one of the main packhorse routes from Sheffield passed through Brinsworth, branching off at Tinsley and running via Tickhill to Bawtry, whence the goods were shipped down the river Idle.

Brinsworth is served by two churches, St Andrew's and St Edward's Roman Catholic. When St Andrew's mission church opened in 1886, the population of Brinsworth, for whom the church was intended, was only 147.

Things began to change in 1890 when Messrs John Brown, who already owned local collieries, decided to sink a new pit in Canklow. Houses were built in Atlas Street, Duncan Street and Bawtry Road for the workers, and by 1901 the population of Brinsworth had risen to 891. There was still an essentially rural atmosphere. Included in the population were nine farmers, a farm bailiff, a nurseryman and market gardener, and a cow keeper. Farmer John Carr was born in 1850, and his descendants are still residing in the village.

The Midland Railway Company opened their new locomotive sheds at nearby Canklow in 1900, the company owning about 60 terraced houses built in Ellis Street. These developments brought the population to 2,007 by 1911.

During the years immediately preceding and subsequent to the Second World War, the rural aspect of Brinsworth was slowly but surely being eroded and, by the 1950s, the village was rapidly becoming a dormitory suburb. The first public house situated on Bonet Lane was called the Angel, but has now been converted into two cottages and named Holly House. The Atlas Hotel was built at the turn of the century by Messrs John Brown for recreation for their workers, and there were stables at the rear of the hotel. There is a modern shopping area in Brinsworth, covering a wide range of goods, and nearby is a child welfare clinic, community centre and a public library.

Elderly people who lived in the tiny village of Brinsworth at the turn of the century would be very surprised if they now stood at the top of Whitehill and looked down the valley. In place of rolling fields they would see a dense throng of roofs, with ribbons of roads winding between them, and instead of having a handful of neighbours they would find approximately 10,000 inhabitants in the 'village'. It is hard to believe all these changes have taken place in less than a century.

Brockholes 🦡

Brockholes – 'Home of the Badger' – lies about five miles south-east of Huddersfield and approximately in the middle of the Holme valley. The main A616 road from Huddersfield to Sheffield runs through the village and affords easy access to various motorway routes.

The village is dominated by a huge rock outcrop, which in 1870 gave the name Rock Mills to the nearby textile mill which manufactured high-class worsted cloth. The mill was demolished in 1975. The directors of the mill built two terraces of sturdy stone back-to-back houses for employees, aptly named Rock Terrace and Rock Cottages. The 'local' is called the Rock Inn.

The river Holme flows through the village on its way to the Humber, passing close to the road at some points, such as the old hump-backed bridge at Smithy Place.

Most roads out of the village lead uphill; at the lower end of Brockholes Lane, situated behind Rock Terrace, we pass the triangular recreation ground, with its tall, graceful poplar trees, planted to commemorate Queen Victoria's Jubilee; here also, in times past, bear baiting took place.

Still climbing Brockholes Lane we come to the village hall, formerly the village day school. The hall, now administered by the Brockholes Village Trust, is well used by several organisations. In 1968 a new, larger school was built behind and above the old day school.

Beyond the village hall a further short climb leads to the lovely church of St George, built in 1863, from where there is a good view of the village centre.

Back to Brockholes Lane and still climbing towards the railway station, we pass the oldest house in the village, dating from Tudor times. Continuing uphill, we pause to look over the shooting range fields to see the 1930s council estate on Oakes Avenue, and beyond that to 'over-Brockholes', now known as Bank End. Hereabouts, a John de Brockholes had a dwelling in 1406, and here also, in the 18th century, a vicar of Holmfirth, living beyond his means, was found to be a coin clipper. He was apprehended, duly tried and executed in York. His son, on the other hand, was given a good job at the Mint!

At the end of Rock Terrace is the post office; on the opposite corner is a florist and greengrocer, where one can also order and purchase fish, flesh and fowl. In place of the former fish and chip shop, there is an Indian take-away, and the former Brockholes Co-operative shop is now the village store, run by a charming and helpful Punjabi family. A busy newsagent-cum-general store and a ladies' hairdressing salon complete the cluster of village shops.

Lancaster Lane passes River Holme Park leading to what was once Lancaster mill, also now demolished. Part of the site has been transformed, since 1982, into a very pleasant wooded caravan and camping park; the old mill dam provides fishing for campers and a home for many ducks and waterfowl. Between Lancaster Lane and the main road, the Brockholes Allotment Society have their gardens. Members of this flourishing society hold an Annual Produce Show. The Bowling Club situated on the main road in the valley bottom is also well supported. Here, too, is another hostelry, appropriately named the Travellers' Rest.

Like all villages, Brockholes has seen many changes from the days when farming, the mining of coal from 'dayholes' in the hillside, and the thriving textile trade were the main occupations; whilst there are some small family businesses and the new business park, most people commute to work.

Although a sighting of the badger is very rare nowadays, the owls still call, foxes roam and herons have been spotted.

Brodsworth ✤

Brodsworth is a pretty, unspoiled farming village, five miles north-west of Doncaster, set in undulating countryside on the way to Hooton Pagnell. The parish of Brodsworth, consisting of Pickburn and Old Scawsby, was mentioned in the Domesday Book.

Before then a church had been erected, possibly by a Saxon, Alsi, who was the lord in the time of Edward the Confessor. He also owned Pickburn and Scawsby, and most likely was the same Alsi, or Elsi, who held Kimberworth, Maltby, Hellaby, and a share of Tickhill. During the 20th century, Brodsworth has diminished in size. It has remained a predominantly agricultural community throughout its existence, although a colliery opened beyond Pickburn in the early 1900s, closing in 1990, during which time a colliery village sprang up in the surrounding area, and was made into a fresh parish of New Brodsworth.

Nestling among the trees on the hillside is Brodsworth Hall, an imposing building designed by a little known Italian architect, Chevalier Casentini, and built of local limestone. It sits in 17 acres of garden, set within an agricultural estate of several thousand acres. The house and gardens have remained virtually as they were when they were built, and the eminent historian, Dr Mark Girouard, described it as 'the most complete example of a Victorian Country House in England'.

Brodsworth Hall was built between 1860 and 1871 for Charles Sabine Thellusson, heir to a family fortune based on banking. The Thellussons were a French Huguenot family who escaped the Massacre of St Bartholomew. Peter Thellusson, father of Charles Sabine Thellusson, came to England in 1750. He bought Brodsworth estate and lived in the old Hall, which stood near to the church but was demolished when the present house was completed. He died in 1797, leaving an extraordinary will locking up his fortune to accumulate to untold proportions. It took 60 years of lawsuits before the House of Lords settled the issue in 1859. In Charles Dickens' *Bleak House*, Jarndyce v Jarndyce is said to be based on the Thellusson will. Following the death of Mrs Grant Dalton in 1988, the Hall passed to her daughter who donated the Hall and its grounds to English Heritage.

English Heritage are carrying out a repair programme on the Hall, which will be kept to a minimum to preserve the present air of 'fading Victorian grandeur'. The Hall will be opened to the public in 1992/93, when it is anticipated there will be a shop and cafeteria. Visitors to Brodsworth Hall will be able to step back in time and see the house and contents preserved exactly as they were in the 1860s.

The opening of Brodsworth Hall to the public is expected to bring many thousands of people per year to the village, and put Brodsworth on the map nationally and internationally, which will mean a great change for the villagers.

Also on the hillside, not far from Brodsworth Hall, is the lovely church of St Michael and All Angels. There is a Norman window, and the Norman style can be seen in the arcade to the old north aisle, and the tower. The church has a 17th century pulpit, adorned with beautifully carved cherubs' heads and foliage, and also a carved chair. The Thellusson memorials are in the church, which they restored in the 19th century, adding the south aisle and chapel, and the porch.

The church has suffered from mining subsidence in recent years, and had scaffolding erected both inside and outside of the building to make it safe, which remained there for many years. Brodsworth church is likely to be restored by British Coal, to bring it back to its former glory.

A former 17th century vicarage is now a private house, known as Gate House. An 18th century laundry and a brew house, which belonged to Brodsworth Hall, are now private residences, and Big Tree House used to be an inn, known as the Three Horse Shoes. There is a Church of England first/middle school in the village.

Glebe Farm barn is being made into a village hall, and this will be a central point where the villagers can meet and hold functions. Brodsworth has an annual gala in July, and a popular Art Festival, run by the local church at Easter.

Burghwallis 🌿

Mentioned in the Domesday Book of 1086, Burg belonged to the Wallis family for many generations, and eventually the village became Burgh-wallis. It is an attractive village situated 8 miles north of Doncaster, higher than its surrounding fields, with woodland adding to its charm.

The present Burghwallis Hall was built by George Anne about 1797, and is said to be partly Tudor. In 1820 the exterior was altered to give the house a medieval effect. It is a picturesque building 'guarded' by a very large Cedar of Lebanon, and has an open view of fields and woodlands. Originally there was a chapel in the attic, enabling the Catholic worshippers to see any approaching visitors, and the priest's hiding-hole from this chapel, was discovered in 1908. Eventually it was destroyed, making way for a chapel in the south west wing, but this was closed in 1888, when the Hall was leased to Protestants, and some of the altar furnishings were transferred to Blenkinsop Castle, Northumberland. The Anne family returned to Burghwallis in 1907, and eventually when George Anne (the last of the Annes) died, he left Burghwallis to his nephew, Ernest Charlton, stipulating he took the surname Anne.

In 1941, the Hall was sold to the Bishop of Leeds for £1,000 by the last resident, Major George Anne, who was the eldest son of Ernest Charlton. The Mansion is now known as St Anne's Convent, being acquired by the Sisters of Charity of our Lady of Good and Perpetual Succour, who care for old and infirm ladies.

The Anne family, who were among the oldest in the area, held Burghwallis for 400 years, and came from Normandy in the 11th or 12th century.

During the 19th century, Michael Tasburgh-Anne died leaving a fortune as dowries to his three daughters. His youngest daughter, Barbara, eloped with William Henry Charlton of Hesleyside, as they were very young and were unable to obtain parental consent. Tying bedsheets together, she climbed from her bedroom window at midnight, to where William waited for her. A post chaise took them to Gretna Green, where they were married by a blacksmith, next by a Protestant clergyman, and finally by a Catholic Priest.

The 12th century St Helen's church has a notable Norman doorway, and by the side of the church is an old cross. There is distinctive herringbone masonry in the walls of the nave and chancel, and the chancel has a lovely vaulted screen made in medieval days, which was restored in 1881. The south door has turned on its ancient iron hinges for many centuries. Buried in the churchyard is a Catholic priest, Abbe Louis de Roux, who escaped from the French Revolution. He was chaplain to an emigre Princess, and they were helped by the Anne family. She returned to France and the guillotine, but he remained, eventually dying at an old age.

Although Burghwallis has no pub, there is a British Legion Club, which is strongly supported. An Armistice Parade is held every year at the War Memorial, and as recently as 1990 a very old member of the Anne family attended the service there. The post office is a modern building, the old post office now being a cottage, and the former smithy, also a cottage, has the Anne coat of arms over the door.

Squirrel Wood, used by the scouts for camping, was given to the village by the Anne family, as was the playing field. An annual gala, started in Jubilee year, is held here in the summer for the children.

Burley-in-Wharfedale 🐝

Set beside the river Wharfe, at the lower end of one of the loveliest dales in Yorkshire, Burley is a very pleasant place in which to live, as the steady rise in population this century bears witness.

Over a thousand years of history link the Burley of today with the tiny settlement of Burhleg, mentioned in the Saxon Chronicle of AD 972, and the Burghelai of the Domesday Book of 1086.

From its earliest recorded days, the village was centred around the church, first known as the chapel of St Michael, with the manor house, the cornmill, the blacksmith's forge, the village inn and a cluster of cottages nearby. The gradual growth of the village along the main street can be traced by several 17th century houses still in occupation, most of them being originally farmhouses with adjoining barns and cottages and all belonging to the lord of the manor.

In the mid 17th century the chapel was rebuilt on the same site and endowed by the Fairfax family. This Fairfax chapel served the village for the next 200 years.

In the 1790s the Industrial Revolution reached Burley, when the Greenholme cotton mills were built. Unlike the 'dark satanic' mills of the fast-growing towns, Greenholme, as its name implies, was in a lovely setting by the river Wharfe and almost invisible from the village street. Originally, most of the mill workers were children brought from London, who were made apprentices. Many, as they served their time, settled in the village in the houses built by the mill owners. Most of these mid 19th century terraces of stone-built cottages have become desirable residences.

In 1848 the mill was bought by W. E. Forster and W. Fison and they had a very great influence on the development of modern Burley. When the half-time system was introduced in 1856, a school was built for the mill children. Later in 1868, when Fison & Forster built the lecture hall (now the Queen's Hall) and presented it to the village, the mill school was moved into the east end of the hall. By 1870 the village had three schools – the National, the Mill and the Township (Nonconformist). Today, two Celtic-type crosses stand in front of the Queen's Hall as memorials to Fison and Forster.

Near the parish church stands a tree which is a recent replacement for the famous 'Great Pudding Tree'. Every seven years until 1787 the feast of the Great Pudding was held, when a huge pudding was boiled and served to villagers from under the tree.

With the advent in 1865 of the Wharfedale Railway the village had greater access to the outside world and by the 1920s between 60 and 70 trains a day passed through Burley. Further growth of the village came with the building of Scalebor Park mental hospital in 1902 providing many new jobs in nursing.

After the Second World War the mill closed and gradually the buildings have become a trading estate, giving employment to many people. The population has doubled since the 1920s, many new houses being built mainly on the south side of Main Street and Bradford Road. The Main Street is still bordered by Yorkshire stone cottages and houses and always the surrounding hills are in view.

Modern Burley is still a thriving village, although many people work in and commute to the nearby cities of Leeds and Bradford. The inhabitants enjoy the benefit of good schools, a further education centre, good welfare facilities and a variety of leisure activities. For the more energetic the moors provide excellent walks and country pursuits.

Cadeby ✍

Cadeby is a small green belt village lying in an area of outstanding country landscape. The village is surrounded on all sides by high quality arable agricultural land, and new development is tightly controlled and confined to small scale infilling within its existing limits.

Documentary evidence for the period between the end of the Roman occupation and the Norman Conquest is scanty, but there is a recorded discovery of a Roman hoard of coins near Cadeby in 1905. Cadeby is listed as Catebi in the Domesday Book of 1086. This name is purely Scandinavian in origin, making it very probable that the place was settled after AD 900. Catebi contains the personal name of Kati, and the whole may be interpreted as Kati's farmstead.

The change in agriculture during the last 75 years is well illustrated in the way the number of farms has decreased in Cadeby. When the Copley estate was sold in 1925, there were four smallholdings and five large farms. Each smallholder was a milk producer and kept pigs. The milk was untreated, apart from being strained, and was collected by the villagers in jugs from the farm door. A pig would be killed each year to provide ham or bacon for the ensuing year. Pig's fry would be distributed amongst the neighbours on the strict understanding that the plate remained unwashed. To wash the plate would bring bad luck. This also applied to the jug containing the beastings (first milk of a cow after

White House Farm, Cadeby

calving), which was also shared with the neighbours to make custards. The smallholders also had other occupations, one working at Cadeby colliery, another coal leading and carting for the villagers, and two having milk rounds. They helped on the larger farms at harvest time and generally enjoyed a reasonable standard of living.

There were five large farms in Cadeby. Today only Cadeby Hall Farm and White House Farm exist as working units. Manor Farm has become the Cadeby inn, Church Farm was demolished and houses erected in its place, now known as Manor Drive. The land surrounding Wildthorpe Farm was purchased by a local farmer, the farmhouse itself was turned into a private residence, and the farm buildings were replaced by bungalows, built in Brackenbury Close.

The 19th century brought about a period of development in the area. The wharves at Cadeby were busy unloading bricks, tiles, linseed cake, lime and limestone. There were also several quarries being worked locally. One large national company is still in operation, producing limestone and associated products.

Cadeby never had an ancient church, though there was a small chapel near the ferry across the Don to Conisbrough. However, it was more convenient to worship at the parish church in Sprotbrough. St John's church at Cadeby was built in 1856 for the Copleys and designed by George Gilbert Scott, the architect of St George's church, Doncaster. It is a pleasing and unusual building, which in basic shape seems to resemble a medieval estate barn, with its steep roofs and tall south porch. This effect is helped by the positioning of the bellcote above the junction of the nave and chancel. At the time of writing, the church is no longer operational.

A large police house was built in 1900, which included two cells. The police constable had to cover a wide area on foot until 1910, when a bicycle was provided for him. The main crime at this time was poaching. After the break up of the Copley estate, the constable went to live in lodgings in Sprotbrough, and was later accommodated in a new police house. The one at Cadeby was converted into a private dwelling, where the marks made by the cell bars are still visible on the window sill.

Over the years the character of Cadeby has changed from that of a closely knit agricultural community to one of a dormitory village. There are approximately 70 houses and less than 200 residents. Apart from two long established farming families, today's residents are in the main professional and business people, who work in the surrounding large towns.

Calverley 🐑

Calverley is situated seven miles from Leeds, four miles from Bradford, on the A657 Leeds to Shipley road. It is of Saxon origin, the name meaning 'a clearing in the wood for calves'. There are still woods, and calves in the fields, as the green belt around Calverley forms a break between the conurbations of Leeds and Bradford. This green belt is jealously guarded.

The old weavers' cottages, built from the locally quarried millstone grit, are the legacy of the woollen trade which, along with agriculture, formed the livelihood of the village for over 600 years. Then, with the Industrial Revolution, mills were built and provided a source of employment for the villagers and the surrounding community. However, with the decline in the wool trade in the 1960s and 1970s, two of the mills were dismantled and brick houses were built on the land; the remainder were sub-divided and used as diverse work units. Consequently, there is very little employment within the village itself and so it has become a dormitory for Leeds and Bradford.

The parish church of St Wilfrid stands at the junction of Town Gate and Carr Road, and the present building dates, in part, from about 1150. The remaining portions of this early church are the nave walls and the blocked up part of a Norman window in the south nave wall. Major restoration of the church was undertaken in 1869/70. The square tower of the church houses the ringing chamber, with its peal of eight bells, which is still in continuous use. The church font is plain and 14th century but its cover is a very good example of Jacobean work, octagonal in shape with two tiers of open-work tracing and foliage, and a spire.

Further along Carr Road is the Methodist chapel built in 1872, and before the Second World War the villagers were either 'Church' or 'Chapel'.

Beyond this lies Victoria Park with its memorial dedicated to the Calverley men lost in the First and Second World Wars. Perhaps it is appropriate that it is here that the Calverley St Wilfrid's Cricket Club plays each Saturday during the summer and, in winter, football matches are held. There is also a thriving bowling club.

One of the more interesting and lesser known buildings in Calverley is the Old Hall. This was the home of the Calverley family until the 17th century. It was towards the end of this period that Walter Calverley, the lord of the manor, ran amok and tried to annihilate his family. At the time he was in financial straits and, through the stress, it is thought he suffered a brainstorm. On 23rd April 1605, he stabbed to death his young son, then turned and stabbed his wife and the son she had gathered into her arms. His wife survived the attack; no doubt the stiffening in the bodice of her dress deflected the blade. Legend has it that the blood stains on the stairs could never be washed out.

Walter rushed to his horse and galloped away to find his third son, Henry, a baby who was being cared for by a wet-nurse. As he galloped over a field, his horse stumbled, he was thrown, and his pursuers were able to capture him before any harm befell Henry. He was taken to Wakefield gaol and sent for trial to the York Assizes but, as he refused to plead, he was pressed to death on 5th August 1605 and buried in York the same day. Rumours abounded that his body was secretly exhumed and returned to Calverley for burial, and that his ghost has been seen.

In 1754 the Calverley estates, which included much land in the village, were sold to Thomas Thornhill. The Hall was divided up into several dwellings and in 1981 the Landmark Trust bought the Old Hall to save it from being sold as separate lots. Fortunately, because the Hall was occupied by tenants, who had no reason to make more than minor alterations or additions, the medieval core of the building has remained intact in most essentials.

Although the population of Calverley is now more transient, the feeling for the 'village' still remains.

Carr & District 🍂

The Industrial Revolution did not properly arrive in South Yorkshire until the first decade of the 20th century, when colliery shafts were sunk. Model villages quickly sprang up and pockets of dense population surrounded each mine. In the triangle enclosed by Dinnington, Thurcroft and Maltby collieries, remained a cluster of small farming communities which, to this day, have been little changed. Surrounding villages have expanded rapidly but, because of the natural divisions caused by woodland and streams, these small communities have remained separate and intact.

Not one of the villages has a shop of any kind, none has a church or a school. Shopping has to be done in one of the nearby mining communities. The children have to attend school outside their village. There are no services of any kind, other than telephone kiosks and post boxes. The roads are narrow and, of course, in winter they can be blocked by snow. There is no pressure from the residents for road widening, because this would attract undesirable traffic. The villages are in industrial South Yorkshire, but were all originally in the West Riding of Yorkshire, a name of which they were proud and sad to lose.

Carr dates from 1319, the name meaning boggy marsh land, which describes the kind of land the village was built on. The beacon at Carr signalled the Spanish Armada and, since that date, has been used traditionally in the nation's network of beacons lit on ceremonial occasions. The last event of this kind took place in 1988, to celebrate the 400th anniversary of the defeat of the Spanish Armada. Hundreds of people flocked to the replica beacon erected for that event. There is an active village group, and events for the village and surrounding areas take place in the hall. This was donated by a former vicar of the area, and functions have to be held to maintain the premises. Of the four villages, it is the only one with a hall.

Slade Hooton, recorded in the Domesday Book, is so called because it is a farmstead on a spur overlooking the Slade valley. It is the smallest of the four villages, with a lovely old William and Mary Hall. Most years the village holds a grand fair with stalls, games, refreshments, and a pig roast.

The earliest date recorded for Brookhouse is 1297. It is named after a large house at the side of the brook, which runs through the main street. This pretty little village boasts a pub and a restaurant, and also has a beautiful cricket ground.

The fourth village is Hooton Levitt, again a farmstead on a spur, with the name Levitt added to it. A knight, William de Levitt, occupied the lands in the 13th and 14th centuries. Hooton Levitt was also mentioned in the Domesday Book of 1086, and is the only one of the four villages which is a parish in its own right. It has a Community Association, which meets in people's homes each month. They arrange a village fair annually, with stalls, games and refreshments, and also organise outings and a Christmas dinner.

The population of Carr is 65, Slade Hooton 50, Brookhouse 100, and Hooton Levitt 120, and overall it has not increased greatly over the last 100 years.

Carr Gate 🦚

This hamlet was initially a collection of houses on the main A650, formerly Bradford turnpike road, three miles outside Wakefield, then having one public building, the Malt Shovel Hotel, which abutted the main road.

The construction of the M1 motorway and the Wrenthorpe bypass, however, left some houses at some distance from the new roads, separated from their public house and also with a long section of the former wide road unused for through traffic. Fortunately the Carr Gate Garden Centre and caravan sales site have blossomed to give the locality a firmer identity.

Carr Gate was on the very edge of the Wakefield Outwood. Ancient highways set out by the Wakefield Enclosure Commissioners in 1793/ 1805 connected the locality with Lingwell Gate, Lofthouse Gate and Outwood Vill. Wakefield Outwood was a thickly wooded area between Leeds/Bradford and Wakefield. Carr Gate, Kirkhamgate, Lingwell Gate and Lofthouse Gate represented the outlet through those woods in the manor of Wakefield, into Ardsley and Thorpe beyond.

Brandicarr Road (formerly Beckbottom Road) was the highway to the west from Carr Gate and it was here that during the 19th century, the strange Prophet Wroe had a magnificent mansion erected by his followers. It still exists, complete with entrance cottage, as Melbourne House, an Elim Pentecostal church residential home. Its elegant rooms lead from a spacious hall, which has an imposing staircase upon which stands a huge grandfather clock.

Residents, dependent upon their viewpoint, either suffer or gain from their proximity to the M1, as some of their rural scene has been eroded. They may also have similar opinions concerning the helicopter pad close by, from which the West Yorkshire police regularly supervise the M1 and other more distant towns and villages.

Carr Gate, in earlier days, was at the head of a gentle incline by which coal was transported using the ancient Coal Road to the river Calder at Bottomboat.

Many years ago there was a mission building on Grandstand Road, but most church people in the locality now travel to more distant churches.

Catcliffe 🦚

Situated approximately four miles from the bustling market town of Rotherham, semi-rural and surrounded by green fields and trees, Catcliffe nestles quietly alongside the river Rother, which once boasted a fine collection of trout. Boating was also enjoyed on the river. An overflow of water has over the years developed into a nature reserve, attracting many bird watchers to see the swans, swallows, herons, grebe, coot, etc., arriving from all over the country.

In the late 19th century, there were less than 100 houses in the village, and no public transport. St Mary's church was built in 1910 of stone taken out of Orgreave colliery. Alongside was the tin Mission church of St Faith, destroyed in the gales of 1962. An old people's centre, Mere Brow, stands off Church Lane, by the side of one of Europe's remaining glass blowing kilns, dating back to the 1700s. It was used in the 1926 strike to serve soup to needy children. Joey Hodson came every year with his circus, and used the kiln for his performances. It now stands a listed building, a proud monument to a bygone industry and era.

The village was split to the north east with the coming of the motorways, which cut through a once beautiful orchard. In spring the trees were covered in apple blossom, pear blossom, and pigs and hens roamed through the grass, with the occasional fox too.

The local school was held in two tiny cottages, down Old School Lane, and later, as the number of children grew, moved to the County Primary and Infants School in Rotherham Road. A School Queen and Captain are chosen each year, and a Gala is held, an active Parents-Teachers Association Group playing its part in the organisation.

The first train to pass through Catcliffe was on the South East Line, Derby to Rotherham, in 1840. To the north the LNER railway was built in 1875. This passes over nine arches, and Banks Pottery is in one of them, owned by Gordon Banks, the footballer. Another holds a betting shop. An open-air theatre group was held in the courtyard, until the stage caught fire and was destroyed, from a spark falling out of a steam engine travelling on the line overhead. The Cobbler and Barber had a wooden hut in the same area.

The Almshouses were erected in Station Road, the money being given to help widows to live, for a reasonable rent, in these premises. They were sold to make one private dwelling, and in later years the money from the sale was added to a Shipley Fund, for widows to benefit at Christmas.

The Doctor's surgery was held in the front lounge of the local greengrocer (Mr Butcher, who started his business with a barrow), then moved to the kitchen of the post office, when patients had to queue outside in all weathers to wait their turn to see the doctor. Unfortunately, this practice no longer is held in the village.

The chemist stands in the Main Street. A Co-operative store and Village Shoppe, butchers and newsagents all used to be in the same street. Some of these shops have closed but have been attractively replaced by trees and grass.

Down by the river Rother, which at one time used to overflow and flood the area, villagers had to be evacuated from their homes every time there were heavy showers of rain. On one occasion, a boat had to be brought from Goole to take people to safety. The course of the river has been altered, and new homes are springing up in the area, flowers, bushes and trees being planted on land which was derelict.

An old people's centre of bungalows, The Croft, stands by the recreation field, a selection of rides for the children, outdoor bowls and football are all played there. Another old people's centre, Chapel Walk, has just been completed on the site of old Frederick Street. Where the Wesleyan chapel once stood, a house meeting was held by a group of friends in the home of Mr and Mrs A. Royle, and so developed the Catcliffe Methodist chapel in 1906. This has a thriving Sunday School, and Sunday worship, and, together with other weekly activities, upholds the Christian witness in the community life of the village and surrounding areas.

Catcliffe was once a hive of industry, with men and women working in various occupations, including strawberry growing, farming and coal mining. Recently two companies have opened on the outskirts of the village, and, apart from these two, the other industries now stand quiet and still, with chimneys no longer smoking or wheels grinding. The only noise is from the motorcars and lorries passing through, or the rumbling of a diesel engine on the railway line.

On an evening, only the birds are singing. So stand and listen to the sky lark trilling, watch the heron and the ducks fly, and the rooks from the nearby rookery cawing, all silhouetted against the evening sky, beneath the trails of the aeroplane, the river quietly flowing by the willows and hedgerows. Who knows, in years to come, with improvements and cleaner waters, trout may be alive and people able to fish in these waters again.

Cawthorne

The village of Cawthorne derives its name from Old English meaning 'cold' or 'bare thorn bush'. It lies four miles from the town of Barnsley, some eight miles from Wakefield and ten miles from Huddersfield. Clustered around its ancient church, the village spills into Tivydale, from which radiates the area known in old documents as 'The Lanes'. Centuries of farming have rendered the land green, masking all traces of former quarries, ironstone workings and coal mines.

Central Cawthorne has seen successive rebuildings. A few houses of the 17th century can be detected, whilst a number of attractive stone cottages bear 18th century datestones. A great number of houses are, however, 19th century buildings in the estate cottage manner, well built of stone, with prominent chimneys of brick. The 20th century has introduced the building of a small estate and a number of private houses, filling in sites such as Tivydale. Today the village is a quiet place, for there are few sources of employment save for a pipeworks and for agriculture. None of the old crafts now exist as occupations, and great imagination is needed to picture the formerly busy village with activity in mines, tanneries and the movement of barges in Barnby Basin. There are approximately 500 houses in Cawthorne at the present time, housing some 1,500 inhabitants.

There are several places of interest in this ancient village. The earliest record of Cawthorne is found in William the Conqueror's Domesday Book of 1086 which stated that the manor was 'three miles long and two broad'. The history of an ancient parish such as this usually centres round its church. The oldest portion of the parish church of All Saints dates back to the 13th century. It has since been repaired and extensively restored. On the south side of the church is a small building known as the parish room. This was once the village grammar school built in 1639. It was last used as a school in 1906 but it is now used and let by the church for various functions.

At the top of Taylor Hill stands the Victoria Jubilee Museum which opened on 31st May 1884 in an old disused cottage, originally a Primitive Methodist meeting house. Because of the Museum's popularity, a larger building was erected as a memorial to Queen Victoria's Golden Jubilee and opened in 1889, by the Bishop of Wakefield. Amongst the many interesting exhibits to be found in the museum is the well known boot of local farmer Tom Parkin, who was struck by lightning whilst working in the fields. Tom came to no harm but his boot is a lasting reminder of the danger of the elements.

Another museum is Cannon Hall Country House Museum. Until it was purchased by Barnsley Metropolitan Borough Council in 1951 the Hall had been the seat of the Spencer-Stanhope family. It also houses the Regimental Museum of the 13th/18th Royal Hussars (Queen Mary's Own). It is open to the public and the grounds are now designated as a country park, attracting thousands of visitors every year.

Whilst at one time the village could boast seven or eight public houses and several shops, there now only remains one pub, two shops, a post office and two craft shops.

Many anecdotes have been passed down through time. One particular one was that of the two farm labouring families, living side by side by Tanyard Beck. They shared one earth closet which was set a little way away from the cottages. The head of one household would take his pipe to smoke whilst using the closet, dropping spent matches down the hole. After a feud, the opposing family decided to take its revenge on the pipe smoker, and poured a large quantity of paraffin down the closet just before he was about to make his daily sojourn there. The result of him dropping his matches down onto the waiting paraffin is left to the reader's imagination!

Chapeltown

There is no mention of Chapeltown in the Domesday Survey of 1086, but many of the recorded names in this area can be traced back to the 12th century. Some of the spellings are quite interesting – Chappel, Chappell, Chappel-Towne. Other local names are Angerum (Angram Bank), Barnes Cross, and Burnt Cross.

On a very early map dated 1637, 'Chapell Towne' is shown on the banks of Blackburn Brook, which flows through present-day Chapeltown. Possibly it expanded round this brook to accommodate water wheels, which were needed to grind corn. They also were used to work the machinery for Chapeltown Furnace, which dates back to at least 1600. The area was heavily wooded, and this provided charcoal for the furnace.

Cowley Manor, originally moated and built like a castle, was purchased by the Earl of Shrewsbury in 1572. It was later demolished by him and rebuilt in a smaller fashion, using the old materials, and this is Cowley Manor as it is seen today. It is on the original lane which ran from Ecclesfield to Chapeltown. Ecclesfield Lane came later in 1637, and, although a more direct way, was only a path across fields.

Howsley Hall was first mentioned in 1436, but is probably older than that. Sir Thomas Rotherham, the Archbishop of York (1424–1500), bought it, and, on his death, left it to his cousin, John Scott. John's daughter, Alice, married Thomas Howsley, whose family had originally owned the Hall, and they inherited it on her father's death. One of their children married a Gerard Freeman in 1594, at which time the family took the name of Howsley Freeman, (Freeman fields can be seen on old maps). The last of the Freemans died in 1837, leaving Howsley Hall Estate to the Right Hon James Stuart Wortley, who sold it to his cousin the Earl of Wharncliffe. The Hall was let to various tenants, including several members of the Chambers family. Mr Chambers and Mr Newton founded Thorncliffe Iron Works in 1793.

Mr Newton eventually resided in Greenhead House, now a restaurant. In 1806, on land leased from the Duke of Norfolk, he built himself a new house called Staindrop Lodge, and this too is now a hotel and restaurant.

The Duke of Norfolk had to pay substantial land tax on all his estates in 1800. To raise the money, he sold a large quantity of land, especially in this area, and a present-day plot of land on Warren Lane once belonged to the Duke of Norfolk. This was part of a deer park which reached as far as Tankersley, and is now the home of the local golf club. The word 'Warren' was the name for a breeding area for deer, long before it was associated with rabbits.

The bringing of the railway to Thorncliffe in 1855 no doubt helped to promote the development of Chapeltown, which had its own station in 1894. In 1897 the line was extended to Barnsley, and the station is used today by many commuters. Newton Chambers and the local coal mines were the largest employers in the area, but now most of this has gone. There is an industrial estate and, as it expands with different companies, it is helping to provide much needed employment, as is the ASDA stores built in the centre of Chapeltown in 1975. There has been a surge of housebuilding over the last fifty years, and Burncross and High Green are now virtually part of Chapeltown.

Collingham 🌿

Collingham is situated on the bank of the river Wharfe some ten miles north of Leeds, at a point where the plain of York first gives way to the Pennines. Indeed, it was at the top of the small hill on the outskirts of the village that a very large Roman villa was discovered in 1854 and called Dalton Parlours. A major archaeological dig took place on the site between 1976–79 revealing clear evidence the Romans had, in fact, built over an earlier Iron Age settlement.

There is evidence to confirm that the parish church started as a small shrine built to the memory of the Christian King Oswini, who was murdered by King Oswi. This foul deed, according to the Venerable Bede, took place in a field near a river at a place called Ingethlingum in AD 650. Many experts believe that this place is now called Collingham. There can be little doubt that the large and rare runic cross, now on permanent display inside the church, has carvings of great artistry which were carried out to commemorate an unusually important event.

The village appears to have slumbered through the centuries until it awoke to national fame because of the deeds of two brothers, who became known as the Collingham Robbers. In 1674 these two scoundrels put into operation a cunning plan for stealing some bags of gold from the richest man in Yorkshire, who lived near Bingley. To avoid detection they compelled the Collingham blacksmith to put the shoes on backwards on their horses' hoofs. Having succeeded in their mission they returned to Collingham by a different route with each horse carrying three bags of gold and both men convinced that they could not be traced. However, their pet dog, which had followed them to the scene of the crime, had been captured and when released had walked back to Collingham stalked by two of the rich man's servants. The gold was found and the two brothers arrested and condemned to death by hanging, with their own apprentice being compelled to carry out their public execution. This youth was so horror stricken after performing this deed that he then took the same rope and hanged himself.

Throughout the 19th century and up to the First World War there were frequent reports of strange apparitions being sighted around an area called Ladywood. It is quite remarkable how, even today, many people walking in this vicinity comment on its peculiar atmosphere. There is no doubt that the Collingham Ghost received much publicity and affected normal village life for, as the well known poem about his activities recounts, no resident dared go out at night for he even 'freeten'd parson as weel as clerk and lots beside'. The Collingham Ghost stayed on around Ladywood despite a well publicised attempt by six residents to drive him out of the village in 1920.

The village has had more substantial visitors including a two night stay by Dick Turpin at the Old Star inn which still stands. The repeated rumour that during his stay the highwayman posted notices offering rewards for his arrest has recently received strong supportive evidence. Likewise, there seems little doubt that Oliver Cromwell spent a night in the original Half Moon inn before the battle of Marston Moor. In more recent times, the well known artist Owen Bowen, who lived in the village, could often be seen painting one of his delightful Wharfedale landscapes which are now so popular.

Prior to the arrival of the railway in 1875 the livelihood of nearly every resident revolved around farming, but the speedy and frequent train service to Leeds soon altered the whole social structure of the village. New homes were built to house the ever increasing number of city office workers who injected a new enthusiasm into the previously somewhat unexciting rural existence. This manifested itself in the form of community activities which were enjoyed by all. Collingham gradually established a reputation for being a village which excelled in putting on large costumed historical pageants in which nearly every resident played some part. These were lavish affairs and attracted large crowds, some of whom came by special excursion trains from Leeds.

Little wonder that the village Memorial Hall, requiring community efforts to finance and build, was the first to be opened in the West Riding after the First World War. This building, considerably enlarged, is still the centre of social and educational activities. Despite considerable growth (population 2,200) and many commuters, village life is bubbling.

Conisbrough 🐚

Conisbrough at the present time is going through a considerable change, mainly due to the loss of industrial employment, which had been coal mining for over 120 years. The village is best known for its 11th century castle, which through Sir Walter Scott's novel *Ivanhoe* has become known world wide. However, the real history of the village would surpass any novel.

St Peter's church at Conisbrough is the oldest building in South Yorkshire, dated about AD 650–700. The present building embodies the extensive remains of a Saxon minster church. It is very similar to Benedict

Bishop church at Monkwearmouth, which is dated about AD 674 in Bede's writings.

Very little is known about the Saxon fort, but it was probably built with the church (which is still standing), or on a spur of limestone that was capped with clay, crowned by a timber palisade and breastwork, and situated some 400 metres from the Saxon township, which is still the village centre. At the time of the Norman Conquest, the manor was held by King Harold and was quite extensive being centred on the church with 28 villages.

The Norman castle was suffering from neglect by the 16th century. The survey of 1537/8 by commission of Henry VIII recorded that the gates of the castle, also the wall between the tower and the keep, had fallen down. The keep floors were falling in and the castle eventually became a ruin. It came under the guardianship of the nation in 1949. A visitors' centre was opened in 1989 and the following year a floodlighting system was installed.

Manufacturing came slowly to Conisbrough. Corn milling gave way to the sickle trade at Burcroft, where for hundred of years there had been a ferry, which enjoyed the title of King's Ferry and operated from the King's Wharf. The river Don drove a water wheel which powered the lathes. About 100 people were employed in this trade for about 150 years. Barges were used on the river to bring wood and steel, they would then take the finished product out to ships, ready to transport them all over the world.

Coal mining started in 1867 at Denaby. It was the farthest east and deepest mine in England at that time. Soon Cadeby colliery started up, just across the river from Conisbrough. On the 9th July 1912, Cadeby colliery suffered one of the worst ever mining disasters, caused by a terrific explosion. Out of 37 men working in the South District, 35 lost their lives. The combined rescue teams from both Cadeby and Denaby collieries, together with W. H. Pickering (a Government Inspector, said to be one of the leading authorities on coal mining of his time), were caught in a second explosion and only two men survived from these teams. The death toll rose to 75. An estimated crowd of 80,000 came to the pit area during the disaster. The King and Queen, who were visiting Hickleton Hall at that time, came to the mine, accompanied by Earl Fitzwilliam and Lord Stanfordham. Coal mining ended at Denaby in 1968 and Cadeby colliery in 1986.

Kilner Brothers opened the Providence Glass Works in 1871, where about 300 persons were employed. They made 'Kilner' jars and bottles, and these also were exported all over the globe. They closed in 1938.

Denaby Powder Works opened in 1889. It was one of the four companies which founded the Imperial Chemical Industries during the First World War. When it closed in 1963 it was making electric detonators and was employing about 200 people.

Conisbrough has survived over 13 centuries of change and hardship, prosperity and poverty and will no doubt continue to do so.

Crigglestone 🌿

Crigglestone parish covers several areas which used to be separate villages, now virtually joined together through new housing. There is Crigglestone, Chapelthorpe, Calder Grove, Dennington, Durkar, Great Cliff and Little Cliff, Hall Green, Painthorpe, Kettlethorpe and Newmillerdam. The boundary to this area covers twelve miles, which is walked once a year by local ramblers.

There have been many changes in the village of Crigglestone, which is four miles from Wakefield, the nearest town. The closing and demolishing of the colliery and coke ovens, which at one time covered half the village, was one of the biggest changes. Part of the colliery area is now an industrial estate and another part a housing estate. There are the usual shops and schools in different areas of Crigglestone and a police station. The railway is now closed, but trains still pass through to Sheffield and London.

Great Cliff and Dennington have now been split due to the M1 motorway. Dennington (Spa) is a small hamlet built on either side of Dennington Lane, so called because of a spring once drunk for its medicinal powers. There were 36 houses and cottages until the motorway came in 1968, but the village is now cut in two with 13 houses disappearing under the motorway. Children used to be able to play on the roadway, and everybody knew everybody else. Now where once was peace and quiet, there is the continual noise of the motorway.

In the area is a cemetery and crematorium which serves the whole district of Wakefield. In the parish of Crigglestone there is now a mail order firm which provides work for many people in the district. The annual flower show and village feast of years ago used to be held on the site where the mail order company is now built.

Calder Grove is part of the parish of Crigglestone, lying in the Calder valley, connected with Crigglestone by a long steep lane. It used to be quite a self contained village with all the usual shops; the butcher and the baker have now gone but there is a Chinese take-away! Many new houses have sprung up all around since the completion of the motorway in 1968, and nowadays this is a commuter area, with easy access to Leeds and London. There used to be the Oak Brewery, which provided some employment, but mostly it was the collieries for the men and mills or domestic work for the women. There is a small church, St John's, but the children always went to another area of Crigglestone to be taught.

A canal runs alongside the river Calder in the valley. Years ago it was a busy waterway with barges continually transporting coal from staithes at Broad Cut. Since the closure of the collieries this trade has stopped and the canal is now used as a base for cabin cruisers and narrowboats, a very colourful addition to the scene. The Navigation inn on the waterside is a very pleasant spot for passing boat traffic to call for refreshments.

Bretton College is within a beautiful area a couple of miles from Crigglestone and is a very popular tourist attraction, famous for its sculpture park.

Cusworth ✍🏻

Cusworth is a small village one and a half miles north-west of Doncaster and in the parish of Sprotbrough. It contains some attractive 17th and 18th century limestone cottages neatly nestled into a south facing hillside and is referred to by some as 'a bit of the Cotswolds in Yorkshire'. The outer area has grown considerably but the village itself is now a dormitory for Doncaster professional and business people.

There has been a settlement at Cusworth since at least the Anglo-Saxon period from which the name is derived. In fact the original Saxon settlement is now protected by ancient monument status and is a large walled paddock known on the old estate maps as Great Ash Croft.

The first recorded entry is in the Domesday Book of 1086 and refers to Cuzeuuorde. The ancient manuscripts relating to Cusworth still survive and the earliest document in existence is a charter dated about 1200 relating to Bernolf de Cuscewrth. Throughout the centuries that followed the estate changed hands and by 1560 it belonged to the Wray family. One prominent owner was Sir Christopher Wray, who was Chief Justice of the King's Bench and who was responsible for building the Elizabethan Cusworth Hall which existed on the site of the present church property in Cusworth village. By 1669 Cusworth had become the property of Robert Wrightson and it is his successors who were responsible for the village and estate as seen today.

In 1740 William Wrightson decided to move out of the old Elizabethan manor house and build the present Cusworth Hall on a hill to the west of the village. Although it has a prominent position and a commanding view of Doncaster, it is still within the confines and approach of the village, thus retaining the 16th century concept of the manor and village being one unit. By marriage into the Battie family of nearby Warmsworth, this created the present family surname of Battie-Wrightson. The last member of the family was Mrs Barbara Pearse (nee Battie-Wrightson) who died in 1989. Her remaining Cusworth estate property she left in trust to maintain St Hubert's church and the walled gardens as a lasting memorial to her family.

The Elizabethan manor house is in the centre of the village and was, for a time, the dower house to the Hall. It later became the estate office and Home Farm and it is now in private ownership. The converted stone barns and adjacent cottages are late 17th and early 18th century and this part of the village, formerly the Homestead, is now called Manor Farm Court. Opposite the manor house is the small church of St Hubert. This was originally a pinfold with various service buildings. When the local authority purchased Cusworth Hall from the Battie-Wrightson trustees in 1961, this resulted in the closure of the private chapel in Cusworth Hall which had been used for public worship. Mrs Pearse then had the pinfold stable converted to a church, the blacksmith's shop into a vestry office, and the cart-shed into a meeting place which is called the Battie-Wrightson Memorial Hall. The church at Cusworth is administered by the Orthodox Church of the British Isles. This was Mrs Pearse's choice because her mother, who was Lady Isabella Cecil, eldest daughter of the third Marquis of Exeter, stipulated in her will that her daughter could not become a Roman Catholic. So, as Mrs Pearse did not favour the Anglican church, the Orthodox church were asked to take over the ecclesiastical oversight.

Behind the church are the walled gardens, terraces and sunken bowling green which served the old Cusworth Hall, which was demolished about 1760 to make way for the property now called Church Cottage and Cusworth Glebe. Although most of the cottages are now privately owned, Cusworth still has the air of a country estate village. In fact the remaining estate property is still managed by the Battie-Wrightson family agent who is resident in the village, so this unique link with the past still survives.

As mentioned earlier, Cusworth is within the parish of Sprotbrough, so it would be natural to assume that the Copley family of Sprotbrough Hall and the Battie-Wrightson family of Cusworth Hall should be good neighbours. So they were until the late 1890s when the Copleys had plans to sink a coal mine just off Sprotbrough Road. This was a long way from their house at Sprotbrough Hall but would have completely ruined the Cusworth landscape and been visible from the windows of Cusworth Hall. Consequently the two families fell out and more trees were planted to screen out Sprotbrough from Cusworth, resulting in what is now known as the Long Plantation. The rift between Cusworth and Sprotbrough continued for many years and only ended in 1926 when the Copleys left Sprotbrough.

Cusworth Hall is now a museum of South Yorkshire Life and was purchased by the local authority in 1961. It has always been a tradition at Cusworth that some ghostly apparition is seen by a close member of the Battie-Wrightson staff within a few months of the squire's death. As the family have now gone it will be interesting to see if it ever appears again!

Darfield 🦢

Darfield lies some five miles east of Barnsley on the A635, which runs from Manchester to Doncaster. A stranger driving through would probably dismiss it as just another of the many mining villages in South Yorkshire. Yet Darfield's roots lie deeper than the coal, which has dominated the lives of the people for so many years.

There have been several finds of Roman coins, and evidence suggests that there was indeed a Roman settlement here. It was a well chosen site, lying between two river valleys, those of the Dearne and its tributary the Dove. The land rises to a high point overlooking the Dearne, and it is here that the church stands proud, visible for miles around.

The church of All Saints is one of the oldest and most interesting in the area. For many years it served seven townships, the names of which are carved in the stone wall beside the steps which lead from the graveyard to the river. It is in the sprawling sloping graveyard that Darfield's claim to national fame can be seen, in the grave of Ebenezer Elliot, the 'Corn Law Rymer'. He wrote these famous words:-

'When wilt thou save the people,
Oh God of mercy when?
The people Lord the people,
Not thrones and crowns but men'.

The road through the village is part of the ancient route used to carry salt by packhorses from Cheshire to Barnsley, Doncaster and beyond. This fact is remembered by one section of this road being called Saltersbrook Road. Saltersbrook was a tiny hamlet high in the Pennines on the Yorkshire border, where there was an inn for the salt merchants to stay on their journey. The road became a turnpike in the early 19th century, and the old toll house, which still stands near the river, is now used as a cafe frequented by lorry drivers.

Darfield expanded with the demand for coal. There have been several mines in the area. Darfield Main, which stands by the river Dove, was sunk in the 19th century and so, for more than a hundred years, local men have worked in the mine. Mine owners built terraced cottages of stone and brick for their workers, and mining became the biggest employer, taking over from agriculture. Yet Darfield is still surrounded by farms and very conscious of being part of a rural environment.

Over the last 20 years, the waste and dereliction generated by the mining industry has gradually been removed. One huge spoil heap has gone completely, and light factory units have sprung up. Another has been landscaped; part was sold to a local farmer and now cows graze on its slopes, and part has been turned into a nature reserve where there are woodland walks and a wild life lake. The pit closed in 1989, and soon most of the buildings will also go, but one shaft will be left for ventilation to underground workings which radiate for miles to other pits. Many still work in the mining industry, but now most people work away from the village in a wide variety of jobs in the Barnsley area.

The population of Darfield is about 10,000. There are three primary schools and a comprehensive school. Although few now work here, Darfield still retains a sense of village life, the people being warm-hearted and generous, working together for the benefit of the community.

Darrington 🐝

Darrington village lies three miles south-east of Pontefract. The Domesday Book states that the manor of Darrington was held by Ilbert de Lacy. There were eight ploughs in use, and the taxable value was 100 shillings, with that of a mill three shillings. A 19th century mill is said to stand on the same site but the sails have disappeared.

For hundreds of years Darrington subsisted on agriculture. An unusual crop was teazles, grown for the Yorkshire woollen industry. As late as the 1920s there was no public transport. Local farmers went to market by pony and trap, only the vicar had a car, the gift of a wealthy parishioner. All residents worked on farms, in the woodyard making equipment for farms, for the blacksmith hooping cart wheels, shoeing horses etc, or for the tailor making hunting pink or sports clothes for the gentry or livery for their servants. There was also a tinner whose wife would travel to Leeds to buy large sheets of tin, which she carried home on a rope suspended from her neck. These sheets were made into milk cans, ladling cans, baths etc. The standard price for repairs to any of these items was tuppence.

The village was intersected by the A1, the Great North Road, until the building of a flyover in the late 1970s. Two inns stood back to back at the A1 crossroads and another, the Spread Eagle, was in the centre of the village. In the 1920s an aged resident used to quote, 'The Crown will lose its honour, the Ship will sink, but the Eagle will continue to fly'. Oddly enough this has happened as the first two were demolished when the A1 was widened.

Nowadays few residents work on the land as the village is a pleasant dormitory for surrounding towns and there is much modern development. This can be seen by the increase in population, from 744 in 1871 to now around 1,650.

The church of St Luke and All Saints stands on a hill overlooking the village. It is of Gothic architecture with a Norman tower. The parish register dates from 1567. The church, churchyard, vicarage (now a private residence), orchard, servants' cottages, church house (known as the dovecote) and the tithe barn were all enclosed in a ring fence. Inside the church there is an unusual stair turret with an arcaded gallery attached to the north aisle. It is probably 14th century and may have

St Luke & All Saints, Darrington

been a watching gallery. Four stalls have misericords, the seats of which must be raised to examine the carvings.

A tablet records the death and interment of Solomon and Elizabeth Dupeer or Dupier. His claim to fame, it is suggested, is that in 1704 he betrayed the Spanish garrison and allowed the British to annexe Gibraltar. The Dupeers settled in Pontefract where Elizabeth built the Buttercross on the site of the old cross of St Oswald. In accordance with her husband's wishes she donated gifts of silver to Darrington church after his death.

The estate of the Sotheron-Estcourts, comprising the majority of dwellings and farms, was broken up in 1944, when many residents availed themselves of the opportunity of purchasing their properties. In one form or another there has been a manor house or Hall since the 11th century but rarely has it been occupied by the manor holder. Part of the Hall remains and is occupied but is surrounded by a modern development.

In 1858 a new church school was built; the children being charged two pence per week. This school with its bell tower survives in addition to the recently built school. Outside the church gates is the pinfold where straying cattle were penned. Here also were the village stocks, whipping post and mounting block. Sadly all that remains is the mounting block.

The reading room, paid for by public subscription and opened by Lord Estcourt in 1903, was used exclusively by men. There they could play billiards, darts, dominoes etc. Copies of the *Tatler*, *Sketch* and *Country Life* were donated by the gentry. Now it is owned by the church and used by village organisations. In 1884 a Wesleyan chapel was built for £800, but this is now used for commercial purposes. An earlier chapel stood on Chapel Hill.

The Yorkshire historian, author and poet, J. S. Fletcher, lived in Darrington for a time. The village was featured in two of his books – *Memorials of a Yorkshire Parish* and *When Charles I was King*. His books were illustrated by the Darrington artist Percy Rhodes, who although having no training and being handicapped by having only a thumb and two fingers on his right hand, left an invaluable record of the village with his pen and ink sketches.

The ecclesiastical boundary of Darrington includes the village of Wentbridge. Wentbridge church was built on the edge of Brocodale, the smallest and one of the most beautiful dales in Yorkshire.

Denaby Main 🌿

Approaching Denaby Main from Mexborough, it is apparent that this used to be a coal mining area. Just before the level crossing, on the left hand side of the road, is mounted the preserved wheel from the old Denaby Main pithead. On it is a plaque commemorating the 203 men and boys who, over the years, lost their lives in the mine.

Today the scene is very different from the one when the village of Denaby Main came into existence in 1868. Since medieval times coal has been worked around the village of old Denaby (it was referred to as 'Dennigbye' in 14th century land charters), and, over the years, various ventures proved unsuccessful, until the coming of Denaby Main Colliery Company.

In 1863, work commenced on sinking the two shafts of the projected colliery, which proved to be very difficult. The considerable problems with water took nearly a year to resolve, which was both expensive and time consuming. By the end of 1868, the colliery was fully working on a commercial basis, and by 1869, a manager had been appointed, with a salary of £150 per annum plus a house. The success of the mine was such that, in 1873, his salary was raised to £400 per annum.

Before the coming of the colliery rural Denaby had a population of 203, with most of them living at Old Denaby, a mile away. With the influx of mine workers, the population increased considerably and, in 1868, the Denaby Main Colliery Company began to construct an entire colliery village. The closely packed rows of terraced houses radiated outwards from the pit, and an odd row would cross-cross the others, forming a maze-like structure of houses, roads, narrow passages and 'entries'. They were not built to give much pleasure or comfort to those who inhabited them, and hygiene standards were poor. There was a high mortality rate in children during the 19th and early 20th century, with up to twenty children a week being buried on occasions. The colliery company also built the local schools, the Parish church and the Denaby Main Hotel.

Recruits for the pit came from all over England, Scotland, Ireland and even Portugal – the youngest being 12 and the oldest 66. In addition to colliery employees, people worked at the glassworks, on the roads and railways, waterways and service industries. The former rural agricultural area became one of grime, soot and smoke.

1889 saw the start of the development of Cadeby Main Colliery by the Denaby Main Colliery Company, which began production in 1893. By this time there were 1,000 colliery houses in Denaby, none of which had baths nor outside WCs, only earth closets. Over the years ownership of the collieries passed into other hands, and in 1947 the mining industry was nationalised. Denaby Main Colliery finally closed in 1968, having produced 50 million tons of coal, and in 1986 Cadeby Colliery also closed.

Arthur Dodd – 'Blind Arthur' – was for many years a knocker-up for the miners, going round the village between 4 a.m. and 5 a.m. For a small weekly sum he would rouse them by rattling their bedroom windows with a long pole, which had a fan of wires on the end. This continued until the miner responded that he was awake. All the names, addresses and shifts were retained in Arthur's head. The 'Scissor Grinder' was well known in the area too, though no-one can now remember his name. Together with his lady companion (presumably his wife) he lived rough, and toured the area pushing a converted pram, on which was mounted a millstone grinding wheel, rotated by a foot treadle. A Mr Kane opened a small wooden shop opposite the pit gates, and from here he sold miners cigarettes as they came off their shift. To save them the cost of matches, he even had a candle burning on the counter, so the miners could 'light-up' before they left.

Built in 1900, All Saints church was opened by the Archbishop of York. It was demolished and rebuilt across the road from the original site in 1975. Many materials from the old church were used, and the inside is a lovely mixture of the old and the new. Interestingly, it is the only Parish church to be built in the Sheffield Diocese for about thirty years. Badly damaged by fire in 1977, it was repaired and re-dedicated in 1979. The font, pulpit and some of the stained glass came from the old church, and there is an outstanding brass plaque, engraved with the names of the 88 men who died in the Cadeby Pit Disaster in 1912.

Adjoining the church is the Miners' Memorial Chapel, built in 1989, of bricks salvaged from Cadeby Pit, and it is the only one of its kind in England. Costing over £25,000, much of the work was done by volunteers. Inside there are many mementos of the mining industry – a miner's helmet, lamp, 'snap' (food) box, pit props incorporated in the ceiling, and a one-piece ton of coal from Manvers Main Colliery, encased in the mahogany glass-sided holy table. However, the most spectacular item is half of the wheel from Cadeby Colliery, which weighs 5 tons and spans 19 feet. Behind the wheel is a stained glass window, depicting various mining events over the years. The peace and tranquillity of the chapel is remarked upon by the many visitors who go there, and in May, 1991, the Duchess of York went to see the building.

Over the years the miners' cottages have disappeared, with semi-detached houses and bungalows taking their place, and there are many grassed open spaces.

Denby 🌿

Denby is of very ancient foundation. It is recorded in the Domesday Book as 'Denebi', meaning 'Farmstead of the Danes', and was founded soon after the Danes had conquered York in AD 682. The village has a special mention in the Domesday survey where it is recorded that 'Ibi est vacaria' ('there is a cattle-house') and this is the only mention of its kind in the whole of the Yorkshire survey in 1086.

The church was not the first one in Upper Denby. A chapel of ease was built around 1672 with money given by Godfrey Bosville of nearby Gunthwaite Hall. In 1839 however Bishop Longley visited the parish and found the church in a filthy and ruinous state and ordered it to be demolished and money raised to build a new one, which is the one seen in Upper Denby today.

Over the years there have been three public houses. The Star and the New inn are both now private dwellings, but the George is still a popular meeting place of both old and young alike. Boxing Day must be one of the most popular days of the year. The Rockwood Hunt meet in the pub car park and, as is the custom, the landlord greets the Master of the hunt with the stirrup cup which is filled with a hot punch. This event brings crowds of people from the surrounding areas.

The village also has its own cricket field, football field and sports pavilion. There is a very active Sports and Social Committee. There is a post office cum general store and a butcher's shop in the village.

The School House at Lower Denby was erected as a charity school by Francis Burdett of Denby Hall who gave £200 for the school and poor of Denby. In 1769 this was invested in property and land at Hoylandswaine and let for £12 6s per annum, half of which was to be paid to the schoolmaster for six free scholars. This building was later converted into a private house. Denby Hall is now a working arable and dairy farm.

A family called Blackburn originally owned Papist Hall and, as the name of the building suggests, the owner of this dwelling was linked with Roman Catholicism. Then there is Tenterhouse Farm. A tenter was a frame or machine for stretching cloth to prevent it shrinking whilst drying so this suggests that it was linked with local textiles, possibly weavers' cottages.

During the 1700s there was a blacksmith's forge and what was the Waggon and Horses public house is now a private dwelling. The present public house, the Dunkirk, is a popular place for eating and drinking. Pinfold House has retained the name of the pinfold where straying cattle were rounded up and kept until their rightful owners claimed them and, upon paying a toll, were allowed to take them away.

It is noted that in the late 1660s there were two famous witches in Denby. Records show their names as Susanne Hinchliffe and Anne Shillitoe. The last known witch of whom there is any account was a Betty Roberts who lived in the village in the early days of the 19th century.

Over the years Upper Denby, with a population of approximately 445 people, has expanded and changed from the typical farming community it once was. More recently parts of it have become home to those who commute to the cities for their work. Lower Denby has increased very little and still has a strong community spirit amongst its inhabitants.

Dodworth

Dodworth was known as a mining village and is on the edge of the Pennines. It has the name locally of 'Honest Dodworth'. The story supposedly originated about a Dodworth miner walking home one night having had a drink too many, who decided for a bet that he would climb a lamp-post in the village. He placed his gold watch on the top of the lamp-post, but forgot about it when he climbed down. The next morning he returned sober to find his watch still there. He was so pleased he shouted 'Honest Dodworth', which it is thought still applies today.

In 1974, Dodworth became part of the Barnsley Metropolitan Borough. It is a township of about 5,000 people. It still retains a rural aspect, with farms and green fields on hand. It has a library, health clinic, shops, church, two chapels and three schools, one being a delightful little church school with many social activities, and a proper home from home atmosphere for the very young.

The weavers' cottages on the High Street were used for weaving in the lower rooms. It is recorded that in 1829 riots took place here, when 500 weavers invaded Dodworth from Barnsley, to try to stop Dodworth weavers from under-cutting prices. Part of these cottages has already been demolished and, although a fight was put up to protect the last one, which is at present a newsagent's shop, it is likely that this will be lost to further development.

Coal mining took over from weaving in the mid 1860s, and the village then became a typical mining area, with the sinking of shafts and the building in later years of miners' houses, but again this has all changed since the contraction of the coal industry, bringing substantial unemployment. The houses were sold off and modernised and, almost overnight, the shafts and mining equipment disappeared. At present over the old colliery workings an industrial estate has been developed, and several firms are expected to move into the area, including a Japanese firm. As a result of this big new housing estates are being built, thus increasing dramatically the population of this close-knit community, and diminishing the beautiful rural surroundings.

St John's church, built by public subscription at a cost of £2,518, was consecrated in 1848 by the Bishop of Ripon. Standing nearby is the beautiful stone vicarage, now far too big for modern vicars and their families and, therefore, having been sold.

The Grange is a large house which belonged to the estate of Thomas Thornely Taylor, who instigated the building of the church. His initials, 'TTT', can be seen on several houses in the village, which were built by him for his estate workers. Also nearby is the Lodge at the entrance to Dodworth Hall, the Lodge being the only evidence of the 'great house', which was the centre of garden parties,ox roasts, etc, where the Thornely Taylors lived. The house was eventually bought by the Coal Board and demolished. Dodworth still has the original 'Old Hall', built in 1621, which is the centre of the village. Sadly disfigured by various uses, at the present time it houses a video shop and a dress shop.

There are seven public houses; most are old, with some historical interest. One in particular, the Travellers' inn, was an old coaching house built in 1746. It was here in 1886 that the village policeman was murdered by a poacher, James Murphy, who lived in the cottage attached to the inn. He was tried and hanged in York.

At the crossroads a soldier, appearing ready to defend the village, stands on top of the war memorial commemorating the fallen of two World Wars.

Come what may, Dodworth is a thriving village, and will continue to be so. Because of its easy access to the M1 motorway and railway station, both within its boundaries, travellers from far and near have no difficulty in visiting this warm-hearted community.

Dungworth & Storrs 🌿

When standing on the hill in Dungworth, from any direction, the beauty of the countryside is breathtaking. Nestling in the valley below is Dam Flask, surrounded by the patchwork green of fields and woods – the heart of the country. Ten minutes away by car is the Derbyshire Peak District, and yet it is only seven miles to the centre of Sheffield.

Dungworth is a small village with only 90 houses, and is connected by two lanes to the hamlet of Storrs, which has approximately 23 houses, so the population in this area is quite small. Before the Second World War the names of Gray, Robinson and Harper dominated the village, but, because residential building was not allowed, the sons and daughters of villagers were forced to move away to find alternative housing. Even-

74

tually, in 1956, the Council built ten new homes, and families from outside the area moved in. There are ten farms in the area. Many of the old stone cottages have been modernised inside, all having been fitted with their own septic tanks. It is interesting to note that during the last 20 years only three houses have been allowed to be built.

In 1935, a huge ball of fire struck three cottages. Some people said that it was a thunderbolt, but whatever it was it caused a great deal of damage, and nearly killed a young boy. It lifted two men and six pigs into the air, burst a water main, and smashed windows in every house in the village. Blue flames were seen to run along the length of the telephone wires, and everyone was terrified by the enormous crash that shook everything. A similar experience was to be repeated years later, when a land mine was dropped in a field at the back of Padley Farm during the Second World War. Half a mile away down the hill from Dungworth is the reservoir, Dam Flask. This was protected by wires and pylons, plus floating barrage balloons to stop dive bombing by German aircraft. One night an enemy plane did manage to penetrate the defences, and dropped two land mines, one falling into the dam, the other into the fields near the cow sheds, destroying Padley Farm buildings, but thankfully no-one was injured.

From 1961 to 1969 the villagers raised money to re-build the old wooden 'bandroom', bought in 1911 and used by the village brass band for rehearsals. Those were the days! The time of real do-it-yourself entertainment and turkey dinners. Years earlier, in the 1950s, the village Methodist Chapel was also altered. A new schoolroom and porch were built on, and inside a 'face lift'. The pot-bellied stove was removed, the organ re-built, and a new portable pulpit installed. The villagers began to get used to raising money for different aspects of community life, and can now look at their achievements with pride. These include the Chapel and the new village hall, which is the centre for many social activities.

In 1964 the Parish Council granted Dungworth a public playground, in a field given by the local firm of Thomas Marshall & Sons. It has a pavilion with changing rooms, and is landscaped with trees and bushes around the children's playing area. When the field was first opened, Dungworth had two football teams playing regularly, but now, with no football team of their own, the field is rented out to Sheffield clubs.

The Royal Hotel is next door to the Chapel, and is the only public house in Dungworth. Between the wars it was run by the Green family, and had a thriving cricket team. 'Knurr and Spell' was played in a field behind the Royal, this being a game played with 'potties', which were placed on a trap and released into the air, the player hitting the 'pottie' with a stick shaped like a hockey stick. Even now you can dig up these little ceramic balls when gardening.

The 'Sermons' (Sunday School Anniversary) was the yearly event in the Chapel calendar which was excitedly looked forward to. Hymns, choruses and anthems were practised weeks before the first Sunday in July, and all the singers and musicians from the village and the Churches around came to augment the choir and orchestra. Platforms were put up in the Church and in Greenfold Farmyard, and almost every house in the village had singers to dinner and tea. People came from miles around to see and hear this joyous outdoor service.

One tradition that is still carried on in this village is 'Kaking Night', which is held on the 1st November. At one time children used to go from door to door, but nowadays both children and adults dress up and wear masks, and are judged in the pub. In days gone by, when the children did go from door to door, the neighbours had the job of guessing who was who, and the 'Kakers' were rewarded with a copper or two, which was spent on fireworks.

Dunsville

The small but developing village of Dunsville, five miles from Doncaster, is situated on a slight ridge overlooking the southernmost edge of the historic Hatfield Chase, once a hunting ground of kings. To the east there is a view of the moors and part of the countryside known as the Levels.

Prior to 1920, it was an estate community, the 'big house' being Park Lane Hall. The hamlet had mainly belonged to the three estate farms and, in addition, there were a few cottages and two houses for the chauffeur and groom. After the First World War, Mr E. Dunn, Manager of the Co-operative Society at Hatfield, developed the areas with the aid of a government grant.

The houses were originally occupied by people moving out of the Sheffield area with a view to their retirement. The rent for a two bedroomed house was five shillings a week, and for a three bedroomed house seven shillings and sixpence, but there were restrictions. No dogs were allowed, no alteration to be made to the external paintwork, which was a uniform black and white, and no alterations to fences or gates unless special permission had been granted by Mrs Dunn. The restrictions continued until the mid-1960s, when tenants were given the option of buying their own property, the remainder being sold to a property company. Since the Second World War, private houses have been added to the original ones, and today estates are being added to extend the northern side of the village.

Park Lane Hall was still occupied privately by Lord Chetwynd. His title was bestowed on him for his munitions production at Chilwell, Nottinghamshire, in the First World War, and it was at this time that the Hall was renamed Wyndthorpe Hall.

After the Second World War it was taken over by the Doncaster Co-operative Society, who sub-let the Hall but retained the farm for dairy production. Later, it changed from a private residence to a residential nursery, but is now a private residential home for the elderly.

There is a group of cottages with the interesting name of 'A Cluster of Nuts'. As far back as 1920 the front of these cottages had hazel bushes. This may have given them the name, but they are marked on an 18th century map of the area, and the name is believed to have come from those days.

In 1920 the first quarry, owned by Mrs Dunn and developed by Mr Dunn, supplied the sand for the village building projects. The entry to that quarry was between the present day post office and the bungalow that the Dunns lived in at that time. Parallel to this, a second quarry was developed, being worked by Mr D. C. Green (a road is named after him). The sand from this quarry was used to fill sand bags in the defence of Sheffield from 1940 onwards.

Water for the village and immediate vicinity is from a bore hole, just outside the village boundary.

Although there is a flourishing Methodist church, which has a popular Boys and Girls Brigade, there is no Anglican church or Catholic church closer than two miles. There is a pub, working men's club and a village hall, which is used for a variety of activities. This was built in the 1970s on land donated by Kenneth Dunn, the money being raised by the residents of Dunsville.

Some of the villagers who have lived in Dunsville for many years have memories of it growing from those first few houses to the present flourishing community.

East Bierley ❧

The village of East Bierley is perched on a hilltop at the edge of Kirklees, on the Bradford border. Though only three miles from Bradford, people have always experienced the greatest difficulty in finding East Bierley and this, perhaps, helps to account for the way it has kept its very real village identity.

The centre of the village is the triangular village green with its stocks, and in springtime a beautiful array of daffodils, crocuses and trees bright with pink and white blossom. Around the green are clustered the school, Methodist chapel, post office, a row of cottages with lovely gardens, and a much older cottage which was formerly the dame school. A former owner, demolishing an inner wall, discovered a 'whipping post' which no doubt had been put to good use.

The oldest thing in the village is the 'Cup and Saucer', beside the pond. These two large stones certainly look like a cup and saucer, but the top stone reputedly once had a cross on top. This is said to have been erected by a Norman lord of the manor, in memory of a peasant who had been killed by his horse. The cross gave its name to Cross House, built in the early 17th century, which stands beside it, and also to the pond. In olden times, religious services were held around the cross, and in bad weather, inside Cross House.

The age of the stocks is uncertain, but one five year old boy at school thought he knew. His description ran 'The stocks are very old, but I do not think they are as old as my teacher'. Beside the Methodist chapel is an old well, last used in a drought in the early 1930s.

Names, too, reflect the village's past. The name of the northern end is The Marsh. A block of flats is Well Green Court, for it was built on the old well green which was no doubt a meeting place for village women. Bierley Bar, at the top end of the village, recalls Victorian times when a bar was placed across the road every evening to discourage 'off-comers', especially would-be suitors! The Granny Croft, a field path, no doubt recalls that this was an old lady's piece of land. Local people always refer to Raikes Lane as 'going down the Ginnies'. Here, a notorious lady named Ginny kept a tavern, very popular with the men of the village but not their wives! As for Cliff Hollins, who gave his name to a lane, no-one is sure whether he was a man or a geographical feature.

The village is rightly proud of its sporting facilities, which include a golf course, football ground and cricket club. The village won the National Village Cricket Competition at Lords in 1979, a day when very few people were left in the village. For younger children there is the recreation ground, but even more popular is the pond, with an abundance of frogs, newts and small fishes in summer, and opportunities for sliding and skating in winter.

Every village has its ghost, and East Bierley is no exception. In the 19th century, Manor Farm was owned by Widow Kaye. Moanings and rattling of keys in the upstairs rooms convinced everyone that the farmhouse was haunted by a boggart. Various members of the clergy were invited along to pray for its speedy departure. The boggart, however, proved singularly resistant to prayer, and the noises continued. One day a neighbour visiting the farmhouse, gave it as his opinion that 'that boggart wants shooting', picked up a shotgun and fired up the chimney. The farm still stands; the boggart was never heard again.

It should not be thought that this is a village which lives in the past. The school and many houses have been attractively modernised, and new buildings blend well with the old. Nowhere is this seen to better advantage than at the Methodist chapel, which retains its Victorian stone exterior, but inside it has been modernised, making it both practical and beautiful, and allowing for five new houses to form part of its building. The village church, St Luke's, is notable for the beauty and superb modern craftsmanship of its internal woodwork, designed and created by Jack Broughton, a local man.

East Hardwick 🦢

East Hardwick is a pleasant rural village just off the A639 road out of Pontefract. The village is situated to the west of the old toll road which was built around 1819. It consists of one winding street down to what was once moorland. There are several outlying farms and three in the village. It is a mixed community consisting of business, professional and retired people. In the past it was purely agricultural, but like everything else 'times have changed'.

The first of its famous inhabitants was Stephen Cawood, who was a well to do farmer and a staunch Parliamentarian. He was living in the village in 1637 at Cawood House, which was sadly demolished in 1964. Stephen Cawood gave 84 acres of land to six trustees to sell and the funds thereof to support the Cawood Trust. As he requested, a school for the poor children was built.

Another famous person who also lived in Cawood House was J. S. Fletcher, author, poet and historian. He wrote *When Charles I was King* – the story of the siege of Pontefract Castle.

At the turn of the century Miss K. Neilson who lived at Hundill Hall was very benevolent towards the villagers. She paid for the church choir to go on an annual visit to the seaside, and invited all the children from the village up to the Hall for a Christmas party. The Hall grounds were used for garden parties in the summertime. In fact Hundill Hall was the hub of the village.

One custom which is still celebrated is Plough Sunday. This is held in January and, after the church service, the WI prepare a Farmhouse Tea in the village hall. St Stephen's church is very beautiful although it is only just over a hundred years old. The Archbishop of York consecrated the new church in 1874. The church bells were rung by Mr W. Smith, three bells rung by one man! Each spring the churchyard is a carpet of daffodils.

The village has several well preserved buildings. There is a lovely Queen Anne cottage, one of a row at the top of the village. The well stands at the junction of the village street and the main road. It is a roofed building with a carved wooden surround, having the head of a griffin at each corner. In the past the water was thought to have curative powers. Close beside the well once stood Hardwick Hall, referred to in the archives as the Manor of Hardwick. This fell into decay and was demolished in 1960. Manor Farm stands close by today.

On the main road there is a private residence which is still known as School House. At one time this was a Roman Catholic private boarding school. Sadly the school in the village was closed in 1986.

East Hardwick village hall is now the centre of all activities that take place in the village. There is plenty to choose from; weekly whist drives, dances, a bell ringing group and the WI.

East Keswick Village

East Keswick 🦚

The parish of East Keswick lies north of Leeds in gently undulating countryside. The village itself is of considerable antiquity. It appears in the Domesday Book as 'Chesinc' or 'Chesing' under Tor, the Saxon lord.

In 1739 one estate was bought by Henry Lascelles. Edwin, son of Henry Lascelles, became the first Lord Harewood. He built Harewood House in 1759 and the estate remained in the family for over 200 years. The Harewood rent book in 1796 details 15 farms, four shops, beer houses, a smithy, a meeting house, and a Quaker burial ground. In 1950 much of the Harewood land and property in East Keswick and the surrounding villages had to be sold to meet death duties.

Lime was first quarried in East Keswick in 1700. In the 19th century East Keswick was famed for the quality of its limestone and flagstone, both being found in large quantities very near the surface. Vast amounts of the lime were prepared and sold to farmers as top dressing. Freestone from the quarries was particularly suitable for building as it had the property of hardening through long exposure to air. Examples of roofs made from large old local flagstones still exist in the village today.

Farming has continued down the ages. There are still eight farms within the parish – arable, dairy, sheep, and also a stud farm. But in recent years some of the farmhouses have been sold off, the surrounding land being leased or sold separately for cultivation.

Methodism flourished in the village in the 18th century and in 1792, following dispensation from the Archbishop of York, a chapel was opened. In the mid 19th century Joseph Lawrence ran a college in East Keswick for the training of young men into the Methodist ministry and he sent ministers all over the world. When Joseph Lawrence died, his students – past and present – determined to build a chapel to his memory in East Keswick. That chapel was opened in the village in 1891.

The church of St Mary Magdalen was built by subscription in 1856. It was built in local stone, which was dressed free of charge by the local stonemason, and was opened in 1857. A Sunday school was started in 1814, and in 1851 a day school was opened which by 1872 was being financed by the Earl of Harewood. It outgrew its original building and in 1914 moved into larger premises.

In 1876 the North Eastern Railway opened a line near the village and this allowed direct running between Leeds and Harrogate and between Leeds and Church Fenton. Sadly, the line was closed in 1961 and so cars and buses became all-important.

Mr Moon, a grocer, built a large shop in the village in 1861. It was three storeys high and there was also a row of houses for his employees. Deliveries to the surrounding villages were made by horse and dray.

The advent of the motor car saw East Keswick become popular as a place to drive out to. The Duke of Wellington, the Star, and the Travellers Rest on Harewood Avenue were and still are well known in Leeds as good rendezvous places.

After the Second World War the first small estate of new houses was built. The village has increased in size over the last 20 years with the addition of many large houses and this has tended to alter its character. The old cottages are being rebuilt and extended, local shops are closing – now only two remain. Most of the residents travel to their work in the cities. The excellent village school was closed in 1990 and children now have to travel to school in Bardsey or to Harewood.

Nevertheless the community spirit still exists. The magnificent village hall was funded over many years by local people and opened in 1986. It is in demand from many organisations. It offers luxurious surroundings, modern kitchen facilities and a snooker room with two tables which is very popular. The badminton hall is in regular use. The cricket team has its pitch and small pavilion within the village and the hockey team plays nearby. East Keswick is a thriving semi-rural community.

Eccleshill

Eccleshill was mentioned in the Domesday Book as Egleshill. Eccleshill's main industry was the manufacture of woollen cloths and the handlooms did not go out of existence until 1870, a good ten years after most of the mills were mechanised.

There are still quite a lot of the three and four-storey weavers' cottages in the village today. Another industry was Manor Pottery. It did not stay in business as a pottery for very long, but carried on as a brick works. At one time there were about seven mills in Eccleshill, which was quite a lot for a small village.

A Mechanics Institute was opened on Good Friday, 26th March 1869, for the education of the working class members of the village. In May 1872 the first board school was opened, in rooms formerly occupied by the Congregational school.

Eccleshill was a very musical place at this time. It had its own brass band, any number of choirs and an orchestral and madrigal society. Not many out of town communities would have been able to boast musicians capable of performing a Mozart quintet, as Eccleshill did in 1873. The flute player was 14 years of age Master Fawcett – a member of one of the most remarkable families in the country. The founding father was Tom Fawcett, a handloom weaver, who came from Horsforth in 1840 to conduct one of Eccleshill's chapel choirs. He played the cello and sang with Bradford Festival Choral Society when it appeared before Queen Victoria at Buckingham Palace. For four years Thomas's son Joseph, who played trombone and organ, conducted a brass band belonging to another mill, in another village. Sir Thomas Beecham paid a generous tribute to Verdi Fawcett, the leader of his orchestra. He drew attention to this family of musicians with Christian names borrowed from the great composers; two Handels, a Joseph Haydn, a Weber, a Mendelssohn and two Verdis. There is still a Mendelssohn Fawcett living in Eccleshill.

The cycling fraternity will be well versed with the name of Baines Cycles, which were made in Eccleshill. Its business was started in 1897 and they ceased operating in 1981. One of the models they built was called 'Baines Super Responsive'. They also made models for racing in the international TTs in the Isle of Man. They were popular with cyclists all over the world.

The Mechanics Institute is now a youth and community centre and a very busy place. Eccleshill has grown, there are now private housing estates and council estates. Old mills are now used by many small businesses. One mill was knocked down and there is an old people's home on the site. The large recreation ground, where local football teams meet to play their matches, was a quarry at one time, but was filled in and grassed over.

One of the village's most famous citizens is the artist David Hockney, born and brought up in Eccleshill, who now lives in America. His mother still lives in the family home.

Edenthorpe 🦡

Edenthorpe is approximately four miles from Doncaster along the very busy Thorne Road, which divides the village in two. Although there is a link road to the M18 running along the back of the village, which takes all the very heavy traffic which used to make crossing the road very hazardous, the road is now so busy, largely due to the big supermarket built a few years ago, that a set of traffic lights have been installed. The supermarket occupies fields used for generations for growing food crops and on which hares used to play watched by residents waiting at the nearby bus stop.

Passing through Edenthorpe there seems nothing of great interest. But, under its original name of Stirestorp (later to become Tristorp and then Streethorpe), it dates back to the Domesday Book!

The Swift family made Streethorpe their residence in the 1600s. Sir Robert Swift is said to have planted the many yew trees growing around the house to supply his people with bows when he was the bowbearer to Hatfield Chase. Streethorpe was held as a manor of Coningsborough Castle by a rent of three bushels of rye.

During the late 19th century the Hall became the residence of Lord Auckland, the son of William George Eden, and 'Edenthorpe' was adopted as a new name for the district.

Lord Auckland was a collector of tropical trees and many were to be seen in the pleasure gardens and parklands. However, in 1928 the Park disappeared when the land was taken for building. In 1922 a fire had gutted the central block of the Hall, which was consequently demolished. The north wing was converted into a house and flats and the south into a house for Lord Montcrief. This wing was later used as a club library and from 1959 as an infants school The north wing was later demolished.

The central section of the hall which was burnt down was said to be haunted by the ghost of a daughter of the owner who lost her life in the fire. Children in the 1930s imagined they had seen her and she was known as the White Lady.

St Oswald's at Kirk Sandall was the parish church and Edenthorpe had a mission hall in Cedric Road, later used as an infants school. St Oswald's is now closed except for one service each year and has been declared an ancient monument.

Up to the 1950s the former lodge of the Hall was used as post office, general store and newsagency. There was also a grocer's shop in Thorne Road and an off-licence in Cedric Road, plus travelling butchers and greengrocers. The Thorne Road shop is now the library with a chemist next door and the off-licence is a Spar shop. The lodge shop was pulled down and two groups of shops built with varying uses.

From the 1950s on, many houses were built, raising the population from a few hundred in 1931 to around 5,000 now. The Manor Farm, where eggs and milk could be purchased daily, was surrounded by houses, but was saved from demolition and declared a listed building.

From being a village with no public house, in the 1950s a club was built, then the Ridgewood Hotel, then the Hollybush and a large house was converted into the Beverley Court Hotel. The Eden Arms is the most recent addition, adjacent to the supermarket and a new housing estate. The mission hall was demolished and an excellent community centre erected on the site in 1986.

When the village was small the people were friendly and welcoming. They worked in the two local glassworks, the mines, on the railways and at the Plant Works, at Bemburgs (now ICI), International Harvesters (now Cases), Parkinsons and Nuttalls sweet makers and in banks, offices and shops. Residents still work in the factories and works still in existence, although many newcomers are white collar workers. Two industrial estates, one at Kirk Sandall and one on the outskirts of Edenthorpe, provide a variety of jobs.

Edenthorpe is still a friendly, pleasant place in which to live. There are still fields, bridle paths and plantations of beautiful trees in which to walk, a good bus service to Doncaster with its very good shopping facilities and one of the best markets in England. The splendid old yew trees still grow around the Edenthorpe Hall School and in some gardens, as reminders of the bowmen of old. They are all under preservation orders so should still be there for our children and grandchildren to admire.

Elsecar ✵

The village is approximately 7 miles from Rotherham, 8 miles from Barnsley, and 10 miles from Sheffield, and has a railway station with a good service to outlying towns and cities. A little off the beaten track, it is still quiet and peaceful, and just a mile away is Wentworth. Elsecar and Wentworth are two closely connected villages. The buildings on the present day 'Elsecar Heritage Trail' were sponsored by the Earls of Fitzwilliam, and visitors are always welcome.

Elsecar is situated in a lovely valley, surrounded by farms, woodlands and hills. It has a reservoir and a lovely park, and was extremely popular in the 1930s with visitors from Sheffield – a day trip to 'Elsecar by the Sea' on special excursion trains was a firm family favourite.

The conservation area at Elsecar is one of the most important historically in South Yorkshire. The fine stone cottages were originally built for the workmen, and have been strictly maintained by the Earl Fitzwilliam Estates Department. In its day Elsecar Colliery was a modern and special place in which to work, and miners came from all over the country to work there.

Elsecar reservoir, completed in 1785, was constructed to provide water for the canal, which originally went as far as the bridge in the village. It was filled from Knoll Beck, a little stream at the bottom of Burying Lane. The canal was extended to reach the Colliery in 1799, and was part of the Rother and Dove canal network.

The miners' lodging house is mid 19th century, designed by a famous architect, John Carr, and provided accommodation for twenty two single men. This has been converted into a smart block of flats, retaining the dressed stone, slate roof, sash windows, and the main door has the same elegant fanlight. The Old Row, built in 1795, comprised 15 miners' cottages, each having a long garden in the front, and a pig-sty and latrine at the rear. Station Row has ten cottages of two and three storeys, built of stone in 1800, with tiled roofs. In Reform Row, the rent was two shillings (10p) a week in 1837 for a cottage, each having a garden and pig-sty.

All the wheat in the district was milled at the Elsecar Flour Mill, built for the Earl Fitzwilliam in 1841. This mill continued to produce stone-ground flour until a few years ago.

After the Chapels, Holy Trinity Church was the last place of worship to be built in the village in 1843. It took two years to build, and cost his

Miners' Lodging House, Elsecar

85

Lordship £2,500. The Milton Hall, used for dances, weddings, meetings, and various other functions, was originally built as a Market Hall. In the Elsecar Heritage complex (in the old National Coal Board workshops), is the original Earl Fitzwilliam's private station. All his guests used to arrive there by train, and be transported by carriage to his mansion at Wentworth. Another of Elsecar's important historical items is the Newcomen Beam Engine, which was installed around 1795, and is one of the few of its kind in the country to remain on its original site. Until 1923, it was operated continuously for draining local mines, and at its maximum output the steam engine could pump out 400 gallons of water a minute.

Emley ☙

Emley village, like many others, is now a mixture of old and new, ancient and modern. The last 20 years have seen the building of three or four modern housing estates. Up to that time, except for a few local authority houses, the village had changed little over many years. It is now a rural village with, as the estate agents claim, unparalleled views and many amenities, yet near large urban areas which are easily reached by good roads. The famous TV mast can be seen for miles around. There is an excellent first school and a football team of national repute, with a floodlit ground.

The village had its origin in very early times. The earliest form of settlement cannot be dated, but the area contains evidence of early man in the form of artefacts of Ice Age hunters. There is little evidence of Bronze Age occupation, but the surrounding district contains quite a number of Iron Age earthworks and Brigantic and Roman coins have been found within three miles of Emley. Any evidence of occupation in Emley itself has probably been destroyed by extensive open-cast mining.

Surprisingly, the manor of Emley, after the Conquest, seems to have still belonged to one Godric rather than to a Norman, and his descendants, the Fitzwilliams, continued to be lords of the manor until 1516. It passed through marriage to the Savile family who still retain it, and live locally to this day.

By 1171 Godric had granted land in Emley to the Cistercian monks of Byland. Later concessions were granted by Sir William Fitzwilliam for the mining of iron stone and the pasturing of sheep. The charter still exists and remains of the bell pits for the extraction of ore can still be seen. Emley was granted a royal charter in 1253 to hold a weekly market, and an annual five day fair from 3rd May. Here the monks were able to sell their smelted iron and their wool. The remains of the market cross still stands in the centre of the village. Emley Feast is still celebrated in May when older residents have visitors and put on a special tea, and the cross is always painted with a new coat of whitewash.

In the 17th century iron was dug and smelted, coal mines were sunk, joiners, wheelwrights, blacksmiths, tailors, weavers, tanners, shoemakers, even a hatter and many innkeepers, all plied their trades. Farming flourished and in 1842 the population numbered 1,575. After that time the population decreased because the new turnpikes bypassed Emley, formerly on the main road to Lancashire. Local towns in the valleys developed their industries. Today the mine is closed and while farming is the major land use locally, most of the villagers go out of the village to work. Only three shops, including the post office, serve the village and only two inns remain.

The church stands in a commanding position in the village, and dates from the 14th century, although built into the walls are stones from earlier churches of Norman times. Legend has it that the church was to have been built on the site of an earlier wooden church but during the night the fairies moved the stones to the present site. The church contains a Norman tympanum, medieval grave slabs and interesting memorials and windows.

A number of interesting large houses dating from the 17th century still exist and numerous old cottages, one with the inscription 'Look to thy house in every degree. As thy getting is let thy spending bee'. Some recently demolished bore the sign of the Knights Hospitallers who used them as a hostel and owned land here. Their cross is now built into the churchyard wall.

In 1826 a certain man sold his wife at Emley Cross for two half crowns. Many old customs still survive, but fortunately not that one. The consolidated charities, which include many old bequests for the benefit of the poor of the parish, still make twice yearly payments to old people and deserving causes. A very successful Agricultural Show, which takes place every August, started as a village flower show in 1877.

The village has thus developed from a small agriculturally orientated community with even its own workhouse and stocks, to a dormitory village largely commuter occupied, with farming and service employment in the village the only local involvement, but still with character and local pride.

Farnley Tyas ❦

Farnley Tyas is situated on the edge of the Pennines in West Yorkshire. First mentioned in the Domesday Book of 1086, it was then called Fereleia. Tyas is a family name from the le Tyeis who held land in the neighbourhood from the 13th century.

Farnley Tyas is noted for its scenic beauty comprising meadows and woodland, vernacular buildings of local stone, wild flowers and birds. It is especially beautiful at Whitsuntide when the woodlands are carpeted with bluebells. Castle Hill, about a mile north-west of the village, stands 900 ft above sea level and the panoramic view from there is breathtaking.

Farnley village was much larger in the 19th century. During this period the maximum population of 900 was recorded. The cottage industry of cloth-making was prevalent. History records weavers, cloth finishers and dyers, and there are still examples of weavers' cottages to be seen. Farnley mill, in 1794, was used for fulling and scribbling.

The main occupation today is dairy farming, the farms being tenanted. The landowner was the Earl of Dartmouth until quite recently, when it was sold to a local family (Sykes). Around 1923 there were as many as 30 farms in and around the village, each having fields at all points of the compass, so that the good land was shared out. Today, there are only five farms and though the land has been reallocated, each farmer still has fields in different directions.

St Lucius' church was a gift of the lord of the manor, the fourth Earl of Dartmouth; the first church in Almondbury parish to be erected by private benevolence. The foundation stone was laid in 1838 and it was completed in 1840. The church spire can be seen for miles around.

Woodsome Hall lies about one mile south from the village centre. This Elizabethan Hall belonged to the Kaye-Dartmouth family. Their motto was 'Kynne Kynde Knowne Kepe' – know and cherish your family and friends. In the 18th century Capability Brown designed a grand setting for the Hall. The present residents are Woodsome Golf Club.

The Golden Cock inn is a listed building, parts of which are thought to be over 400 years old. The bowling club lies some 200 yards down Woodsome Road from the Golden Cock. It was originally a cricket ground. The main building is a wooden structure which is a hospital ward from the First World War. It is often used for social events by the villagers, using it as a kind of village hall.

The Mollicarr Sing is an annual event on Whit Sunday, first held in 1900. It was started by the Zion chapel, Almondbury. The walk starts at 7.30 am, mainly through the Mollicarr, with the singing of hymns at allotted places throughout the walk. It is very informal and everyone is welcome. The woods are at their best; new green foliage and birds in full song.

There have been many characters in the village. One old gentleman, living to a great age, lived on the outskirts of the village. He used to stop strangers to ask them the way to Farnley Tyas, thereby engaging them in conversation, and more often than not found out all their business. An old lady inhabitant used to consider the village supplies her own, and was frequently seen collecting wood for her fire; and potatoes, turnips etc from other people's stocks!

Farnley Tyas has been a green belt area for many years; except for some old people's bungalows and a few council houses, very little building has been allowed. This has resulted in an ageing community. The population now is around 300. The landowners of Farnley Tyas, in recent years, have been given permission to sell the farmers' barns. They are also selling houses which have been tenanted, when they become empty. They have been converted into executive-type housing, much altering the character of the village.

Farsley

Farsley is situated midway between Leeds and Bradford. It formed part of the ancient parish of Calverley and is referred to in the Domesday Book as a manor held by the Saxon Archill. It was originally spelt Fersellei(a) and has gone through various changes to reach the present spelling. It is thought to originate from the Old English 'Fyrs' – a furze of gorse and 'Leah' – a lea or meadow, pasture or open country. It is probable that the village would have been a settlement in 'a clearing with gorse bushes'. After the Black Death, in the late 14th century, a poll tax recorded that there were only 70 people in Farsley, of them only 16 were over the age of 16 years.

Farsley had a long tradition of domestic wool manufacturing which supplemented income gained from agricultural holdings. The homestead or the farmstead was the 'factory' and all family members and apprentices lived together and shared the various duties. Houses had workrooms in the upper storeys for looms, warping, spinning etc. The low living rooms were used as warehouses and the kitchens kept oil and ware and other materials used in the manufacture of cloth. Some of the houses in Farsley still bear evidence of where hand looms were kept.

The earliest known cloth manufacturer in Farsley was John Gaunt, born in 1588. Since his time the Gaunt family have carried on in unbroken succession the trade of cloth manufacturing, now in the hands of the tenth generation. The present day mill of Reuben Gaunt & Sons Ltd still manufactures high quality worsted cloths. With the decline of the woollen industry many of the mills are now used as industrial units with the exception of Reuben Gaunt & Sons Ltd and Hainsworths, on the Farsley border, who are world renowned for their billiard table cloths.

Farsley's most famous son was Samuel Marsden, born in 1764. He was the first missionary to the Maoris in New Zealand, but he is best remembered as the first person to bring wool to this area. It was the beginning of the vast trade which sprang up between Australasia, with its great sheep farms, and the Yorkshire woollen mills. A window in the parish church and an obelisk in the churchyard are in memory of him. In 1982 an 'epic trans-globe dash' brought twelve wool fleeces into the village to be sold at a special charity auction. From the shearing of the sheep in New Zealand to the Samuel Marsden Memorial Garden where the auction was held took 41 hours and three minutes and so earned Farsley a place in the Guinness Book of Records.

The first Baptist chapel was built in 1777 adjacent to Bagley beck, which then ran with pure clean water and in which they used to baptize new converts. The chapel was replaced nearly 100 years later by one at Farsley Green which was then the centre of Farsley. The site of Farsley church was given by Thomas Thornhill, the lord of the manor of Calverley. Building began in 1842 and it became a parish church when by Act of Parliament Farsley was constituted as an independent new parish.

Schooling was sporadic and in the early 19th century children as young as six and seven were in full time employ. However around this time Farsley had a dame school for young children in the home of Mrs Mary Whitaker, and a boys school called Killerby's academy. These were superseded by schools run by the Baptists, Methodists and Anglicans. For financial reasons some of these had to close but others were absorbed into the system which has led to the two infant, two junior and one comprehensive schools which service Farsley today.

Farsley now is a thriving community and with the building of houses the population has increased greatly since the early days. The busy shopping street caters for all needs and coach parties visit to take advantage of the craft and mill shops. Part of Sunnybank Mills is now the studio home of Yorkshire Television's *Emmerdale Farm*.

Finningley 🌿

Once part of a Royal hunting ground, and mostly owned by Cornelius Vermuyden, who drained land in the area during the 17th century, Finningley is a small village lying eight miles south of Doncaster, on the borders of Nottinghamshire, Lincolnshire and South Yorkshire.

A unique feature is the five village greens, the main one having a duck pond, with weeping willows. The village hall was originally a barn, converted into the school about 1836, when the children used the graveyard as their playground. In the 1960s a new school was built, and the hall is now used by the community for all the events held in the village.

The beautiful Norman church of St Oswald has a rectors list dating from 1293. It has many interesting facets, one of which is remnants of glass depicting John the Baptist, above the east window, which date from 1475–1500. Three fragments of earlier glass are also in this window, and comprise a yellow ochre roundel and two pink diamonds. Incorporated in the (1885) porch are a number of stone coffin lids, the incomplete symbols denoting an axe for a woodsman, a sword for a soldier, and shears for a wool merchant.

In the 17th century, the Harvey family owned most of the land in the area. They can be traced back to Robert FitzHerve, who came over with William the Conqueror. The Harvey Arms and Harvey Close bear their name.

The other public house, the Horse and Stag, was a Grade II listed building, but was demolished despite the protests of the local people. The following extract from the parish register shows how this pub, together with others in the area, came by its name:

'These are to certify that I William Ronley of Burton upon Statber, in the County of Lincoln, was parish clerk of Finningley when the Rev Mr Branardiston was the rector of the same; and was an eye witness of the following transaction which happened as I remember. In or about the month of July in the year of our Lord 1707, vis:- Zechariah Botton, riding with his gun on Mr Branardiston's bay horse into Auckley cott field, found five stags herded about 200 yards from the bottom of the long hedge. He fired on them disabling one in the hinder parts, then quitting his horse he caught the stag by the hind leg and called for Jara Wood and myself (who were not far off) for help, but on the stag struggling and braying ye horse took him by the neck and beat him with his fore feet till he lay still. Then we took him alive, layed him on the horse and carried him to the parsonage house at Finningley, into the little court before the kitchen door, where he was killed and dressed by the order of John Harvey of Ichwell-bury Esq who was then present and had given us an order to go about the said transactions. The truth of this I am ready to attest upon oath if required.
Witness my hand this 25th day of June 1739. Wm Ronley.'

The post office has been in the Clarke family for five generations, and they have a wealth of information about this lovely village. The modern post office is approximately 50 years old, with the old post office now a Chinese take-away.

The Royal Air Force came to the village in the mid 1930s. This caused drastic changes in the area, with open fields being turned into runways and hangars. With the larger bombers, it became necessary to demolish the Harvey Hall to make bigger and better runways. An Air Show takes place annually at Finningley, with spectacular flying displays.

Firbeck 🌿

Firbeck is first mentioned in 12th century records as Fritebec, which could mean a clearing in a wood by a stream. Indeed Firbeck is sandwiched between two streams, but is now surrounded by fields rather than woodland, although the pattern of woodland has not changed greatly over the past 150 years.

Although nearby Roche Abbey would have had some influence on Firbeck, from the time of Elizabeth I until this century it was dominated by the Firbeck Hall and Park Hill estates, both of which had their mansions and Home Farms within the village.

The Black Lion Inn, Firbeck

The owner of Firbeck Hall in c1550 was William West, who was Chief Steward of the manor of Sheffield when Mary Queen of Scots was held there. He was a lawyer and famous for his legal writings, which contain vivid descriptions of witches and crimes. In 1935 the Hall became a very fashionable country club, with a swimming pool (now the sunken garden), golf course and aerodrome. The Prince of Wales flew in and famous entertainers of the day were guests. During the Second World War it became an annexe to Sheffield hospitals and then a miners' rehabilitation centre before its take-over by the NHS. It is due to close shortly. There are good specimen trees and a nature trail in the grounds.

Park Hill (originally called Gowkhill, the hall of the hill of the cuckoo) was the home of the St Legers. Legend has it that the first 'Leger' race was run in the large oval field still known as The Racecourse. The first proper 'Leger' was run at Doncaster in 1778. The Park Hill Stakes race was named after the house which Col A. St Leger bought c1761. In 1909 the estate was sold and the house became a girls school. Between the wars it was used as a village centre before being demolished in 1935. The original stables, brewery and cottages still survive, but the ornamental ponds are overgrown and the magnificent garden walls have recently been demolished. A good ice house remains and is listed.

The 19th century estate village was quite self sufficient, the census returns listing a blacksmith, butcher, carpenter, carter, shoemaker, miller, tailor, weaver, schoolteacher, publican and shopkeeper. Now all that is left besides houses are the church, the Black Lion pub, the social club, the village hall and a red telephone box.

At the village centre is the church of St Martin, rebuilt in 1828 in the beautiful magnesian limestone of the district. The style could be called Normanesque. Inside are the memorials to the families of the estates, a notable chancel screen, and a list of incumbents from 1646. Outside are interesting gravestones, including those of Isabel and James Robinson whose ages total 220 years. Many of the stones are now illegible. The main bells in the tower are no longer run, but a set of tubular bells are used. The figure over the entrance is St Peter, to whom the church was originally dedicated.

The social club occupies what was the school, which was opened c1820 and closed in 1938. It had close bonds with the church and Hall, and the old school log makes fascinating reading, sometimes hilarious, at other times pathetic, giving a bird's eye view of life 100 years ago.

During the Second World War the village was virtually taken over by the RAF, the Airfield, as it is still called, being the home of a squadron of light aircraft. The hangar is now used as an implement store and huts can still be seen in Stubbings Wood.

Firbeck has two ghost legends, both about girls who jumped into the mill dam (now Lake House Pond). One, the daughter of William West, reputedly drowned herself when her lover, Sir Ralph Knight, was slain in the Dark Walk, an avenue of yews at the Hall, recently felled. She appears in the Hall grounds and is called the Green Lady. The other, the daughter of an estate worker, got herself 'into trouble' and, knowing that her family would be thrown out of their home, also drowned herself and has been seen on Kidd Lane bridge. She's called Annie.

Fishlake

Fishlake is situated nine miles east of Doncaster and three miles off Junction 6 of the M18. It is equidistant from Thorne and Stainforth, but separated from them by the river Don and the Stainforth and Keadby Canal.

The name of Fishlake carries us back into a time when the river spread itself into a broad expanse of mere and fishermen let down their nets into the water. There was also Long Causeway (now Trundle Lane) which ran between rows of eel ponds, from which the monks of Dunscroft Abbey used to collect supplies of eels.

The oldest building in the village is the church of St Cuthbert, which was granted to Lewes Priory by William, second Earl of Warrene around 1200. Fishlake was then part of Hatfield, but soon became a separate parish. The church was dedicated to St Cuthbert as it was the south-ernmost resting place for his bones during the seven years they were carried round the country to avoid the Danish invasions, before finally being laid to rest in Durham Cathedral. The chief exterior feature is the south doorway, which is still regarded as the pride of the church and dates from the mid 12th century. The rents from church land provide a charity for orphans, which is still available, but fortunately there are not many claimants.

Fishlake school was founded by the will of Richard Rands, rector of Hartfield in Sussex in 1641. The money, £300, was left to the villagers to purchase land, and an annuity to employ a headmaster, who was to be a graduate of Oxford or Cambridge with a degree in Latin. This applied until the early 1900s. The money was to be collected from London by 'two able men of body and fortune and well appointed for fear of robbing'. Henry Brooks, who was to be appointed schoolmaster in 1862, agreed to 'instruct and teach freely and without charge 40 children in Latin, reading and arithmetic and also Christian Religion'. It is still the only endowed school in the Doncaster education area. After the school was built the money left over was put into trust, and grants are available to students and apprentices from the village for their further education. The present day pupils still benefit by receiving oranges on each Shrove Tuesday.

The village is almost an island, being surrounded by rivers and canals, and can only be entered by crossing a bridge. Near the post office is the Landing, which used to be known as Cuthbert's Haven and was used by river traffic travelling between Sheffield and Goole. There was also a ferry which transported horses and carts across the river to Thorne. Barrier banks were built during the draining of the land by the Dutchman Cornelius Vermuyden, in the 17th century. They were designed to keep the water out of the village, but had the opposite effect and kept the water in. Older villagers tell of times when all the fields were flooded, with just the tops of the hedges visible, and of one eccentric who even took his ducks upstairs out of the flood water. The flooding was stopped by a second higher bank being built by prisoners of war at the end of the Second World War.

There are two buttercrosses in the village, but their origins have been lost in antiquity, and whether they were used for preaching or markets is not known. Some say they mark the places where St Cuthbert's body rested. The pinfold, where stray animals were kept, was looked after by one man for very little pay. On the shady side, it is said that tunnels run from the Old Hall to the church and to a house on the old river bank, and were used for smuggling. Until the late 1930s, a fair was held every 11th September.

Fishlake today has a population of approximately 600 and there are many activities. It still remains a rural village with a shop/post office, a butcher's and two public houses. Most of the old trades such as the five mills and the blacksmiths have disappeared and, except for farming, there is very little industry and villagers have to commute to Doncaster or Thorne to work. Until a few years ago, buses only ran to Doncaster on Tuesday and Saturday. This service has now improved, but buses are still infrequent, which helps to make a close community. About 1983, torches were put away when street lights were installed, but the village is still waiting for mains drainage. In the last 20 years there has been quite a lot of building and renovating of older property.

Fishlake may not be easy to find, for the minor roads and even more minor bridges do form hazards to navigation, but it is a place to gladden the eye and please the spirit.

Flanshaw 🐑

The hamlet of Flanshaw lies to the south of Alverthorpe beck and is traversed by a narrow winding road leading from Alverthorpe in the direction of Thornes, which at Flanshaw Lane End meets with the main A638 Wakefield/Dewsbury road. It formerly had a Hall with cottages nearby, which was the refuge of Dissenters or Puritans before 1640. It was demolished to provide, in the post-war period, Flanshaw St Michael's junior school. This was erected overlooking the now disused and filled-in quarry and brickworks of Geo Crook & Sons (Westgate Brick Co).

Acute Terrace, nearby, received its name from the acute angle by which it is inserted into the bend in the road opposite Flanshaw Lodge. This large mansion house and gardens was constructed for John Archer, joint proprietor of a coco matting factory in Alverthorpe Road.

At one time noted for its pastures, dairies and market gardens, inroads of residential development have destroyed much of its character. More recently, further large areas of agricultural land have been devoured by an expanding industrial estate.

Moorhouses Mill, previously Oakes Mill, in the centre of the hamlet, no longer produces woollens but has been divided into numerous small units each serving upholsterers, welders, structural steel factors, vehicle repairers and the like. A metal stitching concern has developed nearby.

Flanshaw was the site of Talbot's confectionary works, in Willow Lane, from which the celebrated humbugs, mint imperials, toffees and Yorkshire mixtures were dispatched throughout the Ridings and beyond. Their enterprise, and the factory with its chimney, ended around 1960.

The main feature which has survived is the magnificent Sirdar factory (formerly Harrap Brothers) whose knitting wools have won world-wide acclaim over many years, largely thanks to that female entrepreneur Mrs Jean Tyrrell (nee Harrap).

The name Flanshaw (once Flanshill) will no doubt persist, attaching as it does to two schools, one in Flanshaw, the other in Alverthorpe, and in the name of the newest pub in the area, the other being the Eagle. Only the distinctive United Reformed church survives as a catalyst for the community.

Golcar & Scapegoat Hill 🌿

Situated about four miles west of Huddersfield, Golcar has been likened to an Italian village, being built mainly on a rocky hill. In the winter it seems a far cry from Italy with the wind blowing down the narrow streets and 'ginnels', but summer is a different story.

Golcar was mentioned in the Domesday survey of 1086 when the manor was held by the Norman de Lacy family. Among the houses are many of the original weavers' cottages, when every household seemed to engage in the textile industry. One of these weavers' cottages now houses the Colne Valley museum, which displays hand weaving and spinning, as well as a gas-lit cobbler's shop where clogs made on the premises can be purchased.

In the late 1800s Golcar was the home of a race track where both flat racing and steeplechasing took place. In 1884 the stand collapsed, preventing further proposed development. Now the area that held the racetrack has been covered by a council estate, though fortunately there is quite a lot of green belt that has restricted development.

The spiritual needs of the area are served by both Methodist and Baptist chapels and a parish church, St John's, built in 1830 in Early English style with a western tower and a broad steeple.

Dialect has regrettably died out now, but yet there is a kind of local pride in being born in Golcar, making you a 'Golcar Lily'. All newcomers to the village are treated with a little bit of suspicion by the older generation and have to serve a kind of probation before they are accepted. From then on the welcome is warm and genuine.

In the upper parts of the village over the last 20 years or so there has been quite a bit of building, providing much needed housing for both young couples and commuters.

Situated as it is between the A62 (the old Manchester road) and the M62 motorway, the position is ideal. This ribbon development has now practically joined Golcar to the village of Scapegoat Hill. This was once a hamlet mainly consisting of small farms and small-holdings. In recent years some of these have disappeared to be replaced by some new desirable and expensive properties.

One development is a new hotel with an hot air balloon club and helicopter access to Manchester airport for guests. At the turn of the century in these rural surroundings a new farm cart was a talking point!

Goldthorpe 🌿

Goldthorpe and district include the three villages of Goldthorpe, Bolton-on-Dearne and Thurnscoe, which for many years have been known as the Dearne Area.

Goldthorpe and Bolton-on-Dearne were part of the Hickleton Estates, and Thurnscoe was part of the Monk Bretton Estates. It was not until 1937 that the townships joined forces, to make the Dearne Urban District Council, until the formation of Metropolitan Councils came into being in April, 1974.

Bolton-on-Dearne was the biggest hamlet, and a school was built there in the middle of the 19th century, to which the children from Goldthorpe attended. With the sinking of Hickleton Main Colliery in 1892, the number of families coming into the area increased tremendously. The schools at Bolton-on-Dearne could no longer accommodate all the pupils, so land was purchased at Goldthorpe, and a school was built there for the local children. Housing also caused a problem, with the influx of people creating the need for more private and municipal accommodation to be built.

The church played an important part during this time, and many activities took place there. Workingmen's Clubs were built, and leisure activities including fishing, football, flower and vegetable shows were pursued by the men. Benefit concerts were put on regularly, for men who had been involved in accidents, or widows and orphans. The community spirit was very good, and, even though there was not a lot of money about, help was always at hand.

Travelling theatres and circuses were always well attended, along with cycling clubs, boxing matches, football, cricket and, of course, dog-racing. The Workingmen's Club organised a popular annual Day Trip.

There were two brickworks in the area, whose products were used for many purposes near and far.

Measles, enteric fever, tuberculosis and diphtheria were prevalent at that time, causing many deaths, as did drowning in the brickwork ponds. A need was seen to provide swimming baths in the area, and one was built at Thurnscoe in the mid 1900s. This was also used for dancing during the winter months, when the water was emptied and a wooden sprung floor was laid. The church and other groups held regular dances, which were very popular.

Because of the increase in housing, industry, etc., in September, 1899, Goldthorpe and Bolton-on-Dearne were granted permission to become an Urban District, and, shortly afterwards, Thurnscoe was also granted this status. A fire brigade was formed in 1908, and mining and ambulance classes were held.

The Workingmen's Clubs were very supportive of the Montagu Hospital being erected at Mexborough, and regularly held concerts and had street collections. A 'Hospital Sunday' was held every year, and the money raised from the street collection at the Parade was given to the fund.

Despite the opposition of some members of the Council, in 1903 a Free Library for the Urban District of Bolton-on-Dearne/Goldthorpe was built, as a result of a donation given by Andrew Carnegie, and this was very well used. Two cinemas and a theatre were built from 1910 onwards, which flourished, but unfortunately, the theatre burnt down, and now the cinemas are shops – one a supermarket, the other a carpet shop.

Three further mines were sunk – Goldthorpe 1909, Barnburgh 1911, and Highgate 1916 – and again the population rose as people came to work in the district. Three railway lines were also built through the area, for passengers and for transporting coal to the then seemingly far away places of Pontefract, or even Hull! There were also small stations, the one at Goldthorpe closing down in the 1950s, but it has since re-opened.

Unfortunately, mines were closed during the 1980s, when the coal was exhausted, and at the present time only one mine remains open. During the 1970s, light Industrial Estates were introduced, which provided a small amount of work, but not on the same scale as mining. It is to be hoped that in the 1990s employment prospects will improve for young people when they leave school, enabling them to remain in the area.

Gomersal

There is a reference to Gomersal in the Domesday Book completed in 1086, where it was recorded that Ilbert de Laci had 14 caracutes of land to be taxed, one of which was Gomershale Dunstan.

By the time of the Civil Wars the woollen industry was already established in Spen Valley. Wool was spun and woven in the cottages of the people or at best in very small workshops. In 1774 the clothiers of Spenborough decided to erect a Cloth Hall to facilitate the buying and selling of cloth. It was built in Gomersal where Burnley's mill now stands. The hall did good service for about 30 years. Spinning and

Gomersal Methodist Church

98

weaving of wool was about this time being concentrated in factories. Children were employed on a half day basis – school for half a day then work in the mill for the other half. By 1838 the working day was at least 14 hours with but half an hour for dinner. Breakfast and tea were taken at the looms. The average expectation of life was 45 years.

Machinery was introduced, bringing for a time unemployment and resentment. This came to a head in 1812 when the croppers (those who 'finished' the cloth) banded together to wreck the machines which worked more quickly than the men. This was the start of the Luddite uprising. Eventually the military were brought into the district and after a battle at Cartwright's mill when several men were wounded and some killed, the rebels knew they were beaten and fled. The ones that were captured were hanged at York. There is a vivid description of this in Charlotte Bronte's book *Shirley*. In 1842 a petition was sent to Parliament demanding higher wages, shorter hours and factory legislation. It was rejected on the grounds that it was too extreme. The rejection was the signal for more riots – the Plug Riots this time. But after a week of upheaval, peace was restored. 'Physical Force' Chartism had failed. However, most of the ideals the Chartists had fought for eventually became law.

There are many large private houses with ground built by the textile 'barons' of those days. Perhaps the best known of these is Red House, built in 1660. Its name derives from the fact that it was built of red brick, which was a rare thing in those days. Red House was the home of Mary Taylor, Charlotte Bronte's schoolfriend. It made such an impression on Charlotte that she put both house and family in her book *Shirley*, the Taylors becoming the Yorke family and the house 'Briarmains'.

Mary Taylor's grandfather was a friend of the great John Wesley and he visited Red House and stayed there many times between 1742 and his death in 1791. People flocked to the window of the back parlour in their thousands to hear him preach.

Methodist preachers often visited the area, speaking at first in the open air but when winter came finding shelter in an old laithe at the top of Coal Pit Lane and then, before chapels were built, in the homes of the converted. The Methodist church built in Latham Lane in 1827 and known locally as the 'Pork Pie' chapel because of its semi-circular frontage, is perhaps the largest of the nonconformist churches. In 1751 the Moravians built a chapel at Little Gomersal and a day school for girls was opened by the brethren in 1758. The church of St Mary was not built until 1851.

Today Gomersal has become a commuter village for people who work in Bradford, Leeds and surrounding towns. As someone said, 'if you work in one of the West Riding towns you'd have to look pretty hard to find anywhere so handy and yet so pleasant as Gomersal'.

Harden 🖉

Harden, called Hateltone in the Domesday Book, lies in a lovely valley. Approach it from Bingley, over the river Aire, up the steeply wooded 'Twines' and so into open countryside. Two miles on is the village, and though modern life and housing have been laid over its long history, village atmosphere still remains.

On Harden moor, two Bronze Age burial chambers and a stone circle date from about 1500 BC. The Romans knew Harden. Braes Castle was built on the site of a look-out post, and two Roman roads lie under the moor's heather, one of which forded the stream at Harden beck. On the moor the Arley Stone, commemorating a Saxon victory over the Danes, marked Harden boundary from 1086 to 1974.

Early in the 13th century, Robert de Birkin gave his Harden lands to Rievaulx Abbey, and the monks held the manor of Harden until 1538. In the hamlet of Ryecroft, in a house still inhabited, the monks brewed beer, and down by the beck, they smelted iron. Slag and ore can still be seen in the vicinity.

In 1636, Robert Ferrand bought Harden Grange (now St Ives) and the family became the chief landlords and builders in the developing valley. On the roof of the oldest part of the Grange is a small tower, originally containing a 'hospitality light', visible in those days for miles around.

Sometime during the Civil War, Thomas Fairfax lived here, and billeted officers in what is now Harden Hall. Built in 1616 as a farmhouse, the Hall possesses an ancient cruck barn, has gables suggesting connections with the Knights of St John, and once specialised in pig-breeding. In 1797, we are told, one youngster weighed 770 lbs at 13 months!

Groups of 17th century cottages lie within the area of the village. At Cockcroft Fold, by the gates of the recreation park, the Bower family for 200 years made shoes for the gentry, and one John married the sister of 'Tabby', the Brontes' nurse.

Harden village centre grew up in the 19th and early 20th centuries, when the Industrial Revolution brought three small mills into the area. One of these is still family-owned and all employ some local people.

The Methodist chapel, 1813, is now two houses, but the handsome 1865 Congregational church and the lovely parish church, dedicated to St Saviour in 1892, stand active at the village crossroads. Interestingly, Harden nowadays covers a much bigger area than before 1914, but the population of about 1,600, is a little more. Many of the worst cottages left by the Industrial Revolution have gone, and modern housing contains smaller families.

There are farmers around Harden, and many real village-born people still live here, but newcomers are mainly business, professional and retired people.

The old Malt Shovel inn by the beck was once a gaol, then part farm, part hostelry. It is now patronised from over a wide area. Leave there and walk along the beck, through the caravan park, and through lovely woods to Goit Stock waterfall, returning by way of old Ivy House Farm or up the lane to the Cullingworth Road.

In 1918, the extensive St Ives estate was acquired by Bingley District Council and it was opened up for the public. There are walks through woods and scrubland, an 18 hole golf course which has hosted big tournaments, and a lovely islanded lake. Though the fishing is private, the ducks respond to offerings from all comers! Alongside the 17th century house stands the 19th century mansion. This once entertained Disraeli. Now it hosts local events and shows, and the St Ives Golf Club. The estate is home to the Turf Research Institute, and a local gardening expert grows his prize blooms in the walled area where once the Ferrand family kept their hunting dogs.

Harlington & Barnburgh

Harlington and Barnburgh sit side by side approximately seven miles from Doncaster.

Harlington is the smaller of the two, and in the 1920s there were nine small farms. Only one remains, Manor Farm. Most of the houses are red brick and quite a few new houses have been built since 1984 but the rural atmosphere is still felt. The larger village is Barnburgh, which can easily be reached from Harlington via Church Lane. The farms and older houses are of stone and the more modern dwellings of red brick.

The ancient church stands in the centre of Barnburgh and is used by both villages, since Harlington has neither church nor chapel. The church is dedicated to St Peter but is known throughout South Yorkshire as the 'Cat and Man' church. This legend has several versions, but the most straightforward one runs as follows.

'In the 15th century, there lived at Barnburgh Hall a worthy knight called Sir Percival Cresacre. He was returning home rather late one night along the bridleway which is now the road from Doncaster. The area at that time was heavily wooded and as he came down Ludwell Hill leading to Barnburgh, a wild cat (or lynx) sprang out of a tree, and landed on the horse's back. So maddened was the horse that it threw the knight off. The cat turned upon the man, then followed a long, deadly running struggle between the two, which continued all the way to Barnburgh. By this time the man was terribly mauled and exhausted. On reaching the church, the knight made for the porch, thinking to get inside and shut the animal out, but the fight had been so fierce that the man fell dying. In his last death throes, his feet crushed and killed the cat against the wall. Thus the cat killed the man and the man killed the cat. So they were found by the search party sent out when the knight's horse had returned home riderless.'

Both Sir Percival and his wife, Alice, are buried in the church. The tomb of the knight has a magnificent oak effigy set in a canopy of stone with, appropriately, a cat beneath his feet.

Barnburgh Hall is no more. It was acquired by the Coal Board during nationalisation of the mining industry, but was demolished in 1969. However, standing in the grounds of the Hall there is one of the few remaining dovecotes in the country. Residents of both villages are anxious that it be maintained. It is a listed building and it is hoped to refurbish it in the near future.

One custom or rite was the 'Barnburgh Tup', derived it is thought from the 'Derby' Tup. At Christmas time, the youths of the village would borrow the 'Tup' (a facsimile head of a ram) from Aunt Ada Bray who lived in a small cottage opposite Centre Farm. They would go round both villages, to houses and pubs, singing the ode to the 'Tup'. There was usually a man under a blanket with the Tup head showing. One youth was the butcher who slew the ram, and the others sang. They collected money as they went along, and this went to old people of both villages. They would travel to surrounding areas on the following night, and all money collected then was divided between themselves.

The annual feast was held on the Bullcroft, which was a walled field opposite Plane Tree Farm, and where the present Coach and Horses now stands. The Jubilee Tree was planted to commemorate Queen Victoria's Jubilee in 1897, and was originally kept in good order by a gardener from Barnburgh Hall. This has now been taken over by the local council who keep it trimmed.

The pinfold, the old home for straying cattle etc, stands on Hickleton Road and was renovated in the 1970s by the parish council. One can now sit there and enjoy the surrounding countryside.

There are two well stocked shops and a hairdresser in Harlington, a general store, post office and filling station in Barnburgh. Between them, the villages can offer three pubs and a working men's club for a pleasant evening out.

Standing on the outskirts of the village can be seen the remains of Barnburgh colliery, but this does not detract from the natural beauty of the area, and there are several enjoyable walks and also a nature reserve where many species of wild life can be seen.

Harthill with Woodall ✤

Harthill is the most southerly parish in Yorkshire, bordered by Derbyshire to the south west and Nottinghamshire to the south east. The parish includes the hamlet of Woodall, three quarters of a mile to the west. Its recorded history begins with the Domesday Book, where it is stated that Hertil (Harthill) was part of the lands given by William the Conqueror to his son-in-law, William de Warenne.

In the church of All Hallows is a memorial to Harthill's most famous son, Edward Osborne, a poor boy, who, like Dick Whittington, went to London to seek his fortune. He was successful and became Lord Mayor of London. He and his family prospered, he was knighted and his descendants were eventually created Dukes of Leeds, and lived for many years at Kiveton Hall to the north of the village. Increasing industrialisation of the area led to them moving away, and Kiveton Hall was pulled down, though the Dukes of Leeds retained their lands and property in this area, until the estate was sold in 1922. Their patronage of the living of Harthill Church was retained by them until after the Second World War. The tombs of the family may be seen in Harthill Church, though the famous silver gilt candlesticks given to the village by Peregrine, Duke of Leeds, are now displayed in York Minster.

Sir Thomas Osborne, the most notorious of the family, lies in a dark corner of the church, a fitting resting place. He was a self-seeking politician, a trickster, and a traitor to the State. With Charles II, he connived to betray Parliament to France, and eventually was imprisoned for five years in the Tower. However, he was released, taking his seat among the peers, and was one of the chief movers in bringing William and Mary to the throne. He eventually died in 1712, of convulsions, a bad old man of 81.

Near the church is a swinging sign, which tells briefly the story of the village. It was made from the timbers of the old belfry, but, unfortunately, was destroyed by fire in the 1950s. However, it has been replaced in its original form.

The history of Harthill was vividly portrayed in the splendid pageants of the 1930s, and again for the Festival of Britain celebrations in 1951. They were written and produced by the then Headmaster of the village school, Mr Harry Garbutt, an enthusiastic student and teacher of local history, and the inspiration of all who took part.

The upper lawn of the old Rectory, with its surrounding flower beds, shrubs and trees, made a superb setting for the actors in their colourful costumes. The floodlighting ensured everyone seated in the raked stand, erected on the lower lawn, had an excellent view. People came from far and near to hear and see these unique dramatic presentations. (Even a West End actor, in the person of Sir Bernard Miles, came.) They are remembered with pride and pleasure by the older members of our community. Mr Garbutt's book, *The History of Harthill*, still graces many local book shelves.

Since the early 1950s, Harthill has grown from a small rural community engaged mainly in farming, mining and quarrying, to a large residential village of 1,600 souls, with most people commuting to work in neighbouring towns. Nevertheless, the strong community spirit has not diminished. Rather it has been extended by the interests and enthusiasm for village life of the newcomers, so that there are now over 20 organisations catering for the social, cultural and sporting needs of all the people, from toddlers to pensioners. There are two pubs in the village, The Beehive and The Bluebell.

There is a Carnival Society, who arrange a yearly event which takes place on the second Saturday in July. Included in the attractions are Shire horses, a parade and floats, stalls and teas. The Carnival Society also organise the Bonfire Night celebrations and are responsible for other functions.

The reconstruction and dressing of one of Harthill's old wells in 1987 was an outstanding occasion. It was dedicated by the Methodist Minister, and celebrated afterwards with song and dance, in the presence of a large crowd of villagers and visitors. Since then the well dressings have continued, one being dressed at Easter and another at Christmas. The well, and its surrounding gardens, (Harthill came second in the Britain in Bloom Competition in 1987), along with the flower beds and lawns that border the roadsides in many parts of the village, will give pleasure to residents and visitors alike.

Hartshead 🪻

The Domesday Book contained the first official mention of Hartshead, but the remains of Walton Cross, about 600 yards north-west of the church, show that a community existed here before the Anglo-Saxons arrived.

The church was originally built sometime before 1120. The Norman arches still stand along with a Saxon font base. The exact date is not known, but 'Kirklees' suggests an earlier church, probably Anglian, some stonework of which remains in the tower.

Kirklees Priory was founded in the reign of Henry II. It is here that the prioress reputedly bled Robin Hood, the semi-legendary medieval outlaw who is reputed to have robbed the rich to help the poor. Although generally associated with Sherwood Forest in Nottinghamshire in the legends which sprang up about him, it seemed likely that the real Robin Hood operated further north – in Yorkshire, most probably in the early decades of the 13th century. He is reputed to be buried where his arrow – shot as he was dying after being bled by his cousin – fell, in the grounds of Kirklees Priory. In the churchyard is a dead yew tree from which Robin is reputed to have made his bows. It is more likely, however, that the tree was used for bows used at Agincourt in 1415.

Rev Patrick Bronte was the vicar of Hartshead from 1811–1815 and his daughter Maria was baptised there on the 24th April 1814. She died young and was the basis for her sister Charlotte's 'Helen Burns' in *Jane Eyre*. Bronte was a friend of Hammond Roberson, who encouraged local landowners to stand up against the Luddites, and it was from this time Bronte constantly carried a loaded pistol.

At the turn of the 20th century Hartshead was a thriving community with mining, weaving and tanning in addition to farming. Unfortunately the pits closed in 1928, followed shortly by the cottage industries of weaving and tanning, so Hartshead has turned a full circle back to the Domesday Book when farming was its only industry.

The first half of the century saw a thriving community supporting a Co-op, post office, a couple of house shops, a cobbler, fish and chip shop, an abattoir, a mobile green grocer, a reading room over the Co-op, an afternoon tea shop near the church, and a thriving Methodist chapel. None of these have survived the years.

There are two hostelries, the New inn and the Grey Ox, now a pizzeria, and a working men's club. The village is now about 200 houses, mainly in two areas with a few houses straggling over the mile and half or so between. Over recent years many new houses have been built. These have increased the population, but decreased community life. Once it was said that if you trod on one toe, all the feet in the village hurt!

Over recent years, a brass band has been formed and a woodcarver is plying his trade. The only survivor from the old community, other than the church, is the village craft fair, held in May.

Hartshead Moor 🐝

Hartshead Moor is midway between the east and west coasts of the North of England and is probably better known in recent years for its M62 service station, opened in 1973. In 1974 an IRA bomb exploded on a coach carrying servicemen and their families on the east-bound carriageway resulting, sadly, in the death of 17 persons. A plaque commemorating this tragedy has been erected near the entrance to the service area.

One of the oldest residences in the area is the Old Field Nook, once owned by the Quaker family of Crosslands. One of the Crossland family, in 1854, opened a sewing class for girls in one of the cottages belonging to Old Field Nook. This was followed by a Sunday school and a boys class, subsequently followed in 1859 by the establishment of a Sunday school in the Victoria Institute, which served as the village hall and place of worship for 50 years. As the numbers grew the Friends' meeting house was opened in 1883.

The old manor house is now a nursing home. In 1835 it was owned by Mr Benjamin Firth and was known as the Manor House Academy. He was a self-made man, a schoolmaster, and about 150 boys were taught there. He published pamphlets costing 6d each headed 'Church versus Dissent or Tory Spite and Virulence'. Later the manor house was the home of the Walker family who were mill-owners in Brighouse and Clerkheaton. Colonel Walker's daughter, Marie Walker Last, who studied at the Chelsea School of Art is a well-known artist who has exhibited all over the world. Her pictures capture the quintessence of the landscape rather than offering a straightforward record of a view.

The Methodists built a small Wesleyan chapel at Hartshead Moor, opposite the manor house, in 1890. The last service was held in 1966.

In the 1920s, when annual tea-parties were held in the local churches, Joseph Seed, a local property owner, who was a thin man with a long white beard like Santa Claus, always bought all the ham fat when the leavings were auctioned. He said the fat was much better than the lean.

The area used to be rich in coal, and mining took place at Whitaker, Highmoor Lane. Whitaker pits were owned by the Low Moor Iron Co in 1886.

Over the last 70 years the shops in the area have gradually closed, and now the community is not served by a single one. The post office used to be in a house where elderly ladies would sit in front of the fire for a gossip after drawing the state pension. There was a Co-operative grocer's and a boot and shoe shop, which also did repairs. A milliner's helped everyone to buy their hats for the Chapel Anniversary and Whit Sunday Treat.

Farming continues to be one of the main occupations. Mr Collins of Pond Farm wins prizes at the Great Yorkshire Show with his dairy animals and in 1987 won the coveted Burke Trophy at the Royal Show.

The cricket field and pavilion was, and still is, the focal point for activities. It is situated on the old Elland to Leeds turnpike road on which the Luddites walked on their way to smash the machinery at Rawfolds, Liversedge, in the 1812 revolt. There was an ambush on Hartshead Moor when valuable machinery was being delivered to Cartwright's mill at Rawfolds.

These days when Bradford League cricket is being played at Hartshead Moor and the wind is in a certain direction conditions can be very difficult for umpires. They have to hope that batsmen will 'walk' after snicking the ball to the wicket keeper. The contact of bat and ball is often impossible to ascertain because of the noise from the motorway just below. However, the views from the wicket are a splendid compensation for this problem.

Hartshead Moor is a lovely spot, which still retains its charm today. On the old turnpike road the two packhorse public houses still remain, but the stables for the horses have long been demolished.

Hatfield 🌿

Hatfield is a lovely village, seven miles east of Doncaster, close to Hatfield Chase. It is a huge area of drained marsh land, and said to be the Haethfelth mentioned by Bede. Part of the Chase was leased by Charles I to Cornelius Vermuyden, who drained the land. Earlier history shows that Edwin, the first Christian king of Northumbria, was slain in the battle of Hatfield Chase in AD 633, by armies led by Caedwalla and Penda, kings of Britons and Mercians. It is thought that Edwin's palace was originally built on the site where Hatfield manor house now stands.

The church of St Lawrence is mainly 12th and 15th century. The west doorways and the tower part of the outer walls of the nave are Norman. The Norman pebble construction can be seen outside much of the building, including the imposing crossing tower, which is 100 ft high, and was rebuilt of white magnesium limestone in 1480–1500.

The vicarage, set in its own grounds, dates back to 1870, and is said to have cost £450 to build. There are other historical houses, the largest being the 12th century manor house, which was originally a medieval hunting lodge. Many kings came to hunt deer in the area. It is one of the finest Norman manor houses in England, with a moat along Manor Road. The second son of Edward III, Prince William, was born there at Christmas 1336, as was a son of Richard, Duke of York, in the 15th century. In 1778 the de Warrene family owned the manor house, which then passed to the Ingrams, from where the Ingram Arms derives its name.

A famous person who stayed in Hatfield from 1356–1359 was Geoffrey Chaucer, author of the *Canterbury Tales*. He was a page in the service of Prince Lionel, the third son of Edward III.

At the junction of Manor Road and High Street, the shops were originally timber-framed buildings, renovated in the 18th century and encased in brick, later pebble-dashed. Next to the Bluebell inn is a private house, formerly an 18th century courthouse. Holly Tree Cottage is a late 18th century keeper's cottage, and there used to be a windmill on Lings Lane.

The population in Hatfield parish in 1931 was 1,820. It has grown considerably during the last 20 years, and in 1990 was approximately 9,000. Though no longer a large farming community, there are still two working farms. The village is well equipped with schools, including a Church of England school, the Chase school for the handicapped and the Hatfield high school, which is the largest. There is a library, post office, about five public houses, a country club and a squash club, many shops and also a marina for canoeing, windsurfing, fishing etc. Caravan and camping facilities are also available.

Modern development in Hatfield is appealing, and has not spoilt the more historic building near the Ingram Arms, which, although itself is not old, has a stunning impact on visitors. Thanks to the M18, very heavy traffic through the village is now largely a memory.

Hatfield Levels 🍂

The Levels is an area ten miles north-east of Doncaster and 15 miles west of Scunthorpe, which derives its name from the various levels of water that were produced when the area was drained in the 17th century.

The flat land of the Levels was formed by the retreating ice sheet of the last Ice Age, about 15,000 years ago. Much of the land is only a few feet above sea level, and before drainage took place the many tidal rivers running through the area kept large parts of it under water. The many villages surrounding the flooded land, such as Hatfield, Thorne, Crowle and Epworth could only be reached by boat. Wedding and funeral parties were transferred from villages to the nearest church across the water, and had to run the risk of a storm blowing up during the journey.

The land above the water, where the villages were built, was rich in wildlife, and hunting was a favourite pastime of the local nobility and Royal visitors. Red and fallow deer were present in large numbers, with wildfowl and fish in the marshlands.

In 1609, an important meeting took place which was to change the Levels area dramatically for all time. Sir Robert Portington of Tudworth Hall was entertaining Prince Henry, eldest son of James I, to a deer hunting expedition. It is said that 500 deer were rounded up and driven into Thorne Mere (one of the large lakes), where the hunting party were waiting in 100 boats. As the deer floundered in the water the huntsmen speared or clubbed the animal of their choice. One of the guests in Prince Henry's party was a Dutch engineer by the name of Cornelius Vermuyden, who had gained considerable experience in land reclamation in Zeeland. The question of draining the Levels area – then known as part of Hatfield Chase – was discussed, and Vermuyden agreed to employ his experience and a large number of Dutch, French and Flemish workmen to do the job. An agreement was made to share the drained land equally between the King, the Participants (Vermuyden and 56 others, mostly Dutch, who put capital into the venture), and Commoners (local inhabitants).

The drainage operation was an enormous undertaking, which involved the re-routing of various rivers – the Don, Idle, Torne – the cutting of a vast number of long, straight drains and the building of flood banks and roads, all with the primitive tools of the 17th century. This operation was not welcomed by local inhabitants, who opposed the drainage by way of riots, murders (of some of the workmen), fires, deliberate floodings and court cases. Despite the opposition, the drainage work was completed in approximately 18 months, which was a remarkable achievement. The reclaimed land was then divided up and distributed amongst the Participants, who came over from Holland and France to claim their land. Although the major work of draining the land had been achieved by Vermuyden, his engineers and his workers, problems connected with the water levels continued into the next century and beyond.

The control and maintenance of the drains at the present day is in the hands of the local Water Authorities and Drainage Boards. A valuable practice in the improved productivity of the land was a system called 'warping', which became increasingly important in the 19th century. 'Warp' is a river or estuary-borne sediment which, by natural or artificial means, settles on land after shallow flooding. Many acres of the land on the Levels was warped, thereby producing rich, fertile farming land.

The peat moors of Hatfield and Thorne have also played a significant part in the economy of the area, the peat having been formed many centuries ago from a combination of heath, moss and various bogland plants. The peat was cut in earlier centuries for fuel. Now it is harvested for the nursery garden industries of Britain and Europe, which has raised controversy over the conservation aspects of large scale cutting of peat. What happens to the 10,000 acres of land when the peat has gone? There have been some remarkable things found in the peat, preserved in perfect condition from many centuries ago. Weapons and tools from the Bronze Age, and pots from the Roman invasion in AD 43, have been unearthed. It is also said that bodies, preserved impeccably, have been found.

Some of the farm houses on the Levels today have strong connections with the time of Vermuyden. Grove House was built and occupied by Vermuyden and his family. Smaque Farm is named after Pierre Smaque, 'a rich Frenchman', who, with his whole family, were forced from Paris by persecution for his faith and who came to live in these Levels. In 1680 he moved to live in Crowtree Hall, which had been built in 1630 by Myneer van Valkenbroch, one of Vermuyden's engineers. Before the chapel at Sandtoft was built, services were held at Crowtree Hall.

A well known family from the time of the drainage was the de la Pryme family. Charles de la Pryme came over to the Hatfield area from Flanders in 1628, to participate in the draining of the area. One of Charles' sons, Matthias, married Pierre Smaque's daughter, Sarah, and they had a son, Abraham, who was born at Crowtree Hall. Abraham de la Pryme (1672–1704) was educated at Cambridge, entered the Church and became curate of Hatfield in 1696. He consequently became vicar of Thorne and a Fellow of the Royal Society. In 1698, he wrote *The Diary of Abraham de la Pryme*, which is considered to be the most important source of information about the history of the area.

The Levels had a thriving community in the early part of the 20th century, centred on the Black Bull pub, on the A18 Doncaster to Scunthorpe road, and the school and the chapel, adjacent to the pub. In the early 1900s an annual carnival was held at the Black Bull and in the fields surrounding it. A procession of people in fancy dress would walk the three miles from Thorne to join in with all the fun of the fair. The Black Bull is still a thriving pub, but the school has closed, and the chapel is converted into a dwelling. The only remaining connection with the feeling of community in the area has been the continuance of High Levels Women's Institute, who met at the school for nearly 40 years until its closure. The Women's Institute now meets in a member's house.

The development of the Humber ports to the east has meant the building of the M180 motorway through the area, thereby splitting the Low Levels from the High Levels, but the land continues to be a fertile farming area, producing abundant crops of wheat, barley, rape, potatoes, peas and beans.

Hatfield Woodhouse 🦢

The village of Hatfield Woodhouse straddles the A614 trunk road. This main road through the village was originally subject to the Selby/Bawtry Turnpike Act of 1793. The village is effectively divided into two almost equal halves by this road, with the school, post office and working men's club on the north side, and the Robin Hood inn, small shopping parade and public telephone on the south side. Small housing estates have been built on both sides of the road, which is now a busy thoroughfare, with a prison on the one-time Lindholme air field and another prison under construction. Areas of land are already the subject of sand and gravel extraction, and many thousands of acres of land adjacent to the village have been irreparably destroyed by the destruction of the raised peat mire of Hatfield Moors.

Hatfield Woodhouse is a small part of Hatfield Chase, which 300 years ago was a Royal Forest consisting of lakes, woods and marshes, and a few dwellings. In 1626 the Dutchman Cornelius Vermuyden drained the fens, making the land fit for agricultural purposes, which turned the people into a community of hard working labourers. The Green Tree inn, which has been well restored, dates back to Vermuyden's time, and was a well known posting inn. Progress was slow, but by the beginning of the 20th century Hatfield Woodhouse had grown into a close knit community of some 200 small farms and cottages. There was a school, two chapels, three public houses, a post office cum general store, five other small shops, two butchers, a cobbler's, later a fish and chip shop, and a village bull who served the local cows. By 1920 almost every house stood in its own garden, or orchard, with a well or pump for water, an earth closet and some kind of out-building.

When the war came, Lindholme aerodrome was built on the outskirts of the village. Lindholme was known at the time of the Saxons, and was the centre of a religious community. A hermit, William de Lindholme, lived a lonely existence in a desolate region which took its name from this man. His grave was discovered near the present Lindholme Hall in 1727. The quietness and solitude is certain proof that the area has altered little since the time of William de Lindholme. It is reputed that Billy de Lindholme's ghost has been seen by residents. It is said that the Black Prince fought a battle at Slay Pits. He lived in the manor house in nearby Hatfield, and is thought to be buried in York Minster.

The old time village is little in evidence in Hatfield Woodhouse now. There is little farming work and, as the village has grown, people go to work in nearby Thorne and Doncaster, which are easily accessible.

The Coronation Tree was planted in the centre of the village in 1902 to commemorate the Coronation of King Edward VII. Unfortunately, in spite of a village petition, the parish council decided the tree was unsafe, and it was chopped down at the end of 1990. However, residents have been promised a replacement and hopefully timber from the original tree will be used to make a seat for the village.

Haworth ҉

A Keighley bard of the 19th century claimed that Haworth was founded by the Chinese Emperor Wang be Wang, 'as com ower in a balloon an browt wi' him all his relations but his grandmuther'! More prosaic historians consider it to be an English settlement about 1,000 years old; the name meaning 'hedged enclosure'. Charlotte Bronte was expressing a common sentiment of the time when she described Haworth as a 'strange, uncivilized little place'. The basic plan of Haworth is simple; the steep Main Street climbs the hillside to the church, beyond which it divides into West Lane and Changegate. North Street connects these two to form a triangle at the top of the village where the green once was.

At the bottom of the Main Street lies the Old Hall, an early 17th century building which is now an hotel but was once the residence of the principal Haworth landowners, the Emmotts. The Hall owns a respectable number of ghosts and stories of secret tunnels for a building of its age. Tucked away at the bottom of nearby Fern Street is the even older Old Fold Hall where the Emmotts are said to have lived before the Old Hall was built. Further to the south on Sun Street is the site of the ducking well, which was removed earlier this century during road improvements.

From the Old Hall the cobbled Main Street (though purists will tell you that these are not cobbles – they are setts) begins its 100 ft climb to the church. The first inn reached is the Fleece where, in about 1850, a local wag named Bill o'th Hoylus End exhibited his 'Great South American War Pig'. The wondrous animal was advertised far and wide and all who could afford the admission fee crowded in to behold . . . a tiny, dejected-looking black piglet. An old Haworth cobbler approached for a closer examination; 'Dust tha call that a War Pig?' asked the cobbler. 'Hast'a ivver seen a war pig i' thi life?' asked Bill. 'Nay, it's warst pig at ivver ah saw!' replied the cobbler. Fortunately for Bill the joke was well received and he went on his way with his pockets full of pennies.

A little above the Fleece on the right hand side was the shop of John Greenwood, now a private house. Greenwood was a little man who wore an extravagantly tall top hat and served the village as tea dealer and stationer for many years. So devoted was he to the Bronte sisters that he would walk to Halifax and back – well over 20 miles – to buy half a ream of paper for their latest manuscripts.

Lodge Street is a pleasant backwater off the bustling Main Street. It takes its name from the Three Graces Masonic Lodge which used to meet here when Branwell Bronte was a prominent member.

Near the top of the street there is a tiny passageway on the right and hard by was the shop of Zerubbabel Barraclough, ironmonger, draper and clockmaker, and monument to our forebears' fondness for scriptural names.

At last the street levels out past the Black Bull inn which catered to Branwell's liking for 'little squibs of rum' and the old apothecary's shop which took care of his craving for opium. Until his death in 1840 the shop was run by Joseph Hardaker who produced a number of volumes of verse, amongst them an early account of the Liverpool-Manchester railway under the grand title of *The Aeropteron or Steam Carriage*.

The Tourist Information Centre was once the Yorkshire Penny Bank and also housed the Bronte Museum from 1895 to 1928.

Just over the crossroads is the manor house where the successive lords of the manor dwelt, but little of the older building remains. Back in North Street is a fine 17th century farmhouse where the Binns family lived for centuries. They not only farmed the land but were the village's carters and carriers as well.

Church Street runs past the house of John Brown, sexton to Mr Bronte and friend to Branwell, past the National school where Charlotte helped to teach the village children and on to the parsonage where Emily and Anne and Charlotte wrote those books which bring hundreds of thousands to Haworth every year.

Below the parsonage is the church; only the tower is original, the rest of St Michael's having been rebuilt by Mr Bronte's successor. So many times has the tower been altered and raised that it was said that the people of Haworth 'mucked it to mak' it grow'.

Between the parsonage and the church lies the old churchyard with its hundreds of gravestones and thousands of burials of the men and women who wrought this village; the hewers of stone, the spinners and weavers of worsted yarn by hand and steam, the clog makers and the bonnet makers and the oat-cake bakers.

Beyond the churchyard little lanes lead on to the moors and there, perhaps, you should go and wander on a quiet day amidst the heather and the gritstone, the streams and the waterfalls to learn whence Haworth draws its character.

Helme 🌿

The small hamlet of Helme with its many-windowed weavers' cottages, its church, the Hall and the new nursing home, is the ideal place for a short circular stroll. Sheltered from the north and easterly winds, it is well wooded and fertile, compared with the bleak and barren moorland not far away.

The hamlet has not suffered from industry and has survived as a small, family community, being little different to what it was 100 years ago. It lies at the edge of the gently descending fields from Cop Hill and on the skyline, West Nab and Deer Hill. A short walk from the centre through the meadows and woods brings you to Blackmoorfoot reservoir. This was constructed in 1875 at a cost of £260,000 and still serves Huddersfield's increasing population.

The name Helme is of Saxon origin and means a cattle shelter. The first records of the hamlet, then spelt Elm, appear in 1421. In 1559 the first record of the community appears in Almondbury parish register, when Barnard of Helme was baptized. To get to this church was quite a walk!

The oldest buildings date from around 1640 and at one of them at Lower Edge, Oliver Cromwell is said to have spent the night.

Helme developed into a larger community with the building of the church and school during the middle of the 19th century. The Brook family who owned the large cotton thread mills at nearby Meltham Mills helped tremendously with the development of the community. The church was built in 1859 in memory of one of the sons of Charles John Brook, who had died at the age of 27. It is said during the funeral, at Meltham Mills church, a rainbow appeared over the hamlet of Helme and the family decided there and then to build a church under the rainbow! The church is unusual in two respects, first that it has no stained glass windows and secondly it is the only church in Yorkshire with a wooden shingle spire. In fact, it is one of only two churches with wooden spires in the North of England, the other being near Lancaster.

Today, Helme has 37 dwellings, no shops, no public house and a very much reduced rural bus service, but it is a haven for anyone wanting to enjoy a peaceful, contented life.

Heptonstall 🌿

Heptonstall is situated on the hilltop above Hebden Bridge and the famous beauty spot of Hardcastle Crags.

It is one of only three places in Britain where there are two churches in one churchyard. The old church dated from 1256 was struck by lightning in the 1830s and is now a ruin. A new church was built close by. The interior was extensively modernised in the late 1950s with a bequest from a local parishioner. There are many graves of interest, including that of 'King' David Hartley. He was the leader of a notorious 18th century gang called the Cragg Coiners. They were so called as they lived in Cragg Vale and 'clipped' gold guineas. They were eventually caught and hanged in York. His body was then brought back and buried in Heptonstall churchyard.

The Wesleyan chapel in Heptonstall is the oldest continually used chapel in the world. It is also unusual in that it is an octagonally shaped building. John Wesley preached there on several occasions.

The local grammar school was founded in 1643 and has been used as a museum housing local artefacts, furniture etc.

There is a Weavers Square in the centre of the main street. This used to be cottages when weaving was done from home. At that time Heptonstall was a thriving, prosperous town, but with the onset of water power everything changed, and weaving was carried out in mills built in the valleys, next to the streams and rivers. Now the Square is used for village fairs, morris dancing, local plays, or just to sit quiet and idly dream.

The village pump is still there. When work was carried out a few years ago a plaque was uncovered on the stone wall behind the well. This contained the names of the local people who were on the parish council at the time it was built. It has since been restored to its former glory. The dungeons and stocks are also still to be seen in Heptonstall – but not used! Many of the cottages and buildings date from the 17th century.

There were originally several public houses in the area. Indeed the vicarage has been built on the site of a disused inn. Today there are only two remaining.

Heptonstall was mentioned in the Domesday Book. All around the area can be seen evidence of historical habitation, from Iron Age encampments through relics of Roman and medieval times to the Industrial Revolution.

Nowadays many of the people who live in the village work in Manchester or Leeds, but the local village carries on much as it has for many decades. The village includes a post office/newsagent's, supermarket, general store and washerette. Not to mention a fish and chip shop, of course!

Every year on Good Friday the 'Paceggers Play' comes to Weavers Square. This tells the story, very loosely, of St George and the various heroic deeds he carried out. Around this time villagers make a local speciality called dock pudding. This is not made with the large cow docks, but a small smooth-leafed one. This only grows in a few areas now. The pudding also contains oatmeal, onion, egg and certain individual secret ingredients! It is eaten with bacon.

Heptonstall has now become one of the main tourist centres of Calderdale. Having said that, it has been a 'tourist centre' for centuries, visited by people such as Daniel Defoe, Dorothy Wordsworth, and even Charles Dickens. Defoe wrote of the 'goodness and wholesomeness of the country which is without doubt as healthy as any part of England'.

Hepworth 🐚

Chipped flints of the Old Stone Age have been found on Pike Lowe hillside facing Hepworth and the stone axes of the New Stone Age discovered hereabouts reveal the presence of primitive man in this moorland region.

The plague was brought to the village by apparel sent from London to a farmhouse known as 'Middle Foster'. There are still a number of triangular patches believed to contain the mass graves of the victims. On the last Monday in June, Hepworth's big feast was first held to celebrate the riddance of the plague and it is significant that this is still held at that time and never on a Holy Day. In approximately 1820 some workmen preparing ground for building cottages in Hepworth discovered human bones and it is assumed that the people of Hepworth buried their own dead at this time to prevent any further spread of the disease. It is known that an 'isolation hospital' was set up near Far Field Head and used during the time of the plague.

Hepworth, or Heppeuurde as it was known, is mentioned in the Domesday Book and people living there housed themselves in cottages made from local stone. There is still a dwelling standing dated 1691, although most of the houses date from the 18th century.

The village's early development was influenced by the woollen industry carried on in the homes of the villagers. Sheep were kept not only for their wool but also for milk. A complaint of 1297 relates to the stealing of milk from 34 ewes; the milk was used for butter and cheese.

The pasturing and shearing of sheep and the spinning and weaving of wool provided the staple industries of the village. Peat was the fuel, local springs gave drinking water, and oats and wheat were grown. The village of Hepworth belonged to the manor of Wakefield and the clusters of houses in the village were called folds.

The village has a river Jordan (which separates Hepworth from Scholes); a Solomon's Temple (a house near to the church has always been called this, but no one knows why) and 'Paradise', the only piece of land in the village where fruit can be grown (or so it is said). Meal Hill was where the Romans brought their hand-mill stones to grind corn for their needs, and Barracks Fold was the place where the people barricaded themselves against the people who had the plague. They erected a fence across the road from their infected neighbours and so the area got its name.

The people met in their cottages to celebrate the Sabbath because the nearest church was Kirkburton and it was too far to go every week. Then a Sunday school was started where the club stands now and people went there instead. By 1852 the Sunday school in Barracks Fold was doing so well that a new building was erected to act as both church and school and the foundation stone of the modern church was laid in 1862.

Hepworth did not enjoy the privilege of being a separate ecclesiastical parish until 1843 and until that date it belonged to Kirkburton parish. All the dead had to be taken to Kirkburton for burial for a long number of years.

The present school in Hepworth was built in 1884 and has steadily increased in numbers as the village has expanded. As in every complete village there is a public house and in Hepworth it is known as the Butcher's Arms. This originally consisted of small cottages and the bar was in the passage of one of them for many years. It has a fine depiction of the Arms of the Worshipful Company of Butchers outside and the Arms also occur on the handles of the beer pumps and a full Achievement hangs on the bar. The colours used in the Arms are blue and silver; these are the livery colours of the company and it is for this reason that a butcher's apron is blue and white.

The Co-operative Society (now sadly closed) was opened in Hepworth some four years before the official first Co-operative movement was opened by the Rochdale Pioneers.

Hickleton 🐾

Lying about halfway between Doncaster and Barnsley, Hickleton is now mainly a commuter village, much admired by folk for its lovely warm-coloured stone cottages and barns which line the very busy A635 road. It is a small community of about 100 houses, a post office, a village club, an 18 hole golf course and five village crosses. The modern way of the world has intruded gently into Hickleton.

Chiceltone, Icheltone and today Hickleton has had a long history. It stands on an old Roman road which runs from Streethouses to Pontefract. There is nothing to see today of Hickleton Castle, which was a motte and bailey structure of wood and lay on the north side of the village. A scale drawing was made in the 17th century, when remains of the site could still be seen. The name has been carried forward into the present day by the naming of Castle Hill Farm and Castle Hill Fold.

The church of St Wilfrid has an early foundation, though what is seen today dates mainly from the 15th century. It was a daughter church to Barnburgh, and once belonged to the monks of Monk Bretton Priory. The road which runs up the hill to the church is still known as Monks Hill. On the eastern edge of the village, fields on either side of the main road show, especially at low sun, the humps and hollows left by the extraction of marl for brick making, believed to have been the work of the monks.

Hickleton Hall and estate was purchased by Sir Francis Lindley Wood, second Baronet of Hemsworth in 1828, and was occupied by the family until the Second World War. It is now a Sue Ryder Home. The present

Hall was built around 1740 to the south of the old Hickleton Palace, which was left to go to ruin. The remains of a curtain wall with mullioned windows, which fronts the main road, and a 16th century dovecote are associated with the old Palace.

Hickleton Brew, a highly individual ale made from an old Halifax family recipe, was traditionally made twice a year in March and September, in the estate brewhouse. The last brew was made in 1989.

The 17th century village school and schoolhouse have now been converted into desirable 20th century homes. A modern school was opened in 1965, but, like many other small village schools, was considered uneconomic and was closed in 1981. Hickleton may be far from the sea, but it does have a link with the Royal Navy. A naval mine-sweeper, commissioned in 1954, was named HMS *Hickleton*. After the vessel was sold in 1967, the ship's bell was presented to the village. Until 1990, the village blacksmith, like his father before him, ran the Hickleton forge.

The Hickleton ghost, a man on horseback dressed in cloak and tricorn hat, is reputed to have been seen twice in recent years, near the cross-roads.

Prior to 1976, the village remained a very small estate village of picturesque cottages and farms. As the estate interest in the village declined, empty properties came onto the market, when farmhouses, barns, stables and coach-houses were converted into private dwellings. A modern estate of houses and bungalows was built in 1976, and in 1987 a further housing development took place on land formerly occupied by the school and playing field.

The Blacksmith's Shop, Hickleton

High Flatts ❧

Even older than Denby village and situated about a mile away is the hamlet of High Flatts. At a height of 1,025 ft above sea level on Castle Hill are the considerable remains of an Iron Age hill fort, with a section of the protective ditch and rampart still in existence. During the 19th century there were several finds of stone axe-heads, flint arrowheads and implements, and there have been several more such finds on this site as recently as 1972.

Records show that for many years the population of High Flatts was made up almost completely of members of the Society of Friends. There is a small part now known as Quaker Bottom. The Quaker community was a thriving one; as well as the traditional occupation of farming these people were involved in the making of cloth. There are remains of various buildings including a dye-house to the side of Low House.

It is said that Friends' meetings started during the mid 1600s in a barn which was on the site of the present meeting house. In 1764 a Quaker boarding school was started. Lessons were held in the meeting house and most of the 50 or so boys were boarded at the farmhouse of Edward Dickinson, probably Low House Farm.

In 1886, at Mill Bank House, a home was opened for the restoration of inebriate women of both the working and middle classes. This home was mainly run and supported by women and continued to run into the early 1900s.

There have been two public houses, one of which was in Pump Row, the terraced houses along the main road. The other was called the White Swan and is now Smithy Farm.

The population of High Flatts is approximately 70. There used to be eleven working farms in the village but there are now less than four.

High Melton ❧

Driving along the main road from Sprotbrough, and passing pleasant countryside, the pretty village of High Melton soon appears.

In the time of Edward the Confessor it belonged to Swein, and after the Conquest was included in the grant to the Lord of Tickhill, Roger de Busli. In the 12th century, High Melton was inherited by Avice-de-Tania (Tilli). In 1153 she founded the priory at Hampole, and erected the church at High Melton, together with some mills. Although there are no mills visible today, one was situated at the bottom of Melton Mill Lane. From the 17th century, Melton Hall was the home of the Fountayne family, later the Montagus.

The estate was split up in 1927 during a two day sale, and High Melton Hall was bought by a Mr Meanley. In 1948, the Hall, outbuildings and 120 acres of ground were purchased from him for £10,300 by the Ministry of Education. After spending a considerable amount of money on the structure, the Hall was opened as a teachers' training college.

St James's church, originally built by Avice-de-Tania, was until the reign of Richard II (1377–1399) known as the church of All Saints. It is built of local limestone, and has a 15th century tower, with curious gargoyles, including a little man in a hat with a horn. In front of the Norman chancel arch is a fine modern screen with a vaulted loft, the rood figures reaching the roof, and the 15th century chapel is enclosed by lovely old screenwork.

The original High Melton Hall appears to have been replaced in the 18th century by Dean Fountayne, although it seems that a structure stood on the site from very early times. The earliest remaining portion is the medieval circular tower incorporated in the present building. In the 18th century the estate was replanned, and farm houses and cottages were built. The village cross originally stood in the grounds at the back of the Hall, near the main road.

During the early years of the 20th century, fallow deer roamed the parkland and a small flock of black sheep were kept. The fleeces of the latter were woven into a brown tweed, and many of the family who lived at the Hall were clad in it. There used to be a bridge across the main road, on the narrow bend, to link the pleasure grounds with Melton Warren Wood and the old gamekeeper's cottage. Melton sported one of the finest partridge shoots in Yorkshire, but this is now much reduced.

In 1926–28, a purpose-built shop and cafe was erected on the main road, selling home-made cakes and scones. In 1948 it became a post office, until its closure in 1987, and is now a private residence. Until recent times, the bus tickets were printed 'Cafe High Melton', although the cafe had long since gone. Across the road from the former shop are some lovely old stone cottages, with leaded-light windows, and just a few yards from there is Hangman Stone Lane, where it is thought there may have been a gibbet at one time. The former vicarage is now a private residence.

High Melton is still a very small village, with little development taking place. There are two working farms, but the majority of the residents commute to the nearby towns, returning to a quiet and peaceful environment.

Hightown 🌿

At first sight, Hightown appears to be an uninteresting straggling village with a mixture of Victorian houses and later ones up the main road, a large and small estate of council houses and some modern private houses, yet it has a long history.

The main road, which is now Halifax Road, was formerly Heigh (High) Street, a continuation of the High Street in Heckmondwike running from Dewsbury, and this is believed to have been a Roman road. There is the base of an Anglo-Saxon cross, now known as Walton Cross, in Windy Bank Lane near Walton Farm, on the boundary with Hartshead. It is thought to be about 800 years old, and still shows typical ornamentation. In Halifax Road, opposite the Mandarin Restaurant, stand the stone posts of the stocks. It is not known how old they are, but they were repaired in 1690. They stood at the gates of Lower Hall, which was a beautiful house built in 1660. Sadly it was demolished in 1939. It belonged to the prosperous Green family who built several houses here in the 17th century.

The Greens became Quakers when George Fox preached at Hightown in 1652, and one, John, was imprisoned in York because he refused to take oaths and died there in 1676. There is still an interesting group of Quaker graves, known as The Sepulchre, in Hare Park Lane dated 1665, 1684 and 1697.

There was less persecution after the Toleration Act of 1689 and a Quaker meeting house was built in what is now known as Quaker Lane, in 1699. It is now a private residence. Quaker Lane is a quiet little backwater springing from the busy Halifax Road and ending at Westgate in Cleckheaton. Once a cart track, its dirt road went past Quaker House, a row of old stone cottages and a meadow, where it split. The left hand part still has the terrace of stone-built houses called romantically Oriental Terrace, linked with a large house further down once called Oriental House. These were built from monies invested in the Orient. To the right of the fork is a public bridleway winding past King George V playing fields, abundant with blackberries in Autumn and used more and more by horse and rider.

The house which attracts most attention is Clough House, which is in Halifax Road just above Quaker Lane. This is also a 17th century house. It was occupied by Rev Patrick Bronte from 1812 to 1815 with his new wife Maria. Here the two daughters who died as children were born. He was the curate at Hartshead church and had lodged at Thornbush Farm near the end of Miry Lane before this. He was at Clough House when the croppers banded together to try to destroy the cropping machines being installed in the large mills. They called themselves Luddites, and met at the Shears inn in Halifax Road to plan the attack. The Shears inn was built in 1773.

There are three other inns in Halifax Road, the oldest being the Shoulder of Mutton near Church Road which was built in 1678. The outside was refurbished in 1990, when the old stone window frames were destroyed. The Old Brown Cow, opposite, was made from three cottages, and the Cross Keys lower down the village near the Shears inn was built about 80 years ago. This may be on the site of an older one on land owned by the Knights of St John, the keys being the emblem of St Peter.

Holmbridge ✾

Holmbridge, as the name suggests, grew up where people were able to bridge the river Holme. It stands at the head of a steepsided valley which runs roughly west to east. In winter time especially, one side of the valley receives far less of the sun's rays and is always known as 'the frozen side' (a polite translation from the dialect!). Some of the cottages date from the 1700s and the valley is noted for its unique style of architecture – four-decker cottages dug into the hillsides. The bottom cottage is approached from the front, the upper cottage reached by a steep flight of stone steps leading round the back. These upper cottages have stupendous views.

The sides of the valley are irregularly patterned with small fields (cloises) surrounded by dry stone walls built of local millstone grit. The two flattest fields in the Holmbridge area are home to the Holmbridge Cricket Club and the Holmbridge Football Club. Old stone farmhouses and buildings dot the landscape, some high up on the edge of the moor. These have now been joined by modern houses, some blending into the scenery better than others.

The prosperity of the valley in the past rested more with the manufacture of woollen cloth than with farming. Many of the old farmhouses have long rows of windows to let in the light so that hand-loom weavers could see to ply their trade. Later many mills grew up in the valley bottom and footpaths abound leading from outlying farms and hamlets to the places where people worked and worshipped. Sadly, the economics of the place have changed and only two working mills and a few shops remain.

Situated opposite the cricket field, the parish church of St David celebrated its 150th anniversary in 1990. Two items which always attract attention are the six ft high, hand-embroidered panel of the Virgin and Child, beautifully worked during the early 1960s by Mrs Sheila Streek, wife of the vicar of that time, and the hand carved altar piece, designed and produced by Mr N. P. Jackson of Northowram in the phenomenally short time of ten weeks. This features individually carved panels showing different scenes of life in the Holme valley.

One of the highlights of the year is the Sunday School Feast. On that afternoon the Sunday school banner, attended by the Hinchliffe Mill Brass Band, leads the children, teachers, relatives, friends and members of the congregation round the village in a procession of witness, stopping to sing a few verses of the chosen feast hymns on their way to Dam Head. Here they hold a United Sing and a short open air service. Afterwards the children, friends and band return to the parish hall for tea, and the villagers take their friends and relatives home. A feature of the tea is the School Cake, a fruity and spicy bread cake.

Holmbridge, situated about one mile from Holmfirth, shares the fame of the BBC TV series *Last of the Summer Wine*. Many of the country scenes are of the lanes and paths around Holmbridge.

In February 1852 Mrs Hirst was reading her bible when Bilberry dam burst. The cry went up to get to higher ground, so she took off her steel rimmed glasses and put them in between the pages of the bible she had been reading. The imprint of her steel frames can still be seen on the bible pages and the book has been named the Flood Bible. This bible is kept in the parish church of St David. There have been five floods recorded in the Holme valley: 1738, 1777, 1821, 1852 and 1944. The two major floods were in 1852 and 1944 which resulted in great damage and loss of life; 81 people died in the 1852 flood, 44 of whom were in the Holmbridge area, including 36 in one row at Hinchliffe Mill Water Street. Bilberry and Middle Digley mills were almost completely demolished and two other mills were destroyed further down the valley together with warehouses, seven bridges and 27 cottages. The 1944 flood, although devastating, was hardly as serious as that of 1852. In this case three lives were lost; 21 industrial premises and 60 shops were damaged.

Holmbridge is a lovely village with the Pennines offering picture postcard views daily. The 'locals' and the 'comers-in' are united in their praise of village life.

Hooton Pagnell 🦢

Lying some seven miles north-north-west of Doncaster at the extreme edge of South Yorkshire, Hooton Pagnell, with its limestone cottages and farms, is one of the prettiest estate villages in the area. The first recorded mention of Hooton Pagnell is to be found in the Domesday Book in 1086, where it is called 'Hotone', the town on the hill. The second part of the name was acquired from the Norman lord of the manor, Ralph de Pagnel.

At the southernmost end of the village is the medieval Hall or manor house, the residence of the Warde-Norbury family. Over the 14th century gateway are the arms of the Lutterell family, who in 1340 commissioned the Lutterell Psalters, a unique and priceless medieval manuscript.

Adjacent to the Hall is All Saints' church, known to have been in existence in 1089. One entrance to the church has a flight of 13 steps, because it is so high above the road. It has several Norman features, and an 18th century marquetry pulpit. However, its most outstanding feature is the carillon, which plays a different tune each day.

On the main street a short distance away from the church can be found the village cross and pound. The cross, which probably dates back to 1253, stands in a commanding position and offers an uninterrupted view of a broad sweep of country reaching up to the Pennines. The pound, almost directly beneath, is a small stone-walled enclosure in which cattle were impounded.

There are now only four working farms, all ranged along the main street, but agriculture no longer dominates the village, and the majority of the adult population commute to surrounding towns. The agricultural organisation of the past is still evident in the tithe barn and the balks, the latter being lanes, wide enough for the passage of farm carts, which were the ancient enclosures of strip farming. They run due east almost from the centre of the village, and are known as Narrow Balk, Broad Balk and Jenny Balk. The tithe barn stands quite close to the church in the stable yard of the Hall, and is of Tudor origin.

The present population of approximately 170 is served by a post office and general store, and a butcher's. There is also a private club, called The Hostel, with a village meeting room. A new school was opened in 1970. The old school, which was built and maintained by the estate in 1866, is now a private residence.

The outward appearance of the village has changed little since medieval times, and great pains have been taken to retain this. With the demise of agriculture, many farm buildings were left unused, and these have been sympathetically converted into private dwellings, as has the old vicarage. Hooton Pagnell has, on three occasions, won the Best Kept Village competition, and the benches, presented by *The Dalesman*, are positioned around the war memorial.

No visit would be complete without seeing the flock of black sheep, usually found grazing in the cricket field. The original flock were brought from St Kilda's, an island in the Outer Hebrides, and their wool is woven into a very durable suiting.

Hooton Roberts

Hooton Roberts is a hillside village above the river Don, situated on the busy A630 Doncaster to Rotherham road.

The church of St John the Baptist dates from Norman times, and has a 15th century tower. Inside there is a stone coffin, on the lid of which is a cross and chalice, and a 13th century window, much restored, showing the figures of a tiny monk and a boy bishop. There is an underground passage (now bricked up) from the church to the manor house, and in the aisle of the church can be seen the slab with iron rings showing its location.

The first Earl of Strafford's widow lived at the manor and, when she died in 1688 at the age of 83, she was buried secretly by torch light in the chancel of the church. There is a memorial to her husband at Wentworth Woodhouse, where he was thought to have been buried. However, in 1895, when work was being carried out near the altar in St John's, three unknown skeletons were found, one appearing to be headless. They were thought to be the Earl, his wife and 16 year old daughter, who had rickets, as one of the skeletons had signs of this disease.

Strafford, (1593–1641) from a great Yorkshire family, was chief

123

adviser of Charles I. He was impeached by the Long Parliament and, with the King's reluctant assent, was executed in May 1641 – 'Put not your trust in princes' he exclaimed when he heard of the King's defection.

As recently as 1964 there were four farms in the village, and two in the parish. At that time there were 45 houses in Hooton Roberts, with a population of less than 200, many people being related. The whole village, apart from the church, the rectory and the Church of England school (attended by twelve children), was owned by the Earl Fitzwilliam of Wentworth Woodhouse. There was a post office and village shop, but no public house.

Visiting Hooton Roberts today, the only sound comes from the traffic passing through, but at the turn of the century it was very different. In September 1902, a young musician staying with the rector's family was listening to the first public performance of his song *Linden Lea*. He was Ralph Vaughan Williams, and composed it sitting in the rectory gardens, where the walls were covered with ivy, and on the lawn were croquet hoops. Vaughan Williams often played croquet at Hooton Roberts.

Now there is very little of the old village left. All the barns, and one farm in the Wapping, are now houses and the ancient tithe barn has become private residences. The beautiful manor house is an hotel, with its lovely green lawns now a car park. The shop and post office have gone, but the little church still watches over the village from the top of the hill.

Horsforth 🐎

Villagers used to boast that theirs was 'the biggest village in England' and still, though it is now called a suburb of Leeds, they are proud of their separate identity and fight hard to preserve it. In feudal times there were five manors, one of which is still represented by Low Hall, now a restaurant, which is basically Elizabethan. Newlaithes Manor, on the hillside overlooking the river Aire, is probably the oldest inhabited building.

Horsforth was mentioned in the Domesday Book of 1086. Although it appears three times in the book, it has three different spellings: Horseforde, Hoseford and Horsford. No-one is sure which was the original ford. The difficulty arises because every road into Horsforth crosses water; Cow beck and Red beck both originate on Yeadon common and form the north, east and west boundaries respectively until they flow into the river Aire, the southern boundary. The most ancient sign of occupation found in Horsforth is the cup and ring stone, found near Low Hall and now moved for safety to the grounds of the picturesque Cistercian abbey at Kirkstall, a mile outside the boundary. Another interesting stone is also outside the boundary and this obelisk, situated near Kirkstall

The Green, Horsforth

Forge, shows that the village is virtually halfway between the capitals of England and Scotland.

Old Horsforth was built of local millstone grit on an outcropping ridge, and many old stone cottages remain, including some three-storey weavers' cottages. One stone on a house in Back Lane carries the date 1691. Many Horsforth householders were 'clothiers', or cloth-makers, and the woollen cloth made by them was sold at special markets in Leeds and Bradford. The church of St Margaret can be seen, on its hilltop, for miles around, as only the woods on Hunger Hills (where residents dug for coal in dangerous bell-pits in hard times) stand above it. Just over a hundred years ago this church replaced the Bell chapel, the outline of which can still be traced on the green (now a garden of rest) at the foot of Town Street. The old gravestones with which it is paved are worth studying.

Perhaps the village's most famous son was Rev Samuel Marsden, who is reputed to have introduced the woollen industry to Australia and New Zealand. He went there as a minister, having worked in Horsforth in the blacksmith's forge at the top of Bachelor Lane, where a hoop stone (used in the making of cartwheels) is preserved as a memorial to him. Horsforth is fortunate in having an active village historical society, which has recently opened a local museum in one of the Georgian houses on the green.

Although there are many modern housing developments, there are still woods and fields in and around Horsforth, and miles of snickets and footpaths used by villagers before the days of motor transport. The trees which line Stanhope Drive were planted as a memorial to those from Horsforth who fell in the First World War. Two hundred and eleven commemorate men and one a woman, Nurse Florence Hogg. Those alongside the ring road are in memory of those who died in the Second World War. The Leeds ring road runs through the middle of Horsforth, almost cutting it in two, but there are two main shopping areas, one in each part. There is also a vigorous life as a community with many clubs and societies representing interests from horticulture to philately, a prestigious music festival, and well-supported flower shows.

Hoylandswaine 🌿

Hoylandswaine is a South Yorkshire village encompassing an area of 2,023 acres, with a population of 850, situated just two miles from Penistone. It stands on a steep rise surrounded by magnificent countryside. Its highest point, 883 ft above sea level, affords panoramic views of wooded hills and productive farmlands to the north. The southern aspect presents, more distantly, scenes of heather covered moorland. In every direction the vista is divided into colourful patchwork by the dry stone walling characteristic of this area.

Hoylandswaine stands on an old salt track, so called because salt was the most important commodity carried along its route from Cheshire to Barnsley and Doncaster. The track has been in existence for at least 2,000 years, but the first mention of Hoylandswaine as a place seems to have been in the Domesday Book of 1086. A thousand years have passed since then and left little mark on the village. There is no evidence of an ancient Hall, no village green, indeed no real village centre, the comparatively modern church, built in 1869, and the slightly older school opened in 1848 being on the northern perimeter.

Little visual evidence remains of the few small industries which have been introduced over the years into the otherwise farming community. A small privately owned colliery at Guider Bottom employed a labour force of 30 at the height of its production, but ultimately it became uneconomical and the last shift was worked in 1969. Evidence of 'day holes' interrupt the landscape here and there, some having been dug for coal, others the clay used in Cawthorne for the making of clay pipes.

In 1806 there were at least 20 nailmakers in the village; in 1881 there were 23, eight of whom were women. By 1900 nailmaking had suffered a decline. Alderman George Senior, Lord Mayor of Sheffield, had been born in Bradfield but lived in Hoylandswaine for some 13 years, and had helped his father make nails in a little shop above the Rose and Crown. In 1906 Alderman Senior demolished the nail shop and built four almshouses. Fortunately not all evidence of our nailmaking heritage has disappeared. Three nail shops stand virtually unnoticed in a cottage garden above the Lord Nelson. Others in Cooper Lane have been converted into a garage.

Towards the top of Barnsley Road was a Quaker meeting house and burial ground. A recent housing development has its access road right through the burial ground. The planners may have met no objections, but previous occupants appear to be upset. Ghosts have recently been sighted in the vicinity.

Hoylandswaine has many musical links and traditions. Two songs sung throughout the area at Christmastime are called the *Swaine Ark* and the *Swaine Anthem* amongst their seemingly numerous titles. The origins of both songs, at least 200 years old, are lost in the mists of time.

From being reasonably self sufficient 50 years ago, Hoylandswaine is now referred to as a commuter village. Certainly very few people earn their living here now. In spite of approximately 100 houses being built during the last 30 years, shops and other amenities have disappeared, such as the 'chippy' and the village cobbler. There remains, however, the church, chapel, school, village hall, post office and just one exceedingly well stocked village store, and the two public houses must not be forgotten or the cricket club and its grounds, a delightful setting for watching the teams in traditional white on a summer evening.

Ingbirchworth

Ingbirchworth is a small farming village situated on the eastern slopes of the Pennine range. At its highest point, about 1,000 ft, it is possible on a clear day to see the Yorkshire Wolds some 50 miles away. It is a bleak place in winter and even when wearing its summer mantle of beauty, the wind creeps around each nook and cranny, plaguing the hardy Yorkshire Tykes who live there. It is the sort of village where people want to live out their lives not only because of the beautiful and picturesque countryside but because of the quality of the local people.

Agriculture and its ancillary businesses have always been the main occupation and some of the farms date back to the 13th century. The village, like most others, is slowly changing with a steady growth in population and dwelling houses. Fifty years ago there were 22 farms, three pubs, the chapel and very few houses. The farms have now dwindled to eight and two smallholdings, the pubs to two, but the houses have increased in number and the present population is around 450.

The chapel and pubs are still the focal points of village life where all the old stories are still told. There is an amusing one about the farm men going into the farmhouse for tea after a day threshing. Seeing no milk on the table, one of the visiting helpers asked for some, whereupon the farmer gave a piercing whistle and a goat came in and jumped onto the table. The milk was certainly fresh and you could say on draught, straight from the goat to the pot. Television took a long time to establish itself and one farmer's wife would never get undressed in the same room as she thought that the people inside the television would see her.

There are many people and places of interest connected with the village and surrounding area, one of them being Grange Farm. At one time it was named 'The Angel Inn' and was a busy coaching house on the route between Halifax and Sheffield. There is a date carved over the door of 1624 but there is proof that there was a house there from a much earlier date. Another inscription over the door is in Latin and means 'Let faith enter and fraud depart'. The house is a perfect example of a well-to-do yeoman's house, having a distaff side where the ladies adjourned and a parlour or talking room for the gentlemen.

In the same parish is the Danish district of Gunthwaite, which for many years was the seat of the ancient family named Bosville, who were very important in this area, holding such rights as the appointment of the vicar of Penistone. Gunthwaite lies amidst beautiful scenery, deep lanes and mysterious woods, but sadly the original Hall was destroyed many years ago. In a clearing on part of the old packhorse bridle path is the most striking building still remaining from the 16th century, an immense timber-framed tithe barn which covers nearly half an acre and is entirely held together by wooden pegs.

For many years at Gunthwaite 'Spa', as it is known locally because of its fearsome tasting waters, there was an ancient practice whereby religious leaders from Wakefield, Pontefract and Doncaster gathered together on the first Sunday in May to bless these healing waters. Local people still keep up the tradition of this gathering.

Ingbirchworth has a present day claim to fame which brings visitors from all over the British Isles. They come to see the many rare birds which visit the reservoir area. The CARE project (Community Action in the Rural Environment) have erected a board walk around the reservoir. The work was done on a voluntary basis, which together with eight other South Yorkshire villages won an award presented by HRH Prince of Wales.

Kilnhurst

In the 14th century, Kilnhurst was developed by the monks of Roche Abbey to provide them with iron. At this time Simon de Montfort lived at Hall's Farm.

Eventually, Kilnhurst was purchased by a John Darley, who died around 1617, aged 75 years. He was buried at Rawmarsh, and his principal heir was his grandson, John Ellis. In 1662, the Ellis family sold this estate, described as 'The Manor of Kilnhurst', to John Hatfield of Laughton en le Morthen. His son, John, sold it in 1717 to Samuel Shore of Sheffield, the Manor passing to his grandson and heir, Samuel Shore, who died in 1828, at the age of 90.

In 1846, Swinton Iron Works was formed on a wharf by the canal on which Kilnhurst lies. It was operational until 1879, after which it declined, when iron gave way to steel. John Baker purchased the derelict site in 1903, and, together with a Mr Bessemer, formed one of the most successful Steel Works – Baker and Bessemer. This company was the first to provide the solid steel railway wheel.

Lying in the centre of a coal mining area, Kilnhurst, too, had its own coal mine, which was sunk in the mid 19th century. As there was no railway in the early days, coal was transported by barge. Another large firm was the Yorkshire Tar Distillers, founded by a Mr Allison, on land bought from Earl Fitzwilliam in 1886. In joint partnership with a Mr Mitchell, the Yorkshire Tar Distillers made many products, including rubber, paint and synthetic materials. Only one of these firms is still in operation, although this has been taken over and the name changed. The Steel Works have now gone, and the colliery yard lies idle.

In Kilnhurst itself, the main street (Victoria Road) was dominated by the Co-operative Society. In 1860 the village was the first to form its own Society. The idea, originally discussed in a room in the joiner's shop, was actually put into operation in 1861. The Co-op dominated most of one side of the road – drapery, grocery, haberdashery. This, too, has gone.

Off the main road from Meadow View, is a very uneven path, which runs from the railway to Bakers 'Pond', known locally as 'Ankle Brekker'. The pond was a popular skating rink in winter, and one young boy, who drowned whilst playing there, was buried in his sailor suit.

In the 19th and early 20th centuries, Kilnhurst was a thriving community, with a number of large prosperous businesses. However, today many of the old houses and shops have gone, leaving behind a smaller community. It still has three public houses and one school, but no railway station.

Although there are many ancient churches in South Yorkshire, the one at Kilnhurst is quite 'young'. Overlooking the village, it was built in 1859, and was called the Chapel of St Thomas.

At the present time small businesses are being established, and perhaps Kilnhurst may once again become a busy, prosperous, community.

Kimberworth 🐗

The village of Kimberworth is approximately two miles from the centre of Rotherham in the county of South Yorkshire and covers almost 3,000 acres of land. It is situated on a hill overlooking the Rother valley, the highest point being over 450 ft above sea level.

Anglo-Saxons were the first known farmers of the land but nowadays there is little farming done in the area as much of the land has been used for building. Evidence of a ridge can still be seen in parts of the village and is thought to have been constructed to keep out the invading Roman army.

With the coming of the Normans, Roger de Busli became lord of the manor and caused a motte and bailey castle, probably made of wood, to be built. The mound on which the castle stood has been preserved and can still be seen, although a housing estate has been built in the area.

Iron ore was mined at Thundercliffe Grange by the monks from nearby Kirkstead Abbey from the 12th century until the Dissolution of the Monasteries by Henry VIII. Mining did continue after this, however, but not by the monks. The present grange still standing on the site was built in the 18th century and at one time belonged to the Effingham family. It was bought and used as a school by the local council but was quite recently turned into flats by a private owner.

The parish church was completed in 1843 at a cost of £1,000. It was dedicated to St Thomas. The clock tower of the church is a focal point for the villagers. There are also Methodist and Congregational churches and quite recently a meeting place has been built by the Salvation Army. There is a Catholic church nearby.

One of the first known schools in the village of Kimberworth was the Academy, which was founded in the early part of the 19th century. The building is still standing and has been converted into a house and two flats. Today, there are two comprehensive schools in the village, one built in 1914 and the second in 1959. The old junior school has been replaced with a modern building. There is also an infants school and the Catholic church has a junior and an infants school.

Many of the village's old buildings have been demolished or fallen into disrepair, including Kimberworth Hall and the 19th century smithy. Barns at the 17th century Manor Farm have been converted into a restaurant and bar, without losing any of the original character. It is now a popular meeting place for old and young alike.

There are two parks in the village. One provides children's amusements and football pitches and the other has bowling greens, tennis courts, miniature golf and gardens. There is also an 18 hole municipal golf course nearby. New housing has increased the population of the village in recent years and it is now a bustling community.

Kirk Bramwith 🦊

The tiny hamlet of Kirk Bramwith lies some six miles north-east of Doncaster, adjacent to the river Don, and bordered by the Stainforth-Keadby Canal and the New Junction Canal. The approach is along a winding country road through open farm land. The village consists of 14 houses, attractively situated along the village street. Many of them are old brick and pantile cottages, but there have been some new additions in recent years.

The focal point of the village is St Mary's church, almost 800 years old and built by the De Laceys of Pontefract after the Norman Conquest. In

1362 Edward III created John of Gaunt Duke of Lancaster, and Kirk Bramwith, its church and all the Pontefract lands were swept into the estates of one of the most powerful families in English history; hence the royal connection and patronage of the Duchy of Lancaster. The Laceys built the first St Mary's church, but most of their work disappeared during the restoration of the 15th century. However, the south door, with its arch of cruel stone hawk heads, the lower half of the tower and the font, are of the original building. The interior furnishings are all hand-carved English oak, containing some of the finest work of the great Yorkshire craftsman, the late Robert Thompson of Kilburn. Thompson's little carved mice, with which he marked his work, can be found on most pieces of furniture. The stained glass windows are worth noting, bearing royal arms of Kings and Queens of England, showing the church's 'royal' connections. A good time to visit the little church is when the snowdrops are in bloom, as they cast a lovely white carpet around this ancient building, the Snowdrop Festival taking place annually in February.

Mainly a farming community of mixed arable, with some cattle and sheep, the lands around the village are surrounded by drainage dykes to prevent flooding, but offering many wild life habitats. Owls, herons, curlews, swans and wildfowl are to be seen on the banks and lanes, plus a very noisy rookery in the churchyard. A lovely walk, clearly signposted, takes you along the banks of the river Don to the pretty village of Fishlake, and then by waterside to the neighbouring town of Thorne.

Kirkhamgate 🐿

The village grew in early days mainly on the south side of the major road and consisted of farmsteads and pit cottages overlooking New Park. The park, owned by Lord Cardigan, extended some three miles in each direction to Gawthorpe, Ossett and Roundwood.

It has a few old farmsteads, some improved with modern interiors. It also formerly had both Wesleyan and Primitive Methodist chapels, the latter of which has only recently been delightfully refurbished. Close by is the village hall which is now more regularly used, but with grey slate roofing and decayed stonework reflects its age.

In recent years the M1 motorway was constructed as close to the village as possible, passing underneath the Batley Road and destroying the village cricket field at a stroke, but revealing a productive coal seam just below the surface. Outcropping of this bed of coal has, to some extent, prejudiced housing development in the region.

The single public house, the Star inn, has the unusual distinction of generous charity giving, whilst at the same time providing the village with a Christmas family outing when the proprietors, as Santa Claus with wife and family, without a reindeer but with horse transport, distribute gifts and hampers to the old folk and children throughout the area.

131

There are two off licence shops, a butcher's, fish shop and a few small undertakings but no larger industrial units. The Asquith farming enterprise ensures the cultivation of much of the arable land in the area and supplies market garden produce over a wide area with the special distinction of perpetuating the best rhubarb growing region in the country. Locals will confirm that, in early winter, one can actually see and hear the forced rhubarb in the act of growing. It is dispatched from here to Covent Garden and virtually every other market in the country during the spring.

The very successful cricket club still thrives some 1,000 yards from the village, but they hope very soon to re-establish their headquarters nearer home.

Close by the village, just across the motorway, is the water purification plant built by Wakefield Corporation. Now administered by the Yorkshire Water Authority, it controls the water supply for a huge area around Wakefield. It has recently been extended.

On the very edge of the hamlet is the Bower House, erected alongside the footpath to East Ardsley. Around 1800, it stood on the very edge of the Wakefield Outwood, an extensive area of woodland between Leeds and Wakefield stretching from Bottomboat in the east to Kirkhamgate in the west. Nooking, a collection of dwellings nearer Kirkhamgate, probably had a similar origin as an encroachment on the forest, but their position to the north-west of Brandy Carr Road indicates they were on the site of the old Roman road. The locals often refer to Brandy Carr Road as 'the new road'. Some old pottery has been found near Nooking and also near Bower House. The area still retains its rural aspect, to the delight of residents.

Kirk Sandall ✑

The village of Kirk Sandall originated from the old hamlet of Sandal Parva. It very possibly played a major part in the nearby battle of Hatfield (AD 633), in which Edwin, the first Christian king of Northumbria, suffered a crushing defeat. The church, the focal point of the hamlet, was dedicated to St Oswald, the warrior king, who succeeded his uncle Edwin. This building was given, with other Warren churches, to the monks of Lewes by the Earls of Warren.

The church is partly Norman, and may have Saxon foundations. It is well known to lovers of old church architecture for its carefully restored medieval oak screens and the roof of the Rokeby chapel, named after a famous 15th century rector, William Rokeby. William, born in 1460, became Archbishop of Dublin and Lord Chancellor of Ireland. He officiated at the christening of Mary Tudor. He died in 1521, his body being buried in the church – in the Rokeby chapel there is a monument to him.

The hamlet consisted of a 'big house', a farm and a cluster of cottages surrounding the church. The Sandall mansion and estate was held in the Rokeby family over a period of 300 years, but was finally sold in 1776 to Mr John Martin.

In 1626, Rev Robert Wood gave property for a schoolmaster to form a grammar school, and by 1827 this had been an elementary school for some years. In 1817, a Methodist chapel was added to the hamlet. Some years later this was sold to Miss Mary Ann Parnell and used as a Church of England Sunday school, and, from 1864 to the opening of the glass works, this was to be the village school.

The new village of Kirk Sandall, situated on the banks of the river Don and Don Navigational Canal, is below the 25 ft contour and comes within the factory zone. It is a quarter of a mile away from the old village, over the other side of the railway and main Doncaster Road, and was originally built to accommodate the glass workers Pilkington's brought with them from St Helen's, when they decided to build their factory on the Sandall site. The site was chosen for its proximity to the canal and railway, and for the sandy terrain which was needed for the production of glass. The factory produced its first glass in July 1921.

The village was to stretch from the outskirts of Barnby Dun along the Doncaster Road in one direction, and back towards Armthorpe Lane in the other. It was well planned in the Garden Village style, with a Catholic church, Congregational church, village hall, recreational club and tennis courts and bowling greens, as well as gardens for people to sit in. The famous glass pub, formerly known as the Kirk Sandall Hotel, was opened in 1934, and was renamed the Glassmaker after extensive alterations in 1956–57.

Kirk Sandall has doubled in size from its beginning, and now spreads to meet Edenthorpe. There is a new church housed between the two villages, in the grounds of the Church of England school. This church still has a rector, Mr Taylor, but the old church is used only once a year in September. Most of the hamlet is now gone, but the odd foundations can still be seen. There is a wood inhabited by squirrels and birds, where bluebells flourish in the spring. The village has a good shopping precinct and a frequent bus service into the local town centre. There are many activities for both young and old, and men still play bowls and cricket on the Pilkington pitches.

Laycock 🐿️

The village of Laycock lies near to the Yorkshire/Lancashire border, two miles from Keighley. It is 768 ft above sea level, with hills above and a deep, wooded valley below.

The oldest houses in the present-day village date back to the 17th century and were built from locally quarried stone. The manor house is thought to have been built in 1697 and has an original stone fireplace. Laycock does not now have an obvious centre, being often only one house deep for approximately a mile along the Main Street. At the west end of the village is a row of remarkable terraced houses built in 1841 into the steeply sloping hillside. These comprise eight houses fronting onto Laycock Lane and six more houses underneath them opening the other way, into Robert Street. These were built for mill workers and are still in use today.

In the late 18th century, a number of mills were built in the Laycock area and this led to the decline of cottage industries such as combing, spinning and weaving. Originally these were cotton mills, as the route into Lancashire was easier for transportation using horses than the descent into Keighley. The middle of the 19th century saw a change in the type of industry from cotton spinning to worsted spinning, bobbin making and paper making, but Laycock's isolation and the difficulty of bringing coal to the mills, led to their general decline. Two particular mills, which endured for 160 years, were in the hamlet of Goose Eye in the valley bottom a quarter of a mile from Laycock. One of these mills manufactured paper for bank notes and the other was a rag house, used for sorting the rags which, together with wood pulp, made the paper.

The people of Laycock were a close-knit community, frequently inter-marrying so that the same family names appear in the records for generations. Dancing round the maypole was recorded up until the 1870s; the local brass band practised in a room over a stable at Gamescar Farm; and Plot Night, Mischief Night and Mumming Night were all celebrated. Children helped with general work and delivered milk etc. The village had its shop with a bakery attached, which even supplied shops in Keighley, and the village joiner was kept busy doing repairs for local farmers.

One local legend concerns William Sharp, of Whorls Farm. Because his close-fisted father, known as 'Old Three Laps', had quarrelled with his bride's father, young William was left literally standing at the altar on his wedding day in 1807. His heart broken, he returned to the farm, went to bed, and stayed there without speaking until his death 49 years later. The room he occupied was some nine ft square, with stone flags on the floor and a window which was fastened shut for his last 38 years. By the time of his death, William weighed about 17 stone; his legs could not be straightened and he had to be buried in an oak chest two ft four inches deep, which needed eight men with strong ropes to lower it into the grave.

In the late 19th century the staple diet was porridge, home-cured bacon and ham, salted meat, home-grown vegetables, and oat-cakes. Lighting was by oil lamps and candles, and water for both drinking and washing was obtained from the wells at points in the village. The only means of transport was by farm cart, and farmers shod their cattle and walked them to market.

Laycock Village Institute was built in 1927 after Sir Abe Bailey, who began his education at Laycock school, offered £600 towards the cost if the villagers could raise an equal amount. This they did, by selling hot toffee and hot peas; a plaque commemorates this gift.

Laycock today is a thriving and attractive village with a blend of some 130 old and newer dwellings. Although it had been receiving piped gas and water for 70 years or so, Laycock was only connected to the main sewerage system in 1961, around the time that a small estate was built at the east end of the village. Laycock is now a conservation area, and all renovations and barn conversions must preserve the traditional character of the village. Unfortunately the only shop and post office closed recently; but the bus service has been improved. Several annual events take place: there is a gala, a gymkhana, a WI fair, and school concerts. The people of Laycock are proud of their village and its traditions.

Letwell 🐝

Letwell is one of the prettiest villages in South Yorkshire. Legend has it that Oliver Cromwell played a part in naming the village. He is said to have visited local landowner, Sir Ralph Knight, glanced at the peaceful scene, and ridden away telling his troops 'let well alone . . .'.

The earliest record of village life goes back to 1160, when Thomas de Letwell, then a sergeant of Tickhill Castle, took possession of an acre of land in the parish. He was given an allowance of threepence halfpenny a day for feeding the hounds in winter. The village church now stands on the land he once tended. During the reign of Henry III, records tell of Peter de Letwell, a knight at Tickhill Castle. He was so poor he is said to have done battle at the tournaments held at Styrrup wearing rusty armour! St Peter's church was built around 1375, but in 1867 all but the tower was destroyed when the sexton got carried away stoking up the boiler, causing a terrible fire. The church was rebuilt by Sir Thomas Woolaston White of Wallingwells.

As one might imagine, wells abound in Letwell. A recent survey suggested that at one time there were as many as 19 either side of Barker Hades Road, the main village street. The wells were the only source of water until 1935, when piped supplies were first brought to the village at a cost of £25,000. The main village pump can still be seen. The stone base stands across the road from the church hall, and is used as a flower tub. The pump now stands on the well outside Manor Cottage. Maintaining water supplies was always a great concern, and, in the early 1930s, there was much consternation when a plumber came along and charged £5 to repair one of the main pumps. When the villagers complained, he replied it was a penny halfpenny for the washer, and the rest for knowing what was wrong and putting it right.

Life in the 1920s and 1930s was idyllic, or so it seems now. At that time almost the entire population was employed on the farms. Two arable farms still remain, but all but a handful of the 110 inhabitants now commute each day to Worksop, Sheffield and even further afield. In days gone by, the village made its own entertainment with weekly dances and concerts in the church hall. On one occasion the population assembled en masse to be taught the Charleston by a pair of professional dancers specially hired from Doncaster.

Today, the village is still a place of beauty. Many of the houses are listed and thankfully cannot be altered. The dovecote stands proudly in the field behind South Farm. It was near to dereliction when villagers rallied round to raise money, forming a Preservation Society in 1982. The group then took on six workers and, with the help of finance from a Government Community Scheme, restored the fabric of this beautiful building. It was constructed of hand-made bricks in the 1700s to provide the village with a source of fresh meat. Octagonal in shape, it is roofed with old red tiles with leaded joints, and a pagoda-style lantern top. Inside there are 200 nesting boxes and a revolving pole, which can be climbed to provide access to the boxes. The restored dovecote, which won an award from the Council for the Protection of Rural England, can be visited, the key being available at South Farm.

Lindley 🦖

Lindley, situated as it is near the M62 on the outskirts of Huddersfield, seems no more than a suburb, but it is in all respects a thriving village. Mentioned in the Domesday Book, the name Lindley is thought to be derived from 'Lin Leah' meaning 'flax clearing', an early link with the textile village it was to become. Lindley possibly grew up as a settlement close to a transpennine drovers' route, then prospered because of its grazing, quarries, its home looms and later its mills, mostly textile but including a prosperous wire company which made its fortune producing mechanised card clothing. The mills and the wire company still exist and Lindley has a measure of fine old houses once inhabited by the wealthy mill owners.

Lindley's best known landmark is its clock tower, built in 1902 in the Art Nouveau style for Mr James Nield Sykes of Sykes Brothers Wire Company in Acre Street. It was designed by Edgar Wood. The mill owner's reasons for building the tower were reputedly mercenary – so that his workers should never need to be late for work! The clock tower was a favourite landmark of Sir John Betjeman, the late Poet Laureate. The theme for the sculpture on the tower is Time, and the eternal virtues of Truth, Purity, Love and Justice.

The tower stands in a commanding position at the junction of five roads, a lasting monument to the Lindley of 90 years ago and the values of a bygone age. The architect, Edgar Wood, was also responsible for a pleasing terrace of houses on Lindley's main street, Lidget Street, for a solid Victorian mansion, Briarcourt, now a home for the mentally handicapped, and for the communion table in Lindley Methodist church, again donated by James Nield Sykes.

Lindley is a treasure trove of back streets and alleyways with typical Yorkshire stone cottages, some over 200 years old and little changed. Church life and its attendant organisations and activities, is strongly represented by the thriving Anglican church, St Stephen's (1830), Lindley Evangelical church and Lindley Methodist church (1745). A former Lindley Zion Methodist Sunday school still stands, although now a carpet warehouse. Opposite is the Mechanics Hall, founded in 1847, which is now the well-used Lindley library.

Although 800 ft above sea level, Lindley nestles amidst the Pennines and on clear sunny days affords views of better known landmarks such as Emley Moor. It bustles with activity, boasting a well-known children's bookshop, an overflowing infants and junior school, six local hostelries and the polytechnic of Huddersfield's School of Education, whose residential tower block mirrors that to the hospital just half a mile away. The students on the campus add greatly to the atmosphere of Lindley village life. A good selection of shops and a number of industrial concerns together with the hospital, a special care unit and a hostel for the mentally handicapped, ensure that Lindley will remain a busy, friendly place to live.

Linthwaite

Linthwaite was not mentioned in the Domesday Book but in 1361 was named as part of the Duchy of Lancaster. The north and west boundaries are clearly defined by the river Colne and Bridley brook, whilst the southern boundary with some deviation follows the line of Blackmoorfoot Road. The eastern boundary was changed in 1937 when local government was reorganised and a considerable part of the township was lost to Huddersfield Borough.

The tithe map of Linthwaite in 1847 reveals a series of 15 widely spaced settlements (five of these were transferred to Huddersfield). These were mainly weavers' cottages where woollen cloth production was undertaken by hand-operated machinery. The building of large factories in the 19th century caused a radical transformation including the construction of rows of terraced housing on or near the major roads and convenient to the new work places.

In 1838 the population was estimated to be 2,852. The great majority of business people were cloth manufacturers at home or in small workshops, 57 are listed at this time. In addition there were six inns and taverns, eleven beer houses, four blacksmiths, two cloth finishers, two dyers, four joiners, three shoe-makers, 17 shopkeepers, three tailors and two wheelwrights.

One of the early manufacturers was George Mallinson, who began employing workers in their homes in 1840. In 1857 he built his first mill, a workshop of three floors, where workers could be gathered on one site and supervised closely, although machinery was still operated by hand. He built his second mill in 1873. This was based on 'modern' lines with power available for all machines. At its peak Mallinson's employed 1,000 workers carrying out every process involved in converting fleece to cloth. George Mallinson was the major supporter of local Methodism, donating £3,000 for the construction of the chapel at Lower Clough.

Dyeing companies were established by George Cock and James Dyson, and the magnificent Titanic mill was constructed by the Crowther family in 1912 for spinning and at one time operated 36 carding sets.

Since the mid 1970s, the textile industry has sadly contracted. George Mallinson's is being used for small units but the Titanic mill now lies exposed to the elements and vandalism. An enterprising pharmaceutical company, Thornton & Ross, has expanded over the last three decades and is a valued source of local employment.

Transport in the mid 18th century was provided by the turnpike road constructed by Blind Jack of Knaresborough, which runs along the top of the hill along the southern boundary, serving the settlements at the top of the village. A new road was constructed in the 1830s to serve the bottom of the village, this is now known as Manchester Road (A62). The adjacent canal had been open as early as 1804, but its usefulness declined with the coming of the railway through the Colne valley (it is just outside the Linthwaite boundary) in 1849. The new road was therefore crucial to the development of Linthwaite.

In addition to the mills and the robust masonry associated with the construction of Blackmoorfoot reservoir, the major building of local interest is Linthwaite Hall. The Hall was constructed early in the 16th century and extended in the 17th. A story about the Hall involves a ghost in the form of a headless horseman who has been seen from time to time.

The village has a number of active church communities. The present church was built in 1828 at the top of the village. Sporting activities are well represented with two cricket clubs, three bowling greens, a soccer club, a tennis club and a golf course. The local comprehensive school – Colne Valley High – is situated in Linthwaite and provides education for 1,500 students. It was the first purpose-built comprehensive school in the West Riding. Members of the public use various school facilities in the evening.

Thanks to redevelopment and a large number of tree planting schemes the appearance of the village is steadily being enhanced.

Linton 🪶

Linton, betwixt Wetherby and Collingham, is well worth a detour to enjoy the atmosphere of a real country pub, the Windmill, with roaring fires in winter and a sunny conservatory and garden in warmer weather. Many pleasant walks are in the vicinity.

Although the village has no church, shop or school, it is one of the most desirable places to live in Yorkshire. It is bounded on one side by an attractive golf course and the river Wharfe. Racehorses are often to be seen being exercised in the village, and a lane beside the Windmill leads to a thriving livery stable.

Linton also boasts one of the finest hotels in the north which, until recently, was a Carmelite monastery. The village has an attractive blend of picturesque old and new dwellings with gardens to delight the eye.

Loversall 🪶

Loversall is a tiny rural village, a mixture of old and modern dwellings, built in a beautiful locality about three miles south-west of Doncaster. Its name first appears historically in Edward I's reign. It still retains its tranquillity in a peaceful pastoral setting, even though it now overlooks the intersection of the busy A1M and M18 motorways.

The villagers are mostly farming people or retired, or commute to Doncaster for work. There is a frequent bus service, but no shop or public house. Before the Second World War, transport to Doncaster used to be twice weekly by carrier. They would even do shopping for you. Then a Mr Prout began a service in his open topped double-decker bus with solid wheels. That must have been a hard and draughty ride!

The attractive small 12th century church of St Katherine can barely be seen from the main road. It is quite isolated from the village itself, and marked by its peace and seclusion. The church is reached by going along the one and only street, through a farmyard and past the old pound enclosure, where lost and straying animals were kept. A rough track is then taken across a field which is usually full of sheep. Inside the church the simple interior of the nave is supported by eight columns of the 13th century. In 1530 John Wirral erected a chapel on the side of the chancel, in which several notables connected with Loversall are buried. Two pairs of misericords stand in the chancel, which may have come from Roche Abbey at the Dissolution of the Monasteries.

In the churchyard stands a 14th century table tomb, unique in appearance because of the unusual mixture of decoration carved on its side. It is thought that a Knight of St John of Jerusalem is buried here, as one did own some property in Loversall. The churchyard is surrounded by an ivy clad stone wall, in which there is a small gate leading to Loversall Hall. Once a medieval Hall, built possibly on a monastery site, it was pulled down and rebuilt in 1809 by the Fenton family. A son, Rev William C. Fenton, is well remembered as the founder of the Yorkshire School for the Deaf in Doncaster. During the First World War, when the Skipwith family were in residence, the Hall was used as a convalescent hospital for soldiers. It is now used as offices, like so many large mansions.

Across the fields towards the village of Wadworth, is an area where Thomas Tofield, whose father was born in Loversall, used to search for flower specimens. He was a famous 18th century botanist, and also a renowned civil engineer. In one of the fields is St Catherine's Well, fed by a strong spring of pure water, now alas covered over. At the well there used to be a stone bath and a small house nearby, which was probably built by William Dixon, owner of the now demolished Alverley Hall. The waters of the spring were reputed to be of considerable benefit for cold bathing in the 18th century. An elderly woman from Loversall was paid to come every day in the summertime to 'assist the bathers and accommodate them with dresses gratis and breakfast afterwards'. Later, Loversall village and district had water piped from this spring through a filter bed to two taps in the village. People can remember tramping through thick snow to the spring to get water when the pipes froze.

Finally it is worth mentioning another notable building standing on Loversall land. This splendid 19th century mansion was built by George Banks, a Leeds wool merchant, and is now St Catherine's mental hospital administration centre, whose future is uncertain.

Luddenden 🐝

Luddenden lies in the bottom of a steep-sided South Pennines valley, from which it takes its name. It is first mentioned in the Wakefield manor court rolls of 1331. The settlement developed around a crossing of the Luddenden brook by the important medieval road called the Long Causeway, which reached upper Calderdale. The brook forms the boundary between Midgley and Warley townships, which are mentioned in the Domesday Book of 1086. The Warley manor corn mill was moved to Luddenden in 1379 to make use of the brook. The boundary here was chosen as the site of a chapel of ease to serve both townships. Just before his death in 1460 Richard Duke of York, lord of the manor of Wakefield, granted land and stone towards the new building.

By 1600 the river was crossed by a bridge and the settlement had twelve houses along with the chapel and the mill. Several inns and alehouses satisfied not only the needs of travellers but also provided meeting places for recreation and business. It was in 1594 at William Hopkinson's alehouse that Michael Foxcroft stabbed Samuel Wade with a dagger. Wade died three weeks later but the family feud, which was about property, carried on for years. Anthony Mitchell, one of the last to be beheaded on the Halifax Gibbet, a sort of guillotine, was arrested in 1650 at another village inn. Midgley township business was conducted at the White Swan inn, built in 1634. It changed its name to the Lord Nelson inn after the battle of Trafalgar. The Murgatroyd Arms, on the other side of the brook, was where Warley business was transacted. This was built by the Murgatroyd family along with its adjacent brewhouse.

The corn mill fulfilled local needs until it closed in 1890. The Murgatroyds, who had owned the mill since 1633, developed part of the site in the late 18th century as a woollen mill. Until the introduction of the textile mill the terraced cottages in the village were occupied by people who spun and wove cloth by hand. The village was well known for its quality of spun yarn, the sole preserve of the women of each household. The 19th century mills in the Luddenden valley were large and numerous, employing many people making a diversity of textiles; worsteds, woollens, silks, cottons, carpets and even paper.

The growth of the northern towns during the Industrial Revolution lead to a demand for good quality building stone. Large quarries were opened around the Luddenden valley and by the 1860s some 40,000 tons annually passed through the village to the canal and railway at Luddenden Foot. This industry was serviced by many horses which were in turn serviced by several village smithies.

From the 1850s Alfred Yates made machine tools and mechanical saws at premises in Halifax Lane. Lower Mill closed as a woollen mill in 1890, but was later used extensively for the manufacture of nuts and bolts for the motor car industry. The factory closed in 1985 and the site has been redeveloped for housing.

The ancient chapel of ease, dedicated to St Mary, was demolished and rebuilt in 1816. Three bishops started off their lives here, one of whom, Robert Ferrar, was burnt at the stake in 1555 at Carmarthen. William Grimshaw, the famous Methodist curate of Haworth, was buried at Luddenden with all his family. His friend John Wesley passed this way to visit the Grimshaws at Ewood in Midgley.

The village in the late 18th century began to flourish as a cultural centre. Calderdale's first lending library was established in 1776 at the Lord Nelson inn. This attracted a coterie of artistic people, one of whom was Bramwell Bronte while he was the clerk at Luddenden Foot railway station. Another was William Heaton, a weaver poet who was born and lived the early part of his life in a cottage next to the churchyard. He taught himself to write by tracing the gravestone inscriptions. In response to the Incorporation of the nearby Borough of Halifax in 1867, some wags at the Lord Nelson inn elected their own mayor. Anyone can be Mayor of Luddenden for one month but the catch is that the new mayor has to buy everyone present at the ceremony in the pub a drink!

The important position of Luddenden declined as new modes of transport passed it by in the main Calder valley, and other places became the centres of local government. New building was drawn away from the village centre when New Road was built in 1820 to bypass the steep old road from the bridge to Midgley. Since the Second World War many shops have closed down. There has also been a physical decline in the village since the war with many old houses being demolished because of public health orders. The housing gap was filled by new council estates sited away from the old centre.

In 1973 the village campaigned for and was designated a conservation area. Since then, planned developments have made the village into a very desirable place to live.

Mankinholes & Lumbutts

Only a quarter of a mile of sloping fields separate these two tiny villages. They are situated in the ancient township of Langfield, which belonged to the manor of Wakefield.

Mankinholes, the older of the two, was mentioned in the Domesday Book, but there was a settlement there much earlier. Its houses all faced south, to keep the daylight as long as possible, when most were occupied by hand-loom weavers. They appear to have grown from the earth, as indeed they have, being built from the millstone grit which abounds on these uplands. They are dark from the years of smoke which used to pour from the many mill chimneys, now largely disappeared.

Mankinholes Hall is now a Youth Hostel and caters for the many walkers, some having come off the Pennine Way, which is about a mile and a half away. In its past it was also a children's home, part of the workhouse. Some of the children would no doubt have worked on the land or in the mills.

There is a cottage called 'Antwerp' which, during the First World War, was occupied by Belgian refugees. They gave the house a name which reminded them of their homeland.

At Pilkington Farm there was once a tenterfield, where the cloth was stretched before being ready for sale. There is now a Quaker burial ground on the spot. Until about ten years ago there was a Methodist chapel in the village. All that is left is the Sunday school building which is now a private dwelling. Methodism is the main form of worship, having taken over from the Society of Friends or Quakers. John Wesley travelled widely on these hills, making many converts, but the Quakers were very strong, meeting in one another's houses. Their first recorded meetings were held in Mankinholes in 1667, in the house of Joshua Laycock. The little tentercroft was rented as a burial ground at a yearly rent of 'one twopence of silver' for a term of 900 years.

The hills are criss-crossed with flagged paths, which are known locally as 'causeys'. These connect the villages and also were once the only way

142

to travel from one town to another, the bottoms or valleys being too wet and muddy for easy travel. The hand-loom weavers used them to take their finished 'pieces' of cloth to sell, usually to Halifax, twelve miles away.

The little village of Lumbutts sits well in a hollow, a 'hanging valley' in fact, and is not really old, being a product of the Industrial Revolution. On the main village street there are eight cottages on one side, and three opposite which seem to huddle together for protection from the east wind. In winter this can whistle down from the moor above, where the dry stone walls enclose the strip fields. Above these walls there is rough ground and short tufty grass.

Two spinning mills have vanished, with little to show for their existence. It must have been a busy bustling place 50 or more years ago. All that is left of one of the mills is part of an outside wall. The window sills are still there to see, and where the floor of the building was, one of the residents has created a beautiful garden. The road which once led there has fallen into disrepair and nature has reclaimed it.

The most striking remains of the other mill is a large water tower which once contained three water wheels, one above the other, fed by a series of dams, to provide the power to drive the machinery. The dams are now tranquil and provide a haunt for gulls, heron and the occasional kingfisher.

Mankinholes Village

The chapel was founded in 1837 and was the result of a quarrel between two factions of the congregation of the Mankinholes chapel. It stands a little away from the village about halfway between the two villages. Its roof is steeply gabled and it possesses some attractive stained glass windows, unusual in a nonconformist church.

Opposite the gate of the chapel is one of the paths leading to the Pennine Way. It is much used, wandering up and over Stoodley Pike, one of the highest hills. This stands at over 1,000 ft and atop stands a monument erected in 1815 to commemorate the overthrow of Napoleon. It can be seen for miles around.

One of the locals, Billy Holt, who left school at twelve years of age to work in the mill as a 'half-timer', was quite a character. He taught himself to paint and to write books. He travelled extensively with his horse *Trigger*, not only in this country but most of Europe too. *Trigger* outlived his master but now lies buried in a nearby field with his own headstone to mark the grave. Perhaps if there are any ghosts, Billy and *Trigger* are roaming the bridlepaths still.

Marsden 🐦

Marsden, or March-dene as it was called in old documents, means boundary valley. It is an apt description, as the village is situated at the head of the Colne valley, seven miles from Huddersfield and 18 from Manchester.

Standedge is a natural place to cross the Pennines because at 1,300 ft it is the lowest point on the watershed. The packhorse road, the earliest known route over Standedge, can still be followed on foot and the first turnpike road made in 1759 by John Metcalf (Blind Jack of Knaresborough) is still to be found by various landmarks in the village.

Marsdeners are known locally as Marsden cuckoos. Legend has it that the villagers liked the song of the cuckoo so much they tried to build a wall around its tree to keep it forever, but just as they got to the level of the bird the cuckoo flew away. The cuckoo is used on emblems and badges for local events and associations.

Close Gate bridge at Eastergate is a famous packhorse bridge dating from about the 17th century; it is now a scheduled ancient monument. Although named Close Gate bridge it is known as Eastergate Bridge, perhaps because Esther Schofield kept the Packhorse inn which stood here more than a century ago and Esther's gate became Eastergate.

The canal tunnel begun by Benjamin Outram in 1798 and completed after his death in 1810 is still the longest and highest canal tunnel in the country, three miles 135 yards long and 645 ft above sea level. It took boats four hours to navigate by means of leggers, who would lay on their backs and push against the tunnel walls with their feet. A shaft 480 ft high brought water from a nearby reservoir and also ventilated the tunnel. In 1845 work was begun on the first railway tunnel through Standedge. Completed in 1848 it was the longest railway tunnel in the world. There are two other railway tunnels here, built between 1868 and 1894, but only one is still used today.

At Tunnel End, near the entrance to the four Standedge tunnels, an aqueduct carries the river Colne over the canal and railway. There are some interesting canal cottages and a fine canal warehouse which is now used as a maintenance depot. The canal reservoir has become silted up in recent years but the canal is under renovation and there is a delightful walk along its banks for many miles.

In the early 19th century Enoch and James Taylor made shearing frames at their blacksmith's shop in the village. The new frames were used in cloth finishing to cut the nap to a uniform level and although the machinery failed to give the quality of finish that could be achieved by hand cropping, many of the highly skilled croppers were thrown out of work. Local croppers and their supporters formed Luddite groups to smash the machines which threatened their livelihood. In 1812 William Horsfall, a mill owner who had brought in soldiers and built barricades to protect his shearing frames, was shot by a group of Luddites whilst riding home from the cloth markets in Huddersfield.

The centre of the village is designated a conservation area and many old and interesting buildings are to be found. Argyle Street has been laid out with flagstones and cobbles between flower beds, with benches for people to sit and watch the ducks on the river Colne. The area in Wessen Court behind the old folk's flats is grassed, with paths to walk along made from the old gravestones. It is here that the tomb of James and Enoch Taylor is to be found, and also the stocks, a relic of punishment in the past.

The village is still a comparatively quiet, peaceful, rural area with a number of farms on the hillside. After a short walk from any part of the village it is possible to be in the solitude of the moors, where wild fruits such as blackberries and bilberries can be picked, where heather blooms in the autumn, and the cotton grass in summer.

Mayfield 🌿

The tiny hamlet of Mayfield is part of the parish of Fulwood within the borough of the city of Sheffield. It nestles between the hills, in the unspoilt open countryside known as the Mayfield valley to the south-west of the city and bordering the Peak district of Derbyshire.

During the 13th century this area was pasturable woodland, known as the Forest of Rivelin, hence the name 'Fullwood' – the Fulwood of today, where the lords of the land enjoyed shooting and fishing.

In 1620 John Fox, a man with considerable possessions in Upper Hallam and the chapelry of Bradfield, was granted permission to purchase and clear a portion of woodland and there he built Fullwood Hall. Situated on the hillside, facing across the valley towards the south, Fullwood Hall still stands. It was the family seat of the Fox family for six or seven generations. It is said the last heir wasted his estate, 'it was the drink that did it.'

Gradually more land was cleared and the small 17th century cottages and scattered farms remaining today were to appear. The soil was good and fertile and by the 18th and 19th centuries the valley was populated with large families, becoming a close knit farming community. A school was built in 1878; it is now used as an Environmental Studies Centre. Children are brought from Sheffield schools to study the delightful countryside and natural habitat. It is also the venue of the Mayfield community centre, the highlight of their year being the Annual Produce Show.

In 1895–96 the Mayfield Wesleyan Reform chapel was built. The fellowship necessitating the building of the chapel was founded in 1873, local inhabitants first gathering in a chamber over a cowshed for worship. The chapel was filled to capacity in those early days.

Two tributaries ripple down the hillside through the valley. One springs from Burbage Moor on Fulwood Head near Ringinglow to the south, whilst the other winds its way down from the moor near Fulwood Booth in the west. Both tributaries join at the lower point of the valley, becoming the river Porter.

There were two water mills in the valley, known as the Upper and Nether Corn Mills. Thomas Boulsover, the inventor of 'Sheffield Plate' owned the wire mill in the 18th century and built a factory for the manufacture of silver-plated buttons and snuff boxes on the river Porter and a small hamlet for his workmen. There is a monument to Thomas Boulsover below the wire mill dam. The Shepherd's Wheel downstream demonstrates how Sheffield depended in the 17th and 18th centuries on water power to drive machinery and is open to public viewing on occasions.

Ringinglow stands on the horizon on the southern side of the valley. It comprises a few cottages, the Norfolk Arms inn built around 1800 and the Round House, an octagonal toll house built 1758–1760. The Round House ceased to be a toll bar when the Ecclesall to Fox House road opened in 1816. The small chapel, built in 1864, was closed in 1985, having been converted since into a dwelling house. Robert Trotter opened up two coal mines at Ringinglow at the beginning of the 19th century. It is said that farmers brought lime from Stoney-Middleton to the Fulwood farms, returning back with coal.

Fulwood old chapel lies in Whiteley Lane on the edge of the built-up area of Fulwood. This chapel was Fulwood's first place of worship, built in 1729. Inside the chapel gates are the original stocks used during the

17th century as a means of punishment; these stood on the green only yards from the site of the chapel.

Whilst Mayfield valley is slow to change and some inhabitants loath to change, some alterations are inevitable with the passing of time. With modern machinery on the farms, manual labour decreases. Over the past 40 years a number of smallholdings have been purchased by city businessmen and restored to distinctive country homes. A one-time farm with a large milking herd is now a riding school for the disabled and was honoured by a visit from HRH the Princess Royal on 15th May 1986. An animal sanctuary occupies land where the flour mill once stood.

Meanwood 🪶

Meanwood lies close to Leeds but still has its own charm. The name Meanwood derives from the Old English for common wood, and indeed in ancient times this was part of a thickly wooded area.

Gradually, however, agriculture was introduced and this was exploited by the monks of Kirkstall Abbey who owned Meanwood from 1230 until the Dissolution of the Monasteries. The monks also introduced small industries including flour milling and stone quarrying. The spread of small industries continued until by the 19th century they included flax spinning, paper-making and tanning. These industries tended to develop along Meanwood beck which supplied the water-power to drive the machinery. As industry developed so agriculture declined although until even recently rhubarb was farmed here!

Today Meanwood has become a suburb of Leeds, but is still well worth visiting and still continues a tradition of village life. It has its Women's Institute (founded 1919), its men's Institute and Village Society, and cricket is still played on the pitch near the Myrtle Tavern.

Meanwood church of Holy Trinity is an interesting Victorian edifice and its peal of five bells rings out over the village. Open space is in abundance; Meanwood Park, with picnic areas and woodland walks and, of course, the beck where children still love to fish. Visit Meanwood also to see its 19th century cottages (Tannery Row especially), the Urban Farm and its tranquil walks.

Meltham 🪶

The village of Meltham is situated five miles south-west of Huddersfield and nestles in the Pennine hills below West Nab. The village is mentioned in the Domesday Book and was named Meltha. 'Melt' signifies a moor covered with cloudberry bushes – so Melt-ham is 'the home amidst the cloudberry bushes'.

The parish church of St Bartholomew is unique in the fact that the first chapel was consecrated in 1651 during the Civil War between Charles I and Parliament, and was the only known church in England to receive episcopal consecration during the period of the Commonwealth. There is also a thriving Methodist and Baptist chapel in the village.

It is well known that King George V and Queen Mary passed through Meltham in 1912 making a rest at a farm on the outskirts of the village – since then the farm has been named Queen Mary Farm.

A few years ago Meltham was a thriving industrial village with several woollen and textile mills, a brickworks supplying silica firebricks for gasworks, a silk mill and a United Thread mill making cotton and sewing silks. The last mill was taken over in 1938 by the David Brown Group, who during the Second World War made munitions and parts for tanks and Spitfire planes. After the war they then produced the world famous tractors. Present day Meltham is mostly residential, with only two woollen mills now in operation and other small pockets of industry.

Meltham had its own railway station, regular trains running between Meltham and Huddersfield, both passenger and goods. The passenger station closed down in 1949, the goods trains ceasing later in 1965. In 1850 a horse-drawn omnibus made one journey every Tuesday from Meltham to Huddersfield. Private buses run by Baddeley Bros and Wilson Haigh started in 1920 (these were called 'Yellow Perils'). Public transport buses took over in 1924.

The town hall in Meltham was built in the late 19th century and was a gift to the village by the Brook family, who owned the United Thread mill. On the death of the last surviving member of this family they also gave to the people of Meltham their Hall and surrounding parkland.

In 1894 Meltham founded its own Urban District Council, elected by the village people. In 1974 the Urban District Council was taken over by Kirklees Metropolitan Council but Meltham still retains a parish council. The present population is approximately 9,000.

A volunteer fire brigade was formed in the 1930s and consisted of six of the council's employees. This is still managed on a voluntary basis today.

Three of the village's customs have been carried on for many years; the distribution of free sweets to the children by the shopkeepers on Collap Monday, the day before Shrove Tuesday; the singing of carols with the band in the centre of the village on Christmas Eve; and the annual Whitsuntide Walk around the village by the different congregations of churches and chapels, accompanied by the local brass band. The Meltham Mills Band was formed in 1845 and has won many trophies and competitions throughout the country, including the British Championship.

There are many sporting organisations in Meltham, including football, cricket, bowls, athletics and golf, each with their own headquarters. Tennis courts are also available in the local park. Cubs and Scouts were formed in the area in 1912 and the first meeting was held in a room above the stables in a local public house. There are also Brownies and Guides in Meltham. Their present joint headquarters was built in 1968 with the aid of public subscription from the people of Meltham. These movements are still flourishing today.

A Carnival was organised in 1977 as part of the celebrations for the Queen's Silver Jubilee. This has now become an annual event and is a popular attraction for Meltham and the surrounding areas.

Mexborough

Mexborough was described in the Domesday Book as Mechesburgh, a meeting place or coming together. It was once a tiny hamlet lying on the northern bank of the river Don, some six miles west of Doncaster, and at one of the few points that the twists of the river could be forded, thus linking the village of Dennaby (now Old Denaby) with Mexborough.

The importance of the ford was such that a nearby hill overlooking the crossing was fortified and a castle built. At this time the adjoining low fields were used in the ceremony of Wapentake, where villagers pledged their allegiance to the local lords of Tickhill.

Today the approach to Mexborough from Denaby takes one up the hill to Castle Hill Gardens, from which point can be seen the area of the river crossing (where a ferry was still in use up to the early 1960s).

The parish church of St John the Baptist, sited a few hundred yards from the ferry, was certainly well established by 1066. Two families of gentry have been associated with Mexborough, the Hornes and the Saviles, the latter becoming the Earls of Mexborough.

Near to the church was sited the George and Dragon Farm. Today in the same area, not a bowshot apart, stand the public house the George and Dragon and the Ferry Boat inn, both within hailing distance of the church.

Prior to the Industrial Revolution, Mexborough had a population of only 403 (1811). The iron works, the potteries, the glassworks and of course coal mining spread the town along the river bank and upwards to the north. Amongst them were the Phoenix and Don Glassworks owned by the Barron and Waddington families, John Reed's Rock Pottery and another pottery called Mexborough Old.

The busy High Street with its family businesses, usually with the owner's homes above and behind the premises, was noted for their quality and bargains. It is now a pedestrian precinct area but still actively engaged in trade with the multiple stores and smaller businesses in full swing and with regular market days on Saturday and Mondays.

A local newspaper was established in 1877 and is still flourishing (*The South Yorkshire Times*). Another highlight of the late 19th century was the building and opening of the Hippodrome Theatre in Montague

149

Square in 1898, brought about through the Livesey family (a modern descendant being the actor Roger Livesey). Unfortunately its creator Mr Sam Livesey died before its completion and he is buried in Mexborough cemetery. Amongst the many stars of the day that trod its boards was Gracie Fields. It was demolished in 1939 and now the only reminder is the sloping auditorium that is the car park alongside the Montague Hotel.

The Mexborough Music and Drama Festival has been an annual event for many years and still attracts competitors from far and wide. The local dramatic society has had many well known actors as members.

Micklethwaite 🍂

Micklethwaite is a picturesque hamlet, hidden on the south side of Rombalds Moor above Bingley, and can be approached from the Aire valley by a road that crosses the Leeds–Liverpool canal and winds up the hillside. The stone cottages, built mainly between the 17th and 19th century, are protected within a conservation area.

The village originated as a Viking settlement in the 10th century and the Domesday Book gives the name as Muceltoit, Norse for 'great clearing'. At the lower end of the village near to Laythorpe Farm, built in 1737, a natural drift mound can be identified, which is reputed to have been important to the Vikings. Translation of Laythorpe indicates 'the place of law or judgement'.

The oldest dwelling is Micklethwaite Grange, probably built for Drax Priory in the 13th century and reconstructed for Robert and Mary Leach in 1695. Legend has it that the east end of the building was destroyed by one of Cromwell's cannons, fired from the Druids Altar rock on the far side of the Aire valley. The Manor House, dated 1601, is an impressive building, sub-divided into three, and situated near the Lower Green. Many of the neighbouring cottages, built in the 19th century, accommodated employees in the textile mills.

Undoubtedly, the woollen trade originated during monastic times, but the earliest evidence in the village, probably dating back to the early 1700s, is a unique stretch of warp peg holes along the walls adjacent to the road. The holes, situated about two ft above the ground and 20 ft apart, accommodated rods, supported by upright posts. The warp threads were wound around two adjacent rods until the required number of threads had been laid down.

Most villagers worked in the textile mills during the 19th century, and by 1871 the population had increased to 426. Two mills had been built on the outskirts of the village. Holroyd Mill built on Morton beck in 1810 as a cotton mill, later changed to weaving and closed in the 1920s. In 1978, the building was developed as a craft centre specialising in hand-made furniture and creative work. Airedale Mills, built in 1869 next to

Micklethwaite Village Green

the canal, included a cornmill and a malt-kiln. These premises are now used for more modern enterprises.

The Free Methodist chapel, built in 1875, continues as the focus of religious and social activities. The tradition of baptism with water from a nearby spring is still maintained. Surprisingly, a second chapel, built in 1854, also flourished for almost 100 years in what is now Overcroft Cottage. Several older residents remember Sunday School Treats, Pie and Pea Suppers and choral concerts, that they enjoyed early in the century.

Poverty was not unknown, although neighbours helped each other, usually 'in kind'. Despite the hard times, older residents look back on a happy childhood. Even late at night some families would go ice skating and sledging, and in summer, walking, picnicking and swimming were popular. Pranks, such as tying strings to door knockers, placing sods on chimney pots and even pouring water down chimneys, are remembered with relish!

Micklethwaite had several shops including a general store and off-licence, a grocer and a clogger. Later, between 1930 and 1952, the Manor House was used as a bakery. The adjacent corner house, the last surviving shop, closed about 1976.

Nowadays, occupations have changed, with marked improvements in the standard of living. The population is about 300, of whom a third live in houses built during the last 40 years. Most people are employed in professional and business occupations, or have retired.

The residents take pride in the appearance of the village and cobbles

151

have been laid in many areas, whilst during summer everywhere is colourful with hanging baskets and flower beds. Restoration of the Lower Green by the residents at their own expense won a 1990 Community Pride Award.

Opposite the chapel, in front of several cottages known as Highfold, stands a red telephone kiosk furnished with linoleum and, usually, a vase of flowers! From here the road climbs steeply, skirting the village green, where the view down the hill and over the roof tops has changed little in nearly 200 years.

Monk Bretton

Monk Bretton, two miles from Barnsley town centre, is still thought of as a village by older residents, though the old village has now been hemmed in by new houses. It was once part of the parish of Royston, and in 1801 had a population of only 480 – today the population is 12,212.

Monk Bretton consists mainly of three streets, making up a triangular shape, High Street meeting Cross Street at the site of the old Market Cross, which still stands from the early 1800s.

Behind the cross is the Cricket Club founded in the 1900s, and two famous players there were the late Johnny Weston and, more recently, Martyn Moxon. At the side of the Cricket Club are open fields, the site of Burton Castle or Folly, belonging to Lord Wordsworth's son. Sadly today, only one stone is left to mark the site.

The Old School building to the right of the cross is now the Library. Here, in addition to books, is a 'Pop-in-Club', Parent and Toddler Group, and activities for children in the school holidays.

To the left of the cross is the Working Men's Club, which had its Centenary Year in 1988. It is the only Working Men's Club left in the county still to be in its original building.

St Paul's church is on the corner of Cross Street and Fish Dam Lane, and the present church was officially opened on 6th May, 1878, by the Archbishop of York. It has a 1,000 year old font, believed to have come from Monk Bretton Priory. The longest serving organist at St Paul's was Ernest Exley. He was organist and choirmaster for 31 years, and also licensee of the Norman inn, across the road from the church. Sunday was a hectic day, when he had to hurry from playing the organ after the service, to get ready for 'opening time'.

Down Fish Dam Lane is the Sun inn, once the home of a famous landlady, Carol Dean, a pop singer from the 1960s.

The biggest employer in Monk Bretton is Redfearns Glass, with an estimated 1,800 employees. It was founded by Joshua and Samuel Redfearn in 1862, Redfearns moving to Monk Bretton in 1946 from their original site in Barnsley. In 1967 they merged with National Glass of Fishergate, York, and the present site is the third largest of its kind in England.

Right of the church and only a short walk downhill is the new Dearne Valley Park, where work commenced in 1981 on land that was derelict. A number of collieries had their own canal and railway systems, and these historical landscapes were incorporated within the project area. A section of the canal has been restored, together with remains of the lock-keeper's cottage and the Old Junction Lock. At Springcliff Wood a lake has been formed, with a wildlife habitat, and there is a landscaped park adjacent to Monk Bretton Priory – Priory Park.

The Priory was founded in 1153 for Monks of the Cluniac Order, by Adam Fitzwein, and, after a series of disputes, Monk Bretton broke away and became an independent Benedictine Monastery in 1281. It was surrendered in November, 1538, to the King's Commissioners, when the buildings were largely stripped, and the north aisle of the nave was removed and rebuilt at Wentworth church, and part of the buildings converted to a private house. In 1932, the Priory came under the care of HM Office of Works. Today it is part of the English Heritage Trust, and visitors can see extensive 11th to 14th century ruins, including a largely intact 15th century gatehouse, and an unusually clear example of monastic sanitation.

Although there is a Lord Monk Bretton sitting in the House of Lords, there is no connection between him and the village. The title was created in 1884, and John George Dobson was the first Baron Monk Bretton of Conyboro and Hurstpierpoint.

Morley ✿

The earliest mention of Morley was in the Domesday Book, as Moreleia (meaning 'field of the moor'). There is still today a church, 'St Mary's in the Wood', on the same site and with a recorded history from Saxon times.

The Wapentake of Morley was formed in the time of King Alfred and comprised four parishes – Birstall, Bradford, Calverly and Halifax. The populous Wapentake of Morley joined with the more thinly-peopled Wapentakes of Ewcross and Staincliffe to form the north-western division of the West Riding of Yorkshire. Later, the Wapentake had its lord of the manor, Ilbert de Lacy, a follower of William the Conqueror. From a very early period Morley appears to have been a place of some consequence. In the 14th century a portion of the Scottish army wintered there.

Like Rome, Morley is built on seven hills. Banks Hill is so called from its position on an 'eminence'. Scatcherd and Dawson Hills were so named from their nearness to residences of old families of that name.

Chapel Hill was named in the 1700s when the old 'New Chapel' was built. Cinder Hill, of ancient origin, is from beds of cinders found in the vicinity of old iron foundries. Hunger Hill, of even greater antiquity, means 'hill of mystery' or Hill of Hun (Gods) before Christianity. Troy Hill remains a bit of a mystery but tops a steep bank, part of old quarry workings. Quarrying Yorkshire stone must have been one of the main industries and some sites are still working today. In 1989 a new school was opened and named Seven Hills School.

Morley remained a straggling village, surrounded by moors and thick woodland. The chief employment was the making of cloth; nearly every house had a spinning wheel and a hand loom. When the piece of cloth was ready for the market it was no uncommon thing for men to carry it on their heads to Leeds, five miles away, and when they arrived they had to stand in Briggate to sell it in all weathers. The staple diet of people at that time was oatmeal porridge and oatcakes. The invention of the Spinning Jenny in the 18th century altered the character of Morley. The first mill to be built in 1790 was Crank mill, run by a steam engine. About 20 more were built in the area during the 19th century and so the village developed into a small town. The mill owners became wealthy and built large houses for themselves, often overlooking their own mill.

A church, St Peter's, was built on land donated by Lord Dartmouth and chapels of all denominations were springing up in the area. In 1886 the town was incorporated as a borough. The prosperous people of Morley were proud of their town and built a large and handsome town hall taking three years to complete and costing £41,277. It was officially opened in 1895 by the Rt Hon H. H. Asquith QC MP, the Morley-born Liberal politician who became Prime Minister and eventually Earl of Oxford and Asquith.

Other notable people born in Morley included Sir Titus Salt at the Old Manor House in 1803. After becoming a noted textile manufacturer in Bradford he later built the mills and town of Saltaire. Manoah Rhodes, born in Morley in 1810, was the son of Joseph Rhodes, a farmer and manufacturer of 'healds and shays' used in the woollen trade. In 1822, only twelve years old, Manoah left Morley and 'walked over' to Bradford (eight miles away) and became apprenticed to a silversmith in Ivegate, staying there 14 years. In 1836 he started his own business and became head of Manoah Rhodes & Sons, one of the largest gold and silversmiths in the North of England.

So the cloth trade grew over the years and by the end over 40 large textile mills had been built in Morley and district. At the same time the borough had expanded and in 1951 Gildersome, Driglington, East and West Ardsley were incorporated and Morley became the third largest borough in England. In 1974 came the incorporation with Leeds. In spite of this people are still fiercely loyal to their own area, so remain the six villages that were their origins.

Morton ✦

Morton is a moorland village, which clings stubbornly to the edge of Rombalds Moor on the opposite side to Ilkley. Relics of early man have been found on Rombalds Moor, but probably the earliest significant remains were those of the Roman road that ran from Ilkley to Manchester passing through Morton on its way. In 1775 a treasure chest was found which contained a large hoard of Roman coins, reported at the time to be one of the most important finds ever made. It was reputed to have contained nearly a hundredweight of Roman denarii dating from AD 54 to AD 238 in a brass chest assumed to be of military origin.

Prior to the Industrial Revolution the homesteads of Morton were the farmhouses and homes of the yeoman farmers and the humble cottages of their workers. On these small upland estates the families toiled over many centuries against natural handicaps like climate and relief, although Morton was better suited than most Airedale communities to arable farming thanks to its sunny south-facing slopes. Oats were the principal crop but most land was given over to sheep rearing, particularly on the common moorland and hill ridges.

When the Industrial Revolution overtook Morton in the late 18th century, farming took second place in the occupational structure of the village as the establishment of the water-powered textile industry attracted workers from all over Britain. The number of people living and working in the village doubled in the first half of the 19th century. Rows of terraced cottages were built, nestling close to the nine mills where the cottagers and their children found employment. After 1890 the depression in the wool industry forced many Mortonians to leave the village and seek their fortunes abroad; 70 families are said to have emigrated to the colonies before 1914. In recent times, as one by one all the mills closed, modern housing has been built on the sites of some of the mills to accommodate those who regard Morton as a desirable dormitory suburb for Bradford, Leeds and Keighley, consequently the village's population is growing once again.

Morton's 'Great Flood' occurred on 12th July 1900. At about 2 pm heavy drops of rain began to fall, quickly followed by a downpour which lasted for over three hours. Morton beck turned into a devastating torrent. The waters collected with immense force on Rombalds Moor above the village, rapidly filling Sunnydale reservoir, which was built to turn the waterwheels of one of the nine mills in Morton valley. The escape weir could not cope with the flow and water streamed over the top of the embankment, uprooting trees and carrying them along like matchwood. The cottages at the top of the village received the full fury; miraculously there was no loss of life, residents got out of upper windows by ladder, but much furniture was washed away. One by one the mills down the valley were damaged, dams burst and property was carried away. The flood continued down to the Leeds/Liverpool Canal but fortunately the final disaster, the possibility of the canal bursting its banks, never happened. The gas main was damaged and villagers reverted to oil lamps and candles.

In days gone by Morton, like other communities in this part of West Yorkshire, was a stronghold of nonconformity. In 1795 there were 28 members of the Methodist Society in the village and fortnightly services and prayer and class meetings took place in members' homes. These were Wesleyan Methodists and in 1828 they built a small chapel, which survives today as part of the village institute. When the congregation grew too large for the small chapel, a much larger chapel was built in 1846 and the old chapel was sold for use by the Non conformists as a British school. When the National school was built, the two schools existed almost opposite each other geographically and in opposition academically for a few years, but the British school gradually declined and eventually closed.

After the end of the First World War, in November 1919, as part of the peace celebrations, the Board of Education gave their consent for a memorial hall to be built onto the back of the former chapel and the chapel was adapted for use as a billiard room and club room. This was for the purpose of a village institute. The institute is the hub of Morton village life and is at present used regularly by all the varied organisations in the village.

Every summer a Gala is held in Morton. Its forerunner was probably the Morton Children's Festival which was started in 1904. Morton Gala is a real community effort and all organisations in the village, including the church and the two chapels, all help. The Gala is the highlight of the year in Morton when 'old Mortonians' and 'off-cumners' come together and have an enjoyable day.

Netherthong 🦢

Netherthong may seem at first to be an inappropriate name for a village situated 700 ft above sea-level, but in relation to its nearest neighbour, Upperthong, the first part of its name – Nether – truly suggests it is lower.

In the centre of the village stands All Saints' church, a Commissioner's or Waterloo church, built in 1829. The Lord Commissioners for the Treasury administered a fund of one million pounds for the building of churches in new areas as a thank offering for the victory at the battle of Waterloo.

There is much evidence around the church of a well established woollen industry in the 18th century; three-storey cottages with long rows of windows – still known today as weavers' cottages. At the top of the house would be a 'taking-in' door, where raw wool was taken in and the finished piece of cloth taken out.

At this time farming and weaving were combined industries; the farm and the land for sheep-rearing were twin pillars of industry, not alternatives. A reminder of the local weaving industry is the wuzzing hole to be seen on a cottage in the village – it is a depression in the stone into which was inserted a metal rod and a wire-basket with chains attached to it; wet wool placed inside the basket was rotated, or wuzzed, until it was dry.

The old houses in the village huddle together, but instead of facing each other, the fronts of one row face the backs of another – an unusual arrangement, but one which gave the occupants the maximum light into the weaving room. Spinning was done by the women and children, at least seven spinners, or spinsters, being needed to spin sufficient thread to keep one weaver occupied.

The Bastille is also a three-storey building, built after the Poor Law was passed in 1834, authorising Union workhouses to be built. The inmates were confined to the premises, married couples being separated, with a master and mistress to control food and lodging.

Wells were an important necessity in any village before the advent of piped water, and at Wells Green one can still see a very good example of a succession of wells. A founder member of the Netherthong WI can remember playing on the green while her mother filled buckets with clear spring water.

Over the years there has been a wide variety of tradespeople in the village – a whitesmith, blacksmith, baker, tailor, brushmaker and a coalman to name a few. Today there is a potter and a sculptor, and three local shops – the butcher, newsagent and general store, and a post office. The public house is aptly named for what was once a weavers settlement – the Clothiers; and another house was formerly a public house called the Queen's Arms until its closure in 1938, a clean patch of stone above the doorway shows where the nameboard was positioned.

A thriving primary school built in the mid 19th century and enlarged three times since then can now accommodate about 200 children. The school is in an enviable position with magnificent views over the surrounding countryside. A stone in the nearby Wesleyan chapel bears the inscription:–

'To the memory of Ann Hobson,
aged 12 years, who died through
fear of whipping by the school
mistress in 1856.'

At one time many people from Netherthong were employed at a large geriatric hospital, formerly a workhouse, situated not far from the village, but this was demolished in 1968 and replaced with a modern housing estate. A mile or so from the village is the smaller cottage hospital, built by public subscription after the First World War and now part of the National Health Service. It has recently been modernised and now caters mainly for geriatric and psychiatric patients – the nearest

Netherthong Village

general hospital is the Huddersfield Royal Infirmary, eight miles away from Netherthong.

Deanhouse Mills, in the valley below Netherthong, were built around 1850, and provided employment for many village people for the next hundred years. But with the slump in the textile industry, the mills were demolished in 1990 and in their place are more houses built in the style of the late 20th century, in natural stone to harmonise with their surroundings.

The most interesting and the oldest building in the vicinity of Netherthong is the Wesleyan chapel, built in 1769, only the sixth Methodist chapel to be built in Britain. John Wesley is known to have preached there.

Netherton ✤

Netherton is a semi-rural hill village five miles west of Wakefield. It forms part of Sitlington parish along with the villages of Midgley, Middlestown and Overton and has a population of around 2,500. It is situated at one side of the picturesque Coxley valley and has the river Calder and the Calder and Hebble Navigation Canal on its eastern border.

Early man is believed to have lived in the area as in 1963 a Mesolithic axe was dug up in gravel near the Star inn. It was found in what were glacial outwash deposits and is now in the Tolson Museum at Huddersfield.

Some doubt arises as to how the parish was so named. However, one of the many theories is that it began as 'Seytel's farmstead' and is recorded in the Domesday Book as Schelintone. According to Smith's *Old Yorkshire*, Netherton means 'lower town'. Over the centuries the 'manor of Shitlington' (now known as Sitlington) has changed ownership. In 1777 the owners of Bramham Park acquired part of the original manor and a draft lease indicates that Netherton was largely occupied by small farmers. Today several working farms remain though not employing so many local people. There were also several sandstone quarries in the area.

Mining is known to have taken place in the area since 1401. The early form of mining was known as 'bell mining' when a hole was dug and then excavated in the form of a bell. There is evidence that there were several of these in and around the village. In later years the local canal was used for the transportation of the coal. Hope Pit was sunk in 1870 and is still working under the name of Denby Grange. This pit was linked with Caphouse colliery (1828), now the Yorkshire Mining Museum, when a railway ran along the top of the village to a point at Calder Grove where it went onward either by canal or rail. Hartley Bank colliery was sunk in 1881 and closed in 1968. As a result many former miners have remained in the village, some living in the council estate built in the 1930s. Today, two large private housing developments have brought the population to its present figure.

Most of the working population today travel to surrounding towns such as Wakefield, Barnsley, Huddersfield, Dewsbury and Leeds and, as the lane through the village is a feeder road to the M1 motorway, there is some heavy traffic at times.

St Andrew's church is Gothic Revival and one of only a few in the country to be built by J. D. Sedding in 1881. It was visited and described by the late Sir John Betjeman as 'an inventive little building'. Of the two chapels only one remains in use – the other built in 1890 is now a family home.

The local manor house – Netherton Hall – is reputed to be haunted by the ghost of a lady in a grey dress. The Hall is said to have been used by Cromwell and the outbuildings as stabling for his horses. It is still lived in today and commands a fine view over Coxley valley. In the old part of the village there is a building which was previously the toll house at Horbury Bridge and which was moved stone by stone in the 1930s when the old turnpike there was taken over by the council, to a site overlooking the Calder valley in the village. Some old cottages round the church have survived – mostly 200 years old – having been restored and an old barn too now forms a fashionable residence.

The old village institute fell into disrepair and was lost to the village but now the fund to build a new village hall is well advanced. It is still possible today to find most things in the village as three shops remain as well as a post office. Gone are the many public houses in the village and only one now remains, the Star.

Joining the village is the hamlet of Midgley, where today there is a large timberyard which has been run by the same family for many generations.

New Farnley

New Farnley is situated approximately five miles from the centre of Leeds on the A58 Halifax road. It is a rural district with surrounding farms and woodland, where pleasant walks may be enjoyed in Farnley Wood and Sykes Wood, the latter adjoining Tong village. In summer people come and enjoy strawberry picking and there are many horseriders who use the bridleways. Leeds City Council and the Ramblers Association have guided walks all around the district.

The Farnley Iron Company was founded in 1844 by the four sons of James Armitage, a woollen merchant who purchased Farnley manor and lands from the Danbys for £45,000 at the turn of the 19th century.

It was because of the demand for workers at the forge that the part of Farnley parish known as New Farnley came into existence. There were not enough men in Old Farnley village for the vast new enterprise, so people were imported. For some reason they all came from Low Moor, Bradford and were for the most part nonconformist in religion.

The Armitage brothers built a school at New Farnley in 1845, which has been demolished during the past 20 years. It was in the school that the first services were held by the curate of Farnley. The tough people from Bradford did not take kindly to the Church of England ministry and after a short period, when a member of the Armitage family was appointed minister, they eventually left this company chaplaincy in the hands of a Wesleyan Methodist.

In 1857 the assistant curate at Farnley parish church seemed to win back 'church' favour and when the huge Iron Church was erected in 1863 he was appointed its first minister, his salary being paid by the Iron Company. This unconsecrated building was destroyed some years ago and replaced by a dual purpose church hall – now known as St James, New Farnley.

New Farnley school has been demolished but in its place there now stands a modern community centre, adjoined by a village green and car park. This is administered by the New Farnley & District Community Association and many activities are centred around it. At the present time, New Farnley village has a general store, a doctors' surgery, fish shop and post office, the latter being a listed building.

Moor Top is a separate little hamlet at the top of the hill and comprises the Woodcock inn and the Lancastrian Schoolroom, known locally as the Moor Top mission room, which is used for church services and social events. There are some modern houses but many of the older properties have been in existence since the turn of the century and have been subsequently modernised from the interior, yet have retained their charm.

Normanton 🌿

The village of Normanton existed in the 7th century as part of the kingdom of Elmet. Three hundred years later the Northmen settled there and called it Northmannatun. The first recorded description is to be found in the Domesday Book of 1086.

In Norman times it was enclosed by a great earthenwork barrier, with a fortified vantage point which is now at the centre of Haw Hill Park and affords the same excellent view of the surrounding countryside as it did in 1086.

The church of today is not the original All Saints but it is built on the same site – some parts of it in the 13th century. At that time it was administered by the Knights Hospitallers who dwelt nearby at Newland Hall. After the Reformation, Henry VIII gave the power of appointing the clergy to Trinity College, Cambridge.

Inside the church stands the tomb of John Freeston, a noted Elizabethan barrister of Gray's Inn, born within the parish in 1512, and a benefactor of Normanton in that he endowed the foundation of a grammar school in his will. The first school stood to the east of the church on Snydale Road and was used until 1887. The grammar school is now perpetuated in a spacious modern building to the west of the church.

Also in the 16th century a famous seaman was born nearby: Admiral Sir Martin Frobisher – knighted for his prowess in the Spanish Main and his exploration of the North West Passage. There is a window in the church which commemorates his passing.

Until the middle of the 19th century, Normanton continued to be a small rural community – its farms within a mile or so radius of the church and its few cottages, school and ancient village cross all close by the church on Snydale Road.

Old Snydale is a village about a mile down this road. In the 17th century it was a mere hamlet and part of the Torre family estate. The Torres, a noble Lincolnshire family, built Snydale Hall, a fine residence, parts of which stand today. James Torre died in 1692 and is buried in Normanton church. Most of the old cottages have disappeared and been replaced by modern houses, but the village still consists of one street with houses on either side and one old public house called the Cross Keys. There are strong but unsubstantiated rumours of a ghost who walks along the road.

In 1840 the first railway train from Leeds to Derby ran through Normanton. Shortly after this a rail link between York and Normanton was established thus creating an important junction. A fine station was erected and large engine sheds were built. A steel foundry was set up and the population increased six-fold. This was closely followed by the development of the coal industry in the area. People from many parts of the south and even from Ireland poured into the district to take up employment.

In 1877 the Baptist chapel was erected as well as several other chapels of various denominations. In 1904 the Catholic church was completed and so the spiritual needs of an ever-growing community were satisfied.

For the next hundred years Normanton's livelihood depended mainly on industry and not on agriculture, although many of the old farms still existed. But of recent times the coal-mines have been worked out, the railway has lost its importance – the station is now merely a wayside halt and, until a short time ago, Normanton was forgotten and fast becoming a depressed area.

Not so now! For Normanton is soon to become the North's Euro Terminal rail link – an inland port – and a West Yorkshire village that will be known throughout Europe.

Norton ☙

Norton is situated between the A1 and A19, on the northern border of South Yorkshire. It is shaped like a foot, a little over a mile long from east to west, with toes in North and West Yorkshire. In times past it was the 'North Town' of the parish of Campsall, which is mentioned in the Domesday Book, and the area was held by Icbert de Laci, whose family was involved in the founding of Pontefract Castle around 1086. The main occupations in the area used to be farming, mining and quarrying. Today local residents commute to neighbouring Doncaster, Pontefract or further afield, in connection with their trades and professions.

There are many traces of Roman and Viking occupation, and there is an archaeological dig taking place in the neighbouring village of Womersley. There are records of a priory in the village by the river Went, but it suffered during the Dissolution of the Monasteries by Henry VIII and only a fragment of wall remains. There is, however, still the Mill House, where the water mill can be seen, and the Priory Farm, both places now being updated and used for domestic purposes.

The ancient parish church of St Mary Magdalene is reputed to have the finest 14th century west tower in Yorkshire, and the fabric holds many features of Anglo-Saxon and Norman origin. In recent years church and chapel have combined for the annual Parish Weekend.

The houses were built either side of the village street, with the older houses being 'gabled on' to the street, but new development has extended its perimeters and filled in many, though not all, former gaps. In spite of the fact that there is not a true village centre, social life is maintained with the aid of both the Methodist chapel where WI, Darby and Joan Clubs and other activities are held, and the mission room, a hall belonging to the parish church, which accommodates the weekly whist drives, playgroup and children's dancing class. Local children are educated within the area from nursery to school leaving age, and a library centre in the middle school is open for eight hours a week.

There is a modern swimming pool and fitness centre in the adjoining village of Campsall, where part of the parkland of the former Hall is now designated a country park and is used for relaxation. Norton has two public houses, the Royal Hotel and the Schoolboy, catering to the needs of locals and visitors alike. With many pleasant walks around the district, industry has not intruded too much on the tranquillity of the village.

Nostell 🦢

Nostell parish is made up of the hamlets of Huntwick, Foulby, Hessle, Wragby, Hilltop, West Hardwick and Nostell. They are all part of the estate of Lord St Oswald. This formidable list houses less than 200 souls.

The history of Nostell goes back into the mists of time. Bede and William of Malmesbury tell us that, on a cold and rainy afternoon in AD 655, the Northumbrian King Oswi spent hours with the hermit of St James of Nostell praying for help against the heathen King Penda, whose superior forces were ranged in battle against him. For his help, Oswi promised that he would build a monastery for the hermit and his followers, his sister Hilda was promised an abbey at Whitby, and Elflida, his small daughter was given to Hilda as a novice. The battle of Winwaed began at dawn next day and Penda's army was destroyed and he was killed. Oswi kept all his promises and Christianity was saved from extinction.

Around this monastic community grew the present parish. Over the centuries work was provided for most of the workers in the area and here their sick were cared for, and travellers fed and housed. What education their children had was received in the monastery.

In the reign of Henry I the priory was renamed the Priory of St Oswald. It was a very important and wealthy Augustinian community; its prior had a stall in York Minster and sat among the bishops in Parliament.

At the Dissolution of the Monasteries, the Prior Robert Ferrer had accepted Protestantism and began to build a new church outside the confines of the monastery. The church has therefore always been a Protestant church. Robert Ferrer became the bishop of St David's in Wales and later Queen Mary burnt him at the stake for what was considered his betrayal of the Catholic faith.

In 1530, before the church was finished, Cardinal Wolsey made his last journey north to his palace at Cawood. He rested at Nostell and next day confirmed 300 people in a church which still had no roof. In a few days Henry VIII sent for him back to London, intending to send him to the Tower. Wolsey was a sick man and died on the way down at Leicester.

Eventually the estate was bought by the Winn family in 1654. They were silk merchants in London and still live at Nostell. The first baronet took the title of Lord St Oswald from the name of the old priory. The family home of Nostell Priory is now held by the National Trust.

Early in the 19th century the Winn family began to mine coal in the village, and when the second shaft was sunk they built a row of 50 colliers' houses. There were two and three bedroomed houses, and in order to have three bedrooms the family had to take a lodger who worked on the opposite shift to the father of the house, so as to utilise the beds as fully as possible. The pit was closed about five years ago and Nostell Long Row has been demolished due to subsidence, leaving a big gap in the life of the village.

A large brickworks is the only source of employment apart from farming. The works are completely computerised and provide very few jobs nowadays. The majority of workers go outside the village to their employment.

The village hall was built to replace an old wooden building which was blown down in 1965. It is badly affected by mining subsidence, as are many houses in the village, and the church. The beautiful Swiss glass in the church windows has been out for twelve years to prevent damage and no date is given for its return. This glass brought many visitors to the church in the past and was a useful source of revenue. In 1991 British Coal removed eleven chosen panels of glass from its storage in York and with the help of the National Trust put a beautiful display in a room in Nostell Priory where hundreds of visitors can admire it.

Nostell boasts a very successful cricket team, but, as is the way these days, the players come from far and wide, even Australia! Visitors to Nostell Priory often park their cars on pleasant summer afternoons and enjoy the game.

The village shop has long since gone, but there is one pub left, grandly named the Spread Eagle. The supermarket is three miles down the road and the post office is a bus ride away.

Notton 🦡

Notton is situated mid-way between Wakefield and Barnsley. It is mentioned in the Domesday Book of 1086. Later records show that monks from Monk Bretton Priory, the canons of Nostell Priory and the Hospital of St John of Jerusalem all held land in Notton at various times.

Round about this time the manor of Notton was owned by Ilbert de Laci. From him the manor passed through various hands to a John

Darcy, who in 1330 was given licence to impark. Parts of this park still remain today, the rest was reclaimed for agriculture during the Second World War. In the 18th century the manor passed to the Wentworth family along with the manor of Woolley and it remained in their possession until this century.

Notton has five listed buildings, three being old stone properties, one an old milestone and the fifth a railway bridge by George Stephenson.

The village also has trust lands, held under a trust deed, which accommodate the village hall, tennis courts, cricket and football pitches and the children's play area. The village green is privately owned; it was bought for the sum of £5 when the Wentworth estate was sold in 1949. It is registered as common land thus ensuring it stays just as it is at the present time.

In Notton Park, which is a wooded area, there are remains of Iron Age workings and at Applehaigh Clough, where there was once a stone quarry, there are two medieval sunken paths which now form part of the footpath walks round Notton.

Up to and during the Second World War the village was mainly a farming community. Village 'get togethers', such as Christmas parties for the children, were held in Mrs Mollett's barn and were thoroughly enjoyed by all. Sunday school and church services were also held in the barn.

The village had, and still has, a post office cum general store, but during the war and just after, traders with horse-drawn carts sold vegetables etc. One such trader was known as the 'Paraffin Man' and sold pots, pans, hardware and of course paraffin for use in the Tilley lamps used prior to electricity being brought to the village.

During the war years one of the favourite haunts of the villagers, and indeed people of surrounding areas, was Woolley Dam. The highlight of week-ends and bank holidays was to take a picnic tea and spend the afternoon at this beauty spot. There was a little shop which sold sweets, crisps and minerals and one of the farms on the edge of the Dam sold jugs of tea. There were rowing boats for hire or one could spend the day fishing. Unfortunately, these idyllic times came to an end when the Dam was drained because of water seeping into mine workings.

In the early post-war years a village gala was held each year in one of the local farmer's fields, with one of the village girls chosen as the Gala Queen. There was a fancy dress parade, children's races and sideshows. Now the gala is held on the village green and is quite a big event attracting people from a wider area.

The village is now very much larger with both local authority and private developments since the Second World War. Some of the farm houses have been sold to private owners with farm buildings also con-verted to private dwellings. Farming is no longer the main occupation of the residents, most of whom now commute to nearby towns to follow their various occupations.

The small prefabricated village hall has now been replaced with a larger modern building with indoor sports facilities. Unlike most villages Notton has no church or school.

Otley 🐝

Otley, Otley–Wharfedale, or Otley the Queen of the Yorkshire Dales as stated in some of the holiday guides. Call it what you will, Otley is a pleasant old market town. It is surrounded by beautiful countryside and the well-known Otley Chevin rises as a background to the town. Magnificent views can be seen from the top; this is known as Surprise View.

There are still many fine old buildings, one being the parish church of All Saints. There was a church here in AD 630. The present stone-built parish church has a fine Norman doorway and houses fragments of Anglo-Saxon crosses. Adjacent to the churchyard is a replica of the Bramhope Tunnel erected in memory of men who lost their lives during the construction of the tunnel on the Leeds–Thirsk railway built 1845–50. Thomas Chippendale, the world famous cabinet maker, was born in Otley in 1718 and baptised in the church in June of that year.

A very popular market is held in the old square every Friday and Saturday. The market dates from Saxon times but history records that it really began on the 1st March 1222 when King Henry III granted the first Royal Charter. There is also a buttercross and many older inhabitants will remember the farmers' wives from nearby dales displaying eggs, butter, fowls etc for sale. It is now used as a resting place in the town centre for young and old to sit and gossip. In the Market Square stands the Jubilee Clock. As the name implies it was erected in 1888 to celebrate Queen Victoria's Golden Jubilee 1837–1887. It has four faces typical of Victorian architecture. On one side of the clock is a memorial stone donated by Belgian refugees in appreciation of hospitality received in the First World War.

A very popular Victorian Fayre is held in December when the whole town turns Victorian. Shopkeepers dress their windows in the old style and a prize is awarded for the most attractive. Everyone dresses up and with the old style lighting in the Market Square it is very easy to imagine being back in the 19th century. Charities benefit greatly from this event. Another relic of the past is the maypole standing on the site of an old market cross. It is now used as a popular meeting place for various cycling clubs in the area. The old village green originally ended at the Market Cross.

On the opposite side of the road stands the Mechanic's Institute, or to use its modern title, the Civic Centre. This was opened in 1871 and was the scene of many entertainments, among them the Farmers' Ball, the Primrose League Ball and the very popular St Patrick's Ball. These grand affairs are no more but it is still well-used and also houses a very interesting museum of bygones, well worth a visit.

Otley is situated on the picturesque river Wharfe, which is spanned by a very old stone bridge of seven arches. This leads to the very popular Wharfemeadows Park enjoyed by visitors and locals alike. There is boating, swimming, bowls and tennis and a much-used children's play area. Close by is the present Prince Henry's Grammar School founded in 1602. A charter was granted by James I and the name of his son, the then Prince of Wales, was used. It is still known by its original title.

In a nearby field the Wharfedale Agricultural Show is held in May. This is the oldest show in England, being founded in 1799, and is one of the highlights of the year.

Years ago Otley had many thriving industries including the foundry where the famous Wharfedale Printing Press was made. The invention of this machine was instrumental in bringing education to the working classes. Alas this foundry is no more but two industries, paper making and stationery and school exercise books manufacture still survive.

Thirty public houses have been recorded. Three are worth a mention. The Black Horse, formerly the Coach inn, is a fine building especially if you lift your eyes to the top. It still has the old yard where coaches left for York. The White Horse opposite is now used as a bank but is not altered in appearance. This also has an old coaching yard and a balcony from which proclamations were made. The oldest pub and one of the oldest buildings is the Black Bull. It is recorded that a party of Cromwell's Ironsides called there in 1648 and drank the place dry.

Owston 🐾

Owston is a picturesque, peaceful village, lying about five miles north of Doncaster, just off the Doncaster to Selby (A19) road. The fact that it is linked to the main road by an approach road of about half a mile in length, ensures that the tranquillity which has permeated the village for many centuries remains comparatively undisturbed.

Owston was originally a Norman feudal manorial estate, and traces of this still remain. It now comprises a hall, a church, a vicarage and several cottages, many of which date from the 17th century. For very many years the village remained untouched, but recently some development and restoration work, tastefully executed, has been carried out; cottages and coach-houses, for example, are now extremely attractive homes.

Owston has a fascinating history; it is known that it existed in the 11th century because it is listed in the Domesday Book (1086). At that time it was termed 'Austun', but in 1150 it was altered to 'Oustun'; the present spelling of 'Owston' was first recorded in 1473.

In the late 17th century the Cooke family acquired the estate, and several generations lived there, and they increased the estate acreage. During their ownership Owston was a centre of sporting activities, especially hunting; the manor had many stables and a covered riding school. Archery, too, was a favourite pastime, as was fishing; fishponds were made in the park. This would not be a difficult undertaking at that time, as in the whole area the land was subject to frequent flooding by the river Don.

Colonel Philip Ralph and Mrs Davies Cooke, the last members of the family to live at Owston, are very well remembered, with great affection, by very many local people. They were very actively involved in the life of the village and the church, and several enjoyable functions were held at the Hall and in the grounds for the benefit of the church and charities. One memorable occasion was an Old English County Fair, in costume, with such events as morris dancing and maypole dancing.

A few years ago the estate was acquired by the present owner, Mr P. J. Edwards. The Hall is now used as a golf club headquarters, and it contains some residential flats. The residents of the village are mostly either retired or business people. One point of interest is that the park land attached to the Hall contains a wide variety of native English and some foreign trees. There are two cottages which are listed buildings; one is opposite the vicarage, and the other near the White Lodge Hotel, both reminiscent of a former era. Other old features remain in the village: the bell, fixed in the bell arch, which, in times past, summoned the estate staff to work, and mounting blocks, for the convenience of horse riders. Adjacent to the vicarage is the old pinfold, where animals which had strayed were enclosed until claimed.

The church, which has a most interesting history, is in an excellent state of repair, and it serves the villages of Carcroft and Skellow, as well as Owston. The original church was built in the 12th century, but re-building and extensions have been done over the centuries. Two features worthy of note are the herringbone masonry, typical of the early Norman period, on part of the original building, and the 15th century rood screen, which is carved with Tudor roses, grapes and quatrefoils.

In the church are several interesting memorials, including the statue of 'Piety', by the famous sculptor, Chantray, the Hatfield Brass, and various tablets. Over the north door of the nave hangs the Royal Arms, painted in the reign of James I; James, who owned the manor at that time, was married to Queen Anne of Denmark, and on this account the Arms include the white horse of Denmark.

The church thrives today as in the past. This is particularly witnessed each year when, for three days in July, the annual Flower Festival is held; this event is very well supported and enjoyed by a great many visitors.

Owston is linked to the neighbouring village of Burghwallis by The Abbe's Walk, a narrow country road. At the side of the road is Squirrel Wood; the Boy Scouts' camp is located in this wood, and full use is made of it in the summer months. No one has actually ever seen a ghost or anything sinister in 'Creepy Hollow', a gloomy spot on a road from Owston to Carcroft, but people walking along there on dark nights, hurry quickly past!

Oxenhope ﹏

One of the best ways to approach Oxenhope is from Denholme on the B6141. There, a breathtaking view is revealed; heather-topped hills and peat moorlands protect and isolate the village nestling in the Y-shaped valley. Despite being only nine miles from Bradford, Oxenhope is still a remote and beautiful valley.

The winters are cold, wet and windy; the bleak 'Bronte country' which tourists expect. The annual rainfall is 45 inches, half as much again as Manchester, and the temperature is described locally as 'two overcoats colder than Keighley', five miles down the valley.

But see Oxenhope on a glorious summer's day! Pick bilberries, listen to the skylarks and drink in the beauty of this hidden upland Pennine valley. The grandeur of the scenery has been preserved as a green belt and a conservation area.

Life in the past was particularly hard, with an inhospitable soil only able to support sheep, some cattle and the hay to feed them. Fuel was obtained from narrow seams of coal at one end of the valley, and peat from the surrounding moor.

Most of the early farming settlements grew on the warmer slopes and spread around the sides of the valley. The farmhouses' narrow mullioned windows afforded maximum light for weaving. Some had a door at first-storey height so that the 'pieces' could be taken out and transported to markets at Heptonstall, Halifax and Bradford, along packhorse routes.

The first mill was built in 1792 so the hand spinners and weavers began to look for work outside the home. Footpaths, formerly linking farms, now led to mills, stone walls marking the fields. There is evidence that 20 textile mills existed during the 19th century, producing worsted. As trade prospered, housing was built in the valley bottom providing, for the first time, a centre to the village.

Two reservoirs, magnificent feats of Victorian engineering, were built in the 1870s by Bradford Corporation Waterworks, submerging farm-houses and three mills in the process. More families were displaced who farmed within the water-catchment area.

When the Oxenhope to Keighley railway was built in 1867, the traditional links with the Calder valley were abandoned. Oxenhope now had access by rail and canal to inland markets and export outlets. The line, closed in 1961, reopened in 1968 as the Keighley and Worth Valley steam railway. This brought tourism to Oxenhope and, occasionally, film companies. *The Railway Children* was made in 1970, using local views and local people.

Oxenhope was part of the chapelry and township of Haworth in the parish of Bradford. Churchgoers walked to Haworth or Bradford, often twice on Sundays. According to Charlotte Bronte, Rev Joseph Grant, her father's curate, wore out 14 pairs of shoes collecting subscriptions for a church in Oxenhope. It was built in 1849, in a restrained neo-Norman style.

As Oxenhope comprises many hamlets, the nonconformists built three Methodist and two Baptist chapels in the 19th century. Since then, chapels have been converted, pulled down or abandoned, but always a new building replaced the old; the most recent being a Methodist church, completed in 1990.

There are over 70 Grade II listed buildings, including the Donkey Bridge, two milestones, a mounting block, a cowshed and pigsty, as well as houses and barns. A building which did not survive was Crock House, unique in this area for its medieval cruck beams. These were rescued, and are being restored for display in Cliffe Castle, Keighley. Only four working mills remain; the rest have been pulled down in favour of a housing scheme, converted into apartments, or merely left derelict.

Such an insular community perpetuates its memories by constantly retelling stories of local characters. One of these, Mad Sarah, terrified the children by chasing them with brooms or a carving knife, screaming, 'Ah'll get tha!' Fearful that demons would come up through the floorboards at night, she sprinkled pepper around herself and sat in the middle of the room brandishing a poker. Perhaps she was safeguarding her fortune in gold sovereigns – on her death in 1933, £20,000 was found to be missing . . .

Oxenhope was always a musical village: Joseph Parker, whose voice was admired by Mrs Gaskell, could have had a career in London, if he had been prepared to leave his village home. At the age of 79, he walked to St George's Hall, Bradford, to sing one solo from *The Messiah*; the audience demanded three encores!

Oxenhope people are frugal; they have had to be. But the farmer who, on finding a dead mouse in a bowl of cream, picked it up and licked it clean, was surely going too far! Their reputation for thrift and saving is summed up in two local sayings: 'In Oxenhope, everyone owns their own house – and the one next door', and 'When a baby is born in Oxenhope, its bottom is spanked with a bank book'.

Visitors are attracted to Oxenhope for the annual Manorlands Garden Party and the Straw Race, which began in 1974, when a couple of local lads suggested a race from the Waggon and Horses pub (1,200 ft), down the valley (650 ft) and up to the Dog and Gun (1,050 ft), carrying a bale of straw and drinking a pint at each of five hostelries on the way.

With its own attractions, and Haworth only two miles away, Oxenhope is able to make its contribution to tourism, with holiday cottages and bed and breakfast facilities, whilst still retaining its character as a Pennine village.

Pool in Wharfedale 🦢

The village of Pool stands on the river Wharfe and its history can be traced back to before the Norman Conquest. The name Pool comes from the Anglo-Saxon meaning pond or marsh. Three families mentioned in the Domesday survey of 1086 were de Caylii, de Pouelle and de Castellay, names which are still familiar to the district today even if slightly different, ie Caley, Pool and Castley.

Pool is well known for its mills. A reference to a woollen mill dated 1673 is recorded in the Otley church register, Otley being three miles from Pool and the nearest town. In the same year bridges over the river Wharfe from Kettlewell to Otley were swept away by flood water; it also swept away Pool Low Fulling Mills. A new mill was built but this was destroyed by fire in 1795, after which a company by the name of Weir & Co started a paper mill. Although the workforce has been scaled down considerably the paper mill is in operation to this day having been run from 1886 to 1981 by the Whiteley family, well known local benefactors.

Pool Bridge was built in 1793; before that date travellers wishing to journey from Otley to Knaresborough had to cross the Wharfe by a ford either at Knot Ford or Castley. Pool bridge was widened in 1815 and bears that date.

The only Pool ghost story is connected with Staircase Lane which runs between Bramhope and Pool and concerns the Dyneley family of Bramhope. For a wager, one of the family after dinner and heavy gambling galloped his horse down the 'Staircase' and it is said that he was killed and that the sound of a horse's hooves are sometimes heard today.

There were three bar houses in the area controlling toll roads. Two of these houses still remain but are now privately owned.

The present church of St Wilfrid was built in 1840 but records show that there was a church on the site as far back as the 17th century. There was a village green and well on land presumably in front of the present church. Feasts were held there and can even be remembered today by some older members of the community. At one end of Main Street, namely 'Stocks Hill', there was a blacksmith's shop and still to this day are wooden stocks.

In the past most of the inhabitants worked in the mills, originally the woollen mill, then paper and also a flour mill which was situated near the river. Some of course worked on the land. Today the village has grown with the building of new houses and most people commute to Otley, Leeds, Bradford, Harrogate and even further afield. The village is only three miles from the Leeds/Bradford airport, which makes travelling to London and the Continent very easy. When the paper mill was taken over in 1981 many people were made redundant so employment had to be found outside the village. In the past farm animals were taken through the main street on foot, today it is the main road from Bradford to Harrogate so there is one continual stream of lorries and cars.

There has always been a keen interest in sports in the village, particularly football and cricket. The cricket team now play in the Leeds League and the football team in the Harrogate League.

The village hall was commemorated to the fallen in the two world wars. This is now a very busy hall used for various activities every day; badminton, bowls, tennis and dancing to name but a few.

Pool National school was built in 1870. A new school was built in Arthington Lane on land adjoining the village hall in 1975 and still houses about 112 pupils.

One mile to the east of Pool is the village of Arthington where there is a house of historical interest known as The Nunnery. This was built about 400 years ago after Henry VIII's Dissolution of the Monasteries. It stands on the site of the old buildings of Arthington Priory; the remains of the old well can still be found today.

Pudsey

Pudsey, known to the Romans as Podechesaie, although now a small town retains the atmosphere of the village it once was. Indeed the area adjacent to the market place in the centre is still officially known as Waver Green though now is the site of the Yorkshire Bank.

Pudsey – a place famous for several things; cricket, the Moravian Settlement at Fulneck, Pudsey Bear, and the birds flying backward to keep t'muck out of their eyes. Whilst cricket is still played at the St Lawrence and Britannia grounds where Sir Len Hutton and Herbert Sutcliffe started their careers, and the church and school still thrives at Fulneck, the dirt which was so evident in the past, with its accompanying smells, has virtually disappeared. Years ago when the woollen mills with their black smoke, the tanneries, shoe makers and chemical works all with their odours, not to mention the tallow candle makers in the centre of the town, were all working, together with the dust and mud from the unmade roads, it's no wonder the comment was made.

Also gone to a large extent are the characters who gave Pudsey its reputation. Before the rebuilding in Pudsey centre which resulted in a tidy row of shops, there was an odd assortment including a wooden building where, amid an all pervading smell of boiled sweets, Minnie Beavers would sell one and a half lbs for 6d. Also remembered is 'Tripey' Ross who sold bags made of twisted paper filled with tripe bits dripping with vinegar. At Delph End, shortened to 'Delphs', where locals went for their week-end walks was a small off-licence where they could stop for refreshment. This little out of the way shop was run by Annie Jones, known by everyone as 'Cider Annie' although most of her trade was actually 'pop'.

A century ago Pudsey was divided by the inhabitants into two areas

Booth's Yard, Pudsey

173

with resulting rivalries, often ending in fights. Lowtown then was a collection of yards and folds, cottages huddled together off the main thoroughfare. Very few are left and one 'fold' has been carefully restored and is now transformed into an area known as Booths Yard with an assortment of shops, a coffee house and a pub. Also a few steps from this yard is the old Trinity Methodist chapel converted to a shopping mall with a large room above which serves as a useful venue for dances and various other events. Brass bands and choirs still retain their attraction.

Religion played a great part in the building of Pudsey. John Wesley preached several times in the area. As the churches and chapels became established the social life of the neighbourhood centred round the events produced there. Not so in the previous century when the inns were the focus of entertainment, especially at feast time with cock fighting and other blood sports taking place. For those wanting knowledge the Mechanic's Institute was built in 1880 and is now the town hall. Several of the chapels and churches have now been demolished or put to other uses, but the fine parish church of St Laurence built in the 1840s stands as a landmark on the horizon for miles around.

The 'top' end of the town in addition to the cottages had most of the larger houses built for the mill owners and other prosperous people. Here also were more open spaces where the inhabitants could spend what leisure time they had.

One such place is the Fulneck valley, or Fallneck as it was known in 1743 when, extending their church from Europe, the Moravians led by Count Zinzendorf chose the site overlooking the valley to build their new settlement and live according to their beliefs.

The building started with the church, followed by the minister's house. Houses for the single brethren, single sisters and widows were built with cottages for the families. In 1753 a boarding school for boys was opened with girls following two years later. Some of these children were orphans and others had parents working as missionaries. The buildings at the back looked out over the 'terrace' and extensive views of the valley. The community still flourishes, the buildings little changed, although the school now has day pupils as well as boarders and also from several religions.

Today Pudsey is a dormitory town for people working in Leeds and Bradford and is surrounded by housing estates and many 'off comed 'uns' have arrived. These people have been incorporated into the spirit of Pudsey.

The first Pudsey Carnival was in 1898 and was a magnificent effort by the entire town to enhance Pudsey's bid for its own Charter which was granted the following year. After several breaks in continuity the Carnival was revived again in May 1988 and Pudsey folk, old and new, working together again made it another success.

Rastrick 🌿

The name Rastrick derives from Old Norse and means 'a resting place on the way'. It is not clear where 'the way' is coming from or going to, but it is known that a Roman road linking Chester with York passed through Rastrick. The site of Snake Hill Ford, where the Roman road crossed the river Calder, can still be seen. Close by is an historic Quaker burial ground, for Rastrick was for many years a stronghold of Quakerism. As the movement grew, larger premises had to be successively built, and the final Friends' meeting house, built in 1869, is a magnificent structure and was referred to as the 'Cathedral of Quakerism in the West Riding'. The premises are now divided into flats.

Rastrick occupies sloping ground on the south bank of the river Calder. It is now mainly residential, with a mixture of Victorian or earlier houses and modern estates and developments. Because of the importance of stone quarrying in the past, the older buildings tend to be of local sandstone. Indeed the last quarry ceased production in the 1970s, but a blacksmith's, founded in 1866, continues in business providing tools and repair services for the quarry industry further afield. The textile industry is much diminished from its former importance, but a large dyeworks still survives. Engineering has for many years been an important employer in the area. The world-famous Blakeborough valves were made in Rastrick for over 130 years until the company went out of business in 1988. Still in business, though, and thriving, is the largest company outside North America making wire coat-hangers – the ones you get when you collect garments from the drycleaners. Another local company was responsible for the impressive architectural glasswork that forms the roof of the Gateshead Metro Centre.

The oldest carved stone in Rastrick is to be found in St Matthew's churchyard; it is the base of a Saxon cross and dates from the 11th century. The existing church building, whose west tower has a circular cupola, celebrates its bicentenary in 1997; the first church on this site dated from the late 14th century. About a mile up the hill, and also in Rastrick, stands New Road Sunday school, which was founded in the early 19th century. It still continues to flourish and is possibly the only undenominational place of worship surviving in the country for over 150 years.

The railway arrived in Rastrick in 1840 and the first station was called Brighouse for Bradford, for it was to be some years before that important city, six miles away, was to have its own station. The name then changed to Brighouse for Rastrick, and finally simply Brighouse. However, the stations, which moved site about 100 years ago, have always been in Rastrick. Shortsightedly, the station was closed in 1970, but there are currently high hopes of it being reopened. It is about 20 years since the M62 motorway opened through Rastrick, helping to relieve the local roads of much heavy traffic.

Recreation is provided by squash, tennis, bowls, cricket and football clubs, but perhaps the most interesting is Castle Fields Golf Club, founded about 100 years ago. Although it is only a six hole course (which is very rare) occupying four acres of attractive parkland, it is probably the oldest golf club in Yorkshire. It is in the English Golf Union, which means that handicaps are accepted nationally. The land originally formed part of the grounds of the adjacent Castle Hill House (the site of which is believed to have been a Saxon settlement or even Roman), where the local author Michael Fairless (real name Margaret Barber) was born, and whose main book was *The Roadmender*. A blue plaque commemorates this. Also of interest is the nearby South Lodge, which was moved stone by stone from its original site over a mile away when the railway sidings were extended in the 1870s.

One feature dominating the landscape at the top of Rastrick, and very clearly visible from the motorway, is Round Hill. Its origin is uncertain – indeed, the experts cannot be sure whether it is natural or man-made.

Undoubtedly, the best way to explore Rastrick is on foot. Away from the main roads, and still waiting to be discovered by the visitor, are old setted or flagged yards and back lanes, and a network of public footpaths. Who knows, you might just come across the brandy snap and ginger biscuit factory tucked away out of sight. This is the small century-old family business that supplies many of the fairgrounds in the north of England.

Ravenfield ⚛

Ravenfield is an attractive village which is situated between the A630 at Hooton Roberts and the A631 at Bramley in a tract of what is, for the most part, agricultural land.

The old part of the village is very pretty and nestles in a hollow below the church of St James close to the site of Ravenfield Hall and adjacent to Ravenfield Park which is a remnant of the private deer park of the ancient family of Westby who are known to have lived at Ravenfield before 1200.

It is known that the village was visited, in 1379, by Poll Tax Collectors who listed 74 taxpayers aged 16 years or over with a total population of about 100 all told. At that time the Squire was John De Coniesburge, a Knight who lived at nearby Conisbrough Castle.

Ravenfield was owned by the Westby family up to the time of the Civil War. However, the Squire was a supporter of Charles I and consequently Oliver Cromwell confiscated the Estate and awarded it to one of his own supporters. With the Accession of Charles II in 1660 the land was returned to its rightful owners. Fortunately the Estate remained intact. The Westby family sold the Estate including Ravenfield Hall to Mistress

Elizabeth Parkin in 1749. She was a wealthy businesswoman who had connections in the local metal trades, was a coalowner, money-broker, investor and landowner. During the 1750s there was much renovation work done on the Hall and grounds. The Architect, John Carr was called in to rebuild the Hall. The old stable and farm buildings were demolished and new ones built alongside Hooton Lane. It was Mistress Parkin who chose the medieval site of Ravenfield Chapel upon which to build a new stone church which is quite interesting, having amongst other things a clock with only one hand and a Minstrels' Gallery. The seating capacity is about 100. St James' church is still in regular use today, although some people think that it is a bit out of the way being situated high up on the edge of the village. It was, however, very convenient for those living at the Hall and as Mistress Parkin was, of course, paying the bills she could choose where she built it. Mistress Parkin died in 1766 and her estate passed to a distant kinsman and protege Walter Oborne, who for many years had been her partner and aide de camp. The estate was then sold to Squire Bosville and until he sold it in 1920 Ravenfield remained an estate village. The estate was then broken up; the park with adjoining land, being sold as a farm. Several tenants then became owner-occupiers and new families moved in.

At one time there was a quarry in the parish which produced the stone used for grindstones in Sheffield. In the old village at least two new farmhouses and farm buildings were completed before the 18th century. A new schoolroom was built in 1848. New Home Farm was built in 1831 but the village changed very little in the 19th century. One of the oldest buildings in the village is what was once the smithy which, until 1979 when it became a private house, had been used as a village shop and beer off-licence and also a post office until 1945.

During the Second World War the Hall was used to accommodate German and Italian Prisoners of War. Huts were built in the grounds and, altogether, there were 1200 of them. In the old cellars the prisoners secretly distilled alcohol and mixed it with gin and/or distilled water and called it 'Ravenfield Special'.

Like many other villages in South Yorkshire, Ravenfield has changed into something very different from the small secluded and picturesque place it once was in 1900. The commercial life of the village has become centred around the crossroads at Ravenfield Common where the local shops, garage, public house and post office are situated. For many years there have also been tennis court facilities on Hollings Lane which were paid for by the villagers themselves from public donations and fund-raising events. Most of the modern residential developments have tended to become clustered around this area too; only 35 new dwellings having been built in the old village since the 1960s. Many other old buildings, including the Hall, have gone; some without trace. Also many hedge-rows, fieldgates and gate-stoops, several ponds, ditches and wells have been filled in including what used to be the villagers' public well at the bottom of Church Lane. Most of the barns have been converted into dwellings and at Woodside Farm which is on Main Street a large pigeon cote has also recently been converted into a dwelling house; although the side facing the road has been preserved and looks almost the same as before. In spite of the changes, Ravenfield is a lovely place in which to live. For the past three years the old village has been entered for the Britain in Bloom competition and has been highly placed each time.

Riddlesden ᘓ

Riddlesden is situated in a very pleasant area astride the A650, approximately one mile from Keighley and three miles from Bingley, in the Aire valley of West Yorkshire. The higher reaches of the village are built on the lower slopes of Rombalds Moor, world famous for the song *On Ilkley Moor baht'at*.

The derivation of the name Riddlesden is authoritatively thought to be Anglo-Saxon. Raedels (council) and Den (Danes) means a place of council of, or with, the Danes. Riddlesden is mentioned in the Domesday Book as a manor which had belonged to the Dane Andulf, but in 1086 it belonged to the King.

In the year 1402 the estate was split into two parts (East and West Riddlesden), one section to the Maude family and the other to the Paslews. Riddlesden includes the village of Morton Banks, which is itself divided into Low and High Banks. The present East Riddlesden Hall, built circa 1640, and West Riddlesden Hall (1687) are both ancient manor houses.

The former, which is now held by the National Trust, has a pond, the 'Stragnum de Riddlesden', which provided fish for the canons of Bolton Abbey as far back as 1320 and which is still a haven for wildfowl. There is also a very large 16th century barn. Frequent historical pageants are held in the Hall throughout the year, together with trade fairs and medieval banquets.

Riddlesden has three well known public houses, the Willow Tree, the Marquis of Granby and the Airedale Heifer. The latter is noted for the fact that the famous Airedale Heifer was housed there. This huge beast was slaughtered in the year 1830 after being severely injured. She weighed over one and a quarter tons.

Religion has always played a significant part in the life of the village, which in its earlier years came under the parish of Bingley. The parish church of St Mary the Virgin was built in 1847 and stands in a delightful setting in Low Banks. It became a separate parish in 1847 when the population was some 700 souls. The first vicar was John Fawcett who was installed on the 5th February 1875. A new infant school was built in the same year and the church school enlarged in 1886. The premises are still in full use together with a further new junior school across the road. Methodism came to this area early around the middle of the 18th century, whilst Primitive Methodism emerged in 1821. Both sections worked happily together but in 1955 they combined to form the Ilkley Road Methodist church. Congregationalism or United Reformed, as it is now called, is a comparative newcomer to Riddlesden but now has a thriving church.

The passage of time has brought many changes in the occupations and interests of the villages. Originally they were yeomen farmers with associated crafts, but two events made great changes. In 1774 the section of the Leeds and Liverpool canal through the village was completed and the Industrial Revolution was soon to follow.

Coal was mined in large quantities and miners and boatmen were much in evidence. Morton Banks Colliery was a source of work as many small pits opened up. The coal was shipped by canal barge and exchanged for lime which was brought back for use in agriculture and building work. Two local families were much involved in this process; the Oldfields, who owned some of the barges and who still run a coal business, and the Scotts, who were chiefly boatmen at the time. Limekilns were worked in the village; one road, alongside the canal, was known as Limekiln Lane (now Scott Lane).

Cottage weaving, formerly a staple occupation, was transferred to the mills. Gradually the village expanded and began to cover the lower slopes of the moor as encroachment from Keighley increased, so that current occupations now cover a broad cross section of our modern mobile age.

In former times much of the life of the village was connected with the places of worship, with their Sunday school trips and Whitsuntide frolics. Some went by canal barge (specially cleaned) to Skipton for the day. There was a maypole on the green in Low Banks and at Fanny Fair, outside the Marquis of Granby, a roundabout swung halfway across the canal.

Today the motor car has, to a large extent, changed much, but in many ways church activities continue with outings and rambles, whilst the memorial hall, built in 1919 to commemorate the end of the First World War, has a Veterans Association and other activities. An annual event of note in the recent Riddlesden calendar is the Gala, held in June and run by an enthusiastic team of devotees, which has raised thousands of pounds for charity.

The mine shafts and the limekilns have long since disappeared. On part of the land which they formerly occupied stands a fine modern school with a rural aspect. The very few remaining canal barges are now used for maintenance and repair work. The canal itself is now the realm of pleasure cruisers who do great business, particularly during the summer months.

Many ghost stories are told, particularly concerning former residents of the Halls. The Grey Lady was possibly a Paslew whose husband imprisoned her in her bedroom and allowed her to starve to death after finding her with her lover. Her lover incidentally was walled up on the premises. The White Lady was drowned in the fish pond after being thrown from the house. There is also the Scottish merchant's ghost. He, so the story goes, sought shelter at the Hall during a blizzard and was murdered for his money by the Steward of the Hall, who was subsequently hanged in York Castle in 1790.

Roberttown ✍️

Today Roberttown is a thriving community but it wasn't always like that. Two hundred years ago it was described as a 'hamlet' in the township of Liversedge in the parish of Birstall, situated near the high road between Leeds and Huddersfield. From these early times the hard working people spun and wove cloth in their dwellings, thus the woollen trade grew and developed causing 'much traffic' passing through the village taking the finished cloth by packhorse to the cloth halls of Leeds and Huddersfield.

The bar house was built in 1819 and the turnpike road opened when visitors arriving by stage coach could refresh themselves at the coaching inns, a famous one being the Yew Tree inn. The Royal Mail used the hostelries to change horses. In the 1700s one of the hazards of travel was the footpad and the highwayman 'Swift Nick' Nevison roamed the area.

In the late 1800s a great unemployment hit the village, when John Wright from Lancashire brought hands and apprentices to weave cotton cloth. The building of the five storey cotton mill with its tall chimney became a landmark where cotton spinning continued until the Second World War.

Conditions improved for a while, to be upset by the economic depression of the 1840s, when the Chartist movement was born in London. Soon there were many Chartists in the area – a meeting was held at the Old Yew Tree inn which resulted in the biggest Chartist gathering – 250,000 attended on Roberttown Common. The crowds which gathered for this meeting presented no problems to the Roberttowners who were able to cope and offer hospitality at its many inns and in its cottages. They were used to catering for big crowds which attended the Roberttown Races held annually at midsummer for three days on the common, the men of the turf and famous racegoers putting up at the Star.

Religion played a great part in the lives of the dour spinners and weavers and after the many visits of John Wesley, the chapel to celebrate 100 years of Methodism was built in 1830. Rev Hammond Roberson, who had arrived in the area in 1795, was determined to bring the Anglican church into the valley and was responsible for the building of All Saints' church at Roberttown. This was consecrated in 1845 and with the chapel has played a great part in village life. Church schools were built later.

Roberttown is still a village, though the population has increased, many houses and efficient modern factories being built where once fields and cottages stood. It has its churches, schools, clubs, inns, shops, post office and community centre. The building of the M62 motorway has made Roberttown almost part of the commuter belt. Hollybank school for the handicapped is situated on the edge of the village and a seat presented by the Women's Institute is a resting place on the common for those who wish to sit and enjoy the view.

Rossington

Rossington, whose name suggests Anglo-Saxon origin (settlement of people of the moor), is situated near the Great North Road. However, evidence exists of Roman occupation, as a large Roman fort and temple lie under the approach road.

In the Middle Ages, Rossington was part of a large manor, which included many other villages on the south side of Doncaster. From 1472 ownership passed to the Crown and then to the burgesses of Doncaster, who built farms and houses for the poor and proved very good managers of the land. In 1838 Rossington was purchased by a wealthy Leeds woollen manufacturer, whose family were in possession until 1939. Up to this date the only landowner, apart from the manor, was St Michael's church. The railway main line to London and the South, opened in 1849, cuts across the area. New Rossington lies on the east side and Old Rossington on the west, but there is no real divide between the two. St Michael's church in Old Rossington, and the four different denominations in New Rossington, support and co-operate with each other in services and social functions.

St Michael's church was built in the Middle Ages, probably on the site of a former Anglo-Saxon mud and wattle church. It served also as a community and market centre and was, until 1650, the village school. The church still retains its control of the modern St Michael's junior school and, although it was virtually rebuilt in 1844, many Norman features were preserved. By the church door there used to be the grave of James Boswell (died 1702), known as the 'Gipsy King'. Born a gentleman, he went to live in encampments in Sherwood Forest and helped gipsies to improve their way of living, and to gain the goodwill of local farmers. Gipsies passing through the area often came to pay their respects and would take away a piece of the gravestone, so that in time it disappeared.

The old village post office is housed in one of the remaining 18th century dwellings, not far from the railway. Opposite stands the village pump, dated about 1850. It is unique to the Doncaster area. During development of the mining village, when the water supply was cut off for pipe cleaning, villagers came here to draw water.

A great change came when coal was discovered on the west side of the village, the first coal being brought to the surface in 1915. A well planned mining village, known as New Rossington, grew up with shops, schools, churches of four different denominations, and public houses. As with most mining villages, there existed a community spirit, which partly remains today. Many think this was enhanced by the shape of the village. The streets of well appointed houses were built in concentric circles, with a green in the middle. The houses ended at the Station Hotel and, when the gates were closed at night, people felt secure inside their little world. Neighbours and friends were always there to share joys and sorrows. They still are, but people no longer leave their door unlocked when they go out. On the wall near the bus terminus is the Hospital Bulletin Board, no longer used. News of hospital patients from Rossington was phoned to Mr Addy, the chemist, who would post it on the board nightly for the benefit of relatives and friends unable to visit.

A welfare hall provided leisure pursuits, dancing, amateur drama, male voice choirs and a youth club. There was a tennis club, cricket and football teams, also a library, billiards hall and a cinema. On Sunday mornings Mr Price, the bellman, would cycle round the village ringing his bell and calling out details of events and meetings for the coming week. Sunday was also 'walking day', when groups of people, mainly young, would wander about the old village greeting each other. There was no vandalism. The cinema is now closed and many activities are no longer indulged in. A regular bus service to Doncaster encourages many to leave the village for their recreation. Work available for the men was in mining, railway work and engineering. For the girls there was shop and office work. Many local men continue to work at the colliery.

It is interesting to note that electricity did not come to the village until 1952. Up to that time methods of housework were old fashioned, and television is still considered a novelty by many of the older people.

Old Rossington is no longer mainly a farming community, as much farm land has been sold off for housing and new houses continue to be built. The inhabitants mostly commute to Doncaster or further afield for their work.

Ryhill

Ryhill with its long main street of tidy houses and well-tended gardens, is one of West Yorkshire's nicest and friendliest villages.

The name Ryhill, meaning 'the hill where rye was grown', in the early 1800s was just a tiny hamlet providing for the needs of local farmers. It was once the property of the monks of Nostell Priory, to whom rents were paid.

With the Industrial Revolution came the demand for coal and transport. Mills sprang up all over Yorkshire and mines were sunk in and near Ryhill. Wintersette reservoir was built and Barnsley canal widened to transfer the coal. Soon the pressure for more coal and faster transport became so great that a railway was needed.

Large numbers of men arrived to build the railway. More houses were built and a new water supply laid – until now the people drew their water from spring wells. Some men brought their families and this meant schools and churches were needed. Ryhill now had three churches, two Methodist and the beautiful parish church of St James which is still in use today. In 1970 a fire broke out in St James' and caused great damage, but by the following year thanks to its parishioners the church was once again restored to its former glory.

The little hamlet had by now become a village. The demand for coal was so great that Ryhill had not one but two railway lines and two stations. The Empire Music Hall opened and also Kelso's Portable Theatre. These were later replaced by the Imperial Picturedome with its silent films and piano accompaniment, which, in its turn was replaced in 1913 by the Empire Picture Palace. The Palace became so popular that it installed an organ which rose up out of the ground and the audience sang along with the music. It lasted until 1959 when it finally closed, possibly because its patrons considered threepence and one shilling too much to pay for the privilege of sitting for three hours on hard wooden seats.

The old Imperial Picturedome is still standing but its patrons alas have changed. When it was purchased in 1945 by a local pork butcher he converted it into a piggery. Time marches on.

These were good years for Ryhill. On Friday nights dances were held in Felkirk school or in the church hall, and on Saturday nights long queues formed outside the Picture Palace for the early and late shows.

In summer families took their picnics down to Wintersette reservoir and in winter, when the ice had frozen hard, they skated there. A local man took his handcart, on which he had set a small stove, down to the reservoir and sold pies and peas to the skaters.

Things took a turn for the worse when the demand for coal dropped. Then the coal ran out and the mines closed. The railways were no longer needed and they closed also. They were replaced by several private bus companies and later by West Yorkshire Passenger Transport. The closing of the mines and railways brought unemployment to Ryhill although some people were offered work elsewhere. Others went to Wakefield and Barnsley to find employment, but times were hard.

In 1966 a Leeds firm opened a branch of its 'High Class Gents and Ladies Tailors' in a disused chapel and employed 50 women. Their standards were high and demand for their products ranged from Royal garden parties, to Ascot and all the major golf tournaments. The British contestants and BBC commentators who took part in the 1972 Olympics were supplied with uniforms by them, as were many well known celebrities. The factory closed down in 1987.

Ryhill survived in spite of everything and the population instead of decreasing, is increasing. The village itself is full of life. In recent years a new library and health centre have been built. There are bowling greens, tennis courts, cricket and football pitches. Classes are held weekly in the parish hall for those interested in sewing, typing, art and aerobics, and the Women's Institute and Mothers' Union are thriving.

The popularity of Ryhill is due, in no small way to the friendliness of its people. Meet them at a bus stop, in the shops or on the street and they will smile and speak to you. You will not remain a stranger here for long.

Saltaire 🐑

Saltaire is a charming place to visit, not only because of its present appearance, but also because of its extremely interesting past.

Begin your visit at the bottom of the valley in Roberts Park, where stands the statue of Sir Titus Salt, a Victorian manufacturer of great vision and compassion, attributes not prevalent amongst most of his contemporaries.

Titus Salt was born at Morley on the 20th September 1803. He gained experience in the wool trade and eventually joined his father's business as a woolbuyer. In 1830 he married Caroline Whitlam of Grimsby and they had eleven children. Ever alert to new methods and materials, he found fame and fortune manufacturing alpaca wool, rather than sheep's wool.

It was during his term as Mayor of Bradford that an outbreak of cholera killed over 400 people in the city and he determined then to move his mill and his workers out of Bradford and build a model village. It was officially opened on his 50th birthday in 1853, and by 1876 it had 775 houses, bath and wash houses, 45 almshouses, a hospital, church, educational institute, school, Sunday school and park.

Look around the delightful park, Shipley Glen, a local beauty spot, and the open moorland is not far away. Head back into Saltaire, crossing the footbridge over the river Aire. It was this river plus the 'Salt' of Sir Titus that gave Saltaire its name. Make your way up Victoria Road.

On your left is the enormous honey-coloured bulk of 'The Mill', once the hub of Saltaire. Today, sadly, much of it is unused and neglected, but parts have been restored and are now used as shops and offices. Work on the mill began in 1851 and the building was carried out to unbelievably high standards and with what is now called 'environmental sympathy'. The edifice is crowned by a tall chimney modelled on an Italian bell tower – shades of the Piazza San Marco!

The block of buildings to your right have been used as stables and offices and also as a home used from time to time by the Salt family on their visits from their homes at Methley and Lightcliffe.

Set back from the road, still on the right is the United Reformed church. This was built by Sir Titus in 1858/9 and cost just over £16,000. This too has Italian connections; it is said to be a replica of a church in Italy and is considered one of the best examples of Italian architecture in the country. It is well worth a look inside, as is the mausoleum built on the side.

Alongside the church runs the Leeds and Liverpool Canal, once a great transport route from the manufacturers of Yorkshire and Lancashire to the port of Liverpool and the markets of America and the rest of the world. Today the canal is a favourite tourist attraction, there are boat trips in the summer and the banks have been made pleasant for walkers. The railway also runs through Saltaire, putting the city of Bradford and the Yorkshire Dales within easy reach.

Continuing up Victoria Road, cross over the railway and notice the well tended allotments of the villagers on the left. The houses to the right and left of the road were built for the millworkers, notice the roofs at different heights, breaking what could be monotonous rows. The wash-houses provided for the villagers contained six washing machines, wringing machines, drying frames and hot-air closets. People were supposed to use these houses for all their laundry, but many women put out their lines across the streets and air-dried their washing, in defiance of Sir Titus. Incidentally, the streets are named after the Salt children, Charlotte Street, Fanny Street and so on.

You now come to two large buildings facing one another across the street, forming a square, Victoria Square. The building on the left was built as a community centre, to compensate for the fact that Sir Titus, a strict teetotaller, would not allow a public house to be built. The Institute as it was known, had a library and reading room, a conversation and smoking room (for those over 21 only), a concert hall, a billiard room, a science laboratory and a gymnasium.

The building on the right was the dining hall for the mill, but was also used as a school for the children, up to 700, many of them working part-time in the mill. These premises are now occupied by Shipley College of Further Education.

On the right you come to a row of small houses set back from the road, with a pleasant garden in front. These are the almshouses, built to accommodate selected retired workers who were allowed to live in the houses rent free and were given a small pension.

Opposite the almshouses is the Sir Titus Salt Hospital, originally a dispensary and first-aid room for the mill, but in its heyday it boasted three wards. It is now a rest home for the elderly.

In this short walk you have seen the major buildings of a scheme set up by a great and enlightened industrialist, far ahead of his time. On the day of his funeral in December 1876 all the mills in Bradford closed as a mark of respect.

Saltaire today has been enveloped by the suburbs of Bradford, but it is still a super place in which to spend a day, wandering. The present inhabitants are mainly elderly, the houses considered too small for families, but young marrieds are buying houses here now, ensuring the continuity of this unique place.

Scarcroft 🌿

Scarcroft is one of a cluster of small villages lying along the A58 from Leeds to Wetherby. It sits on the highest point of the road and commands lovely views in all directions. The old name Skardecroft has led to a theory that it was the croft of Skardi, a Norseman.

The history of the village goes back much further than this. There are traces of a Roman road in a field west of the A58, and mounds known as Pompacali are still something of a mystery. Suggestions have been made that they are the remains of a prehistoric stockade for animals, or a Roman camp, or a medieval quarry. Further evidence of Roman occupation is that a number of Roman coins have been discovered and local legend has it that Roman soldiers washed their wounds in a pure spring at Hetchell.

Once a small community of around 200 inhabitants concerned almost entirely with farming, the village has grown to more than 2,000 inhabitants and has become a fashionable residential dormitory of the city of Leeds. Today's residents are no longer involved in farming, although there are three large milk producing and mixed farms and a large hen farm. Scarcrofters these days are mostly business and professional people working in Leeds or commuting throughout the country on a daily or weekly basis.

In years gone by older inhabitants remember an annual feast or fair held in August. There was no village green in those days and this feast was held in a field behind the village pub – the New inn. The present day pub is set well back from the main road and its large green area in front is used for all kinds of local rendezvous and meetings. Nowadays the village boasts a very fine golf course and a grand Village Show held each September in the village hall.

There is no church or school in Scarcroft and villagers are divided by parish boundaries – some attending St Peter's in Thorner and the rest going to church/school in Bardsey with all the social and religious activities associated with church and school life.

In a cottage in Ling Lane, Miss Barker was killed as she was plucking a goose. This same lady, who each Sunday walked over the fields to church in Thorner, is reputed to haunt the area and the sight of her is claimed by several locals.

On a lighter note it is believed that Dick Turpin jumped over the toll bar gate on Wetherby Road. This same toll gate is part of Leeds transport history. It was established in 1826 to pay for the new road from Leeds to Wetherby and the charge was a halfpenny per hoof. The toll house is mentioned in the 1841 census return and still stands at the end of Thorner Lane as a listed building.

The oldest remaining buildings in the village are Moat Hall Farm and Scarcroft Water Mill. Parts of Moat Hall Farm date back to the 13th century and the moat was plainly visible at the beginning of the 20th century, but has now silted up and has been filled in. Scarcroft Water Mill is a large building housing a water wheel driven by water from Scarcroft beck and corn was still ground there up to 50 years ago. The mill was built in 1810 but sadly the farm house and buildings are now derelict and the mill is badly in need of repair.

A large stone house was described in 1837 as a newly built public house and was known as the William IV inn. The house was modernised in 1906 and is now used as offices by Yorkshire Electricity. The headquarters of YE are now in the grounds of Scarcroft Lodge.

Scarcroft Grange is mentioned in 1687, but a fire in the 18th century removed all the original stonework, and during the Second World War the house was occupied by the military and Russian repatriates and deteriorated very much. It has now been modernised and made into dwellings.

There are two old milestones remaining in the area. One is hidden in the hedge at Bay Horse Lane, giving directions to Otley, Pontefract and Tadcaster, and the other is on the east side of a waste triangle where Milner Lane joins Thorner Lane and this gives directions to Wetherby and Leeds in 'old' miles (the present day mile is equal to one mile and a third in olden day mileage).

Perhaps our only other remaining vestiges of fame are that there are two extremely rare wild plants surviving in the Hetchell Nature Reserve – one is a thistle and one is a toothwort.

Scholes 🌿

Six miles out of Leeds along the A64 to York is the signpost to Scholes.

Home Farm is the first of the five working farms in the village and has diversified over the years from growing corn to rhubarb and now to Pick Your Own soft fruits. Look amongst the farm buildings and the stables housing the horses for the Riding for the Disabled Organisation and see the two up, two down brick house. This was the dream home of a young man who could only build it after his work on Saturdays. Brick by brick with the help of friends he eventually finished the house and took his bride home to the house that is still known as Saturday Cottage.

The greatest change to village life was the coming of the railway. You can see the station, opened in 1876, now transformed into a restaurant and pub, 'The Buffers'. You can stand on the platform next to what was the station master's house and imagine the hustle and bustle when the train brought the commuters home from Leeds. New houses and shops were gradually built, especially along Station Road, a tree-lined avenue beautified by horse chestnut trees, each one planted in memory of a soldier from the village killed in the world wars. This road leads to the school, library and parish council offices. Behind lie the quiet waters beloved by anglers, once the clay pits of the local brickworks. Many of the houses in Scholes and beyond were built with bricks from Scholes Brickworks, owned and managed by the Chippindale family.

Main Street starts by the council offices and leads down to the Coronation Tree. Here you will see several old houses and terraces, some with lovely names; Snowdrop Cottage, Badger Terrace, Parrot Row and Cluster of Nuts. The road curves round what was once a deer park where medieval lords hunted and deer was 'exported' to Pontefract Castle. Being in the parish of Barwick in Elmet, Scholes did not have its own church until 1875 when the little church was built to hold up to 75 people. By 1960 it was obvious that a much larger building was needed so the new church was built, providing a fascinating contrast in style.

Next to the village hall used to stand the manor house. This was demolished when it became unsafe and a complex of sheltered housing bungalows now occupies the site. A small 'Manor House' hall provides a meeting place and the amenities of washing machines, a visiting hairdresser and chiropodist, which combined with coffee mornings, organised outings, meetings and bingo make life pleasant for all Scholes pensioners.

The Barleycorn was built in the 1930s, the house next door being the former beer house. This house too has experienced changing times, from beer house, butcher's, grocer's shop and now a doctor's surgery.

Of the five farms there are two which open directly on to the main street, one on either side of the road. The old granary can still be seen at Green Lodge Farm, for many years the meeting place of the Methodists before their chapel was built in 1878. The chapel has a beautifully carved stone front piece which incorporates a badger. This animal was part of the coat of arms of the Grey family who lived in Morwick Hall on the York Road. The family used to walk across the fields on Sunday mornings leading their servants and tenants to church or chapel. At the end of Main Street stands the Coronation Tree – a lime tree – planted to honour King Edward VII.

This is the Scholes you can see but what perhaps is not obvious as you drive through is its caring community spirit. There are many organisations, all of whom help each other's charitable activities. The Community Care Organisation, for instance, has volunteers who collect the housebound once a month and take them to where other volunteers have cooked them a lunch and sit and talk with them. This organisation also provides help and respite to anyone in the village in need and runs weekly coffee mornings in the manor house.

Shelley 🌿

Shelley is situated about six miles south of Huddersfield on the A629. A hundred years ago Shelley was just a compact little village on a shelf of land – with small hamlets to the east, west, north and south of it. The village church built in the period around 1866 is situated amongst lovely green fields with a Victorian vicarage alongside – this now an old people's home. Opposite the church is a garden centre complete with rose gardens and restaurant in which one can dine and see the most beautiful views of the Holme valley and Pennine moorland.

Shelley Hall, not far from the church, is a 17th century building beautifully restored by the present occupants and sited near what was once the manor house and the pinfold. The latter was last in use in 1860.

In the fields to the north of Shelley and almost on its boundary lies Gryce Hall, the home of Lord Saville, a descendant of the Savilles who were landowners throughout the centuries and the servants of kings.

A hundred years ago most of the men in the village were farmers or miners. Handloom weaving has also been a cottage industry for centuries and evidence of it can be seen in the long rows of upper windows in many of the cottages.

Methodism has been strong in Shelley for more than 200 years, as can be seen in the little chapel in Barkhouse Lane. John Wesley preached from its pulpit when on his tour of the North of England. At the present time Shelley is having to come to terms with modern day house-building on one of its south-facing hillsides. Shelley Park is an estate of about 200 houses with planning permission for up to 350 more, which will make it a village within Shelley village and bring, with the development, the modern problems of cars, roads and access points.

Shelley had mills in the 1800s and throughout this century, where cloth was woven, and corsets (or stays as they were known) and rugs: the home of the famous Tumble Twist rug is Shelley. With the demise of the small mills nothing is left of the industry except rug-making.

On 1st January each year the custom in Shelley is to walk the boundaries of the village, and around 100 young and old set out from the village hall and perambulate through the fields and lanes, passing through places with such names as Goose Pasture, Spink Royd Ings, Cinderhills, Ibbetson's Brow, Allen Wood, Tullas Close, Breary Close Shrog and Hepworth Hobstrides.

There are four hamlets on the fringes of the village. Roydhouse (meaning a house in a clearing), Brookhouse (probably a house by a brook, or dyke as it is known in these parts) and Woodhouse (a house made from timber before we used stone in Shelley). Ozzings was another early settlement; it goes back to the 1300s and was once inhabited by a lady called Ozan-de-Shelley.

Towering over the village is the very high Emley Moor TV mast, at night illuminated by many lights and a landmark for miles around. With the Holme Moss TV mast winking its warning lights from the south-west we really feel in communication with the north from this small village.

There is not much night-life in Shelley – three or four cosy pubs, and a village hall with a busy programme of dancing, bridge, keep-fit, women's meetings, Scouts, Guides and so on. Football and cricket teams are well supported.

The 1881 census return for Shelley listed occupations of the villagers. For example, 196 adults were involved in cloth making, 37 men were miners, 47 were farmers or farm labourers and there were also black-smiths, railway platelayers, cloggers, carpenters, stay (corset) finishers, washerwomen, servants, wheelwrights, tailors and seamstresses. Present day Shelley would have a job to find a weaver or miner and farmers can be counted on the fingers. Almost everyone commutes to the towns of Huddersfield, Holmfirth, Leeds or Sheffield.

Shelley is facing many changes though it still has its small post office and two well-stocked shops, and the school set in green fields, Shelley is still a lovely place to live.

Shepley ⚜

Poor, proud and peevish! This is how the people of Shepley have been described by those of the neighbouring village of Shelley.

The description could be true. 'Poor' – more than likely. As far back as the 13th century, certain lands were granted by Matthew of Sheplye (otherwise spelt Shepleie, Schepelay, etc) to the monks of Roche Abbey (between Doncaster and Sheffield), who would be committed to their vows of poverty. Later the village, long involved in the textile trade, was largely developed during the 19th century, with the coming of four worsted cloth mills, a maltings and brewery, and a number of quarries. Workers in these industries experienced plenty of poverty, as did the families of men and children who went down the pits of neighbouring villages.

'Proud' – certainly! No doubt Sir Matthew de Shepley, as he became, lord of the manor and steward to the Earl of Warren, of the Lordship of Wakefield, and his successors, were proud of their positions and their holdings. Certainly, could they have looked 700 years on, they would be proud as well to know that their Hall, of which 1542 is but the earliest mention in a 19th century local history, partly still stands. In the Hall, as it is at present, an elaborately plaster-decorated ceiling shows 1609 as a date of renovation.

The 19th century textile workers, poor as they were, could be proud that two of the mills produced worsted cloth of the very highest quality. The local textile trade resulted in over 30 tailors' shops existing in

Shepley – wooden annexes to the workers' cottages in which the tailors made up suits from this cloth. Some of the tailors were 'higglers', travelling round the country to sell their goods.

Shepley could be proud of its brewery. Like the mills it is gone now, but the excellence of the beer was attributed to the purity of the spring water that went into it. It is said that the brewery master, Seth Senior, started it up with only a sovereign in his pocket, and that the Sovereign inn, nearby, marks this rather than defies the area's Cromwellian support two centuries previously.

Today, Shepley is proud that it has a railway station, on a line still open, in spite of a long succession of closure threats and reprieves – the reprieves due to the tenacity of the local rail users' association. It is proud of its monthly village magazine, produced without a break for 20 years by a voluntary team. It is proud also that it is one of the few places to boast a public croquet green; and that there are well over 20 local organisations.

Shepley Village

Shepley is by no means a 'chocolate-box' village. In earlier days it was probably, like most small communities, fairly compact, the most important building being the Hall, with nearby stone farm buildings, a granary, and other houses. One still standing bears the date 1642 on its lintel. Inside this house was revealed a few years ago part of a medieval timber-and-wattle dwelling.

The village had stone-built ribbon development thrust upon it during the 19th century when, in 50 years, its population doubled to 1,200. It stretched then about one and three quarters miles; and still does. Many newcomers have arrived, but recent development has mostly been infilling, largely by brick-built houses, although lately there has been planners' insistence on a return to stone as a building material.

Two churches flourish: the parish church of St Paul, built in 1848, and a new Methodist church which, attractive and versatile, replaces the two that once existed in Shepley. Two miles away is a still-used Quaker meeting house: the Friends were at one time very active in this area, and a house on the outskirts of Shepley combined, during the 17th and 18th centuries, the functions of Quaker dwelling and meeting house. A 'gentle ghost' is associated with this building – a lady dressed in Quaker grey.

With a population now of roughly 3,000, Shepley was, until a few decades ago, a very self-contained village. Most people lived and worked here, and a train ride to Huddersfield was an event reserved for birthdays and holidays. There were once 24 'spice' (or sweet) shops, and other local traders well satisfied people's needs. Now, although there are one or two light industries, it has a predominantly commuter population, the wage-earners going daily to Huddersfield, Wakefield, Sheffield, Leeds and Manchester.

And 'peevishness'? But naturally villagers are peevish when people cannot distinguish Shepley from neighbouring Shelley!

Shibden ❧

Shibden is a valley of scattered development, with no village as such. Originally called Schepeden, (sheep-dale), Shibden has a soft-featured landscape, though its hillsides were once worked for coal, iron and clay. Many wealthier landowners had their own coal mines and the clay was used until recent times for pottery and sanitary ware.

The 17th century was a time of prosperity, brought by the expanding clothing trade, when wealth was spent building new homes and enhancing older houses. Many of these Jacobean Halls and homesteads remain today.

Shibden Hall is of course the best known, standing in its 90 acres of rolling parkland. The house was begun in the 15th century by the Otes family; since then it has been occupied by the Savilles, the Waterhouses and the Listers; the last private owner – John Lister – died in 1933. Now the Hall and adjoining Folk Museum make a wonderful historical heritage for all to visit.

The Spa Well at Spa House was visited by hundreds of 'May Day Pilgrims' from about 1780–1840. Field House was built on land once owned by the Knights of St John of Jerusalem, who used the rents from the house and land to support their charitable works.

Shibden Mill inn was built on the site of Shibden corn mill, which for six centuries ground corn for the people of Northowram. The mill dam (now filled in) once had a ducking stool, then in latter years was used as a boating lake.

Scout Hall is a very large imposing mansion on the hillside above Simm Carr. Built in 1680, it was famous for its 365 panes of glass in 52 windows. Stories abound about first owner John Mitchell and his gaming parties, race meetings, drinking orgies and his eventual death, when he donned wings and jumped off the overhanging escarpment behind Scout Hall. Today the Calderdale Way crosses the valley close to Scout Hall.

High Sunderland was perched on the bleak hill top from 1274 until its final demolition in 1951. It reputedly fitted the description of Emily Bronte's Wuthering Heights. Black Boy House, near High Sunderland, gained notoriety in more recent times as the birthplace of the infamous murderer, John Cristie, born 1898, hanged in Pentonville, 1953.

Stocks Brewery and an associated coal mine were located at Shibden Head. It is said that between the two World Wars, if the beer ran out at the local Stump Cross pubs, the 'Paraffin Man' would use his horse and cart to fetch another barrel from the brewery.

Salterlee school was first established in 1877. The 'new' school was opened in 1888 next door to the original building, which later became the mission church, attached to Northowram's St Matthew's until its closure in the 1960s. Today the school is thriving as never before.

Throughout the school's life detailed records have been kept, providing a wealth of information, varying from how many house martins nested in the eaves, to what impact evacuees had on the area in both World Wars. First World War evacuees came from as far afield as Belgium, while in 1939 they were from the East End. Two of these little Cockneys allegedly rolled a boulder down the hill behind the school. It crashed through a window, necessitating the covering of all windows with wire mesh, which is still there today. Interesting too, is the fact that three of the few bombs to fall on Calderdale were dropped in Shibden. The craters are visible yet, in fields near the school.

This is a peaceful haven, guarded by the tall poplars standing beside the stream. Birds and small animals abound, the hillsides yield a harvest of bilberries and wild flowers are prolific in the meadows. Surprisingly this rural delight is but a couple of miles from Halifax town centre; no wonder the residents wish to preserve it. Although they would fight an intrusion by any major developers, they are keen to encourage people to appreciate the valley's beauty and walk its paths. Even the sheep are returning to Shibden – this unspoiled Valley of Sheep!

Silkstone
& Silkstone Common 🦚

Nestling in a valley lies Silkstone, a village known to the Romans. It is said to receive its name from the Roman word 'salix' on account of the willow trees that surrounded the village. Today there are still areas of woodland providing pleasant walks. In the Domesday Book the spelling is Silchestone.

At the south end is a hill leading to the common land where the villagers took their stock to graze. It was here, in 1854, the railway station was sited and the village of Silkstone Common was born. The hill still separates the two villages.

A church, built in 1090, was granted to the monks of Pontefract. Dedicated to All Saints, it is the mother church of the district and known as 'The Minster of the Moors'. It has a beautifully carved medieval screen and a modern tapestry worked by some of the women (and one man) of the parish. The registers of Silkstone church date back to 1549.

The monument to Sir Thomas Wentworth, who died in 1675, is considered to be one of the finest examples of a knight in armour of the Restoration period. There is also a memorial plaque to Joseph Bramah, engineer and machinist, who was born in the parish in 1749. Two of his inventions were the water closet and the fountain pen.

Whilst digging foundations for a house, the charred remains of the old beacon were found on Beacon Hill on Silkstone Common. From here, there is a panoramic view over Silkstone and the surrounding countryside.

In the past coal mining has dominated the two villages. In 1838 at Huskar Pit, Silkstone Common, 26 children, aged from seven to 17, were drowned. This tragedy was instrumental in the passing of an Act prohibiting women and children working underground. A monument to the children stands in Silkstone churchyard and in 1988 a sculpture was erected at the entrance of the dayhole where the children were drowned.

On one of the oldest railroads in the country, horse-drawn waggons took coal from the pits at Silkstone Common, down to Silkstone and thence to the canal at Cawthorne. The sleepers can still be seen and the old waggon way linking the two villages is still a popular walk. At the Crystal Palace Exhibition, 1851, a three cwt piece of coal taken from the Silkstone seam at Huskar Pit was on display and caused a great sensation.

In 1910, Pyrah Armitage went down a mine shaft at Silkstone Common and was never seen or heard of again. Older miners say that whenever anything was mislaid they would say 'Pyrah's got it'. Now the pits are closed and only a handful of miners left. Both villages have expanded and because of their proximity to the M1, jobs are varied and diverse.

Village education was provided as long ago as 1754 when Rev John Clarkson left the rent of two portions of land for the instruction of nine poor children. The endowment was increased and a school, house and garden built. The school was rebuilt in 1862 and in 1939 replaced by the council school. The old endowed school is now used by the play group. In 1850, Mrs Clarke, in memory of her mineowner husband, gave money to build the National infants school, now a hairdresser's and a bakery. Silkstone Common had to wait until 1913 for its own school.

Opposite the church is Pack Horse Green, named after the string of packhorses driven by John Harrop. In 1793 he drove the first stage waggon between Manchester, Barnsley and Doncaster. In his later years he kept the Ring o Bells. It was here, in 1843, the first miners' union meeting in Silkstone was held.

Since 1861, Old Silkstone Band has led parades, performed at village events and won competitions. Their carol playing round the villages is part of Christmas tradition.

In the process of being erected are boundary stones depicting scenes of local historical interest. This project won the Ford United Kingdom Conservation Award, putting Silkstone, where it has always been, on the map.

Slaithwaite ✤

Slaithwaite is situated in the once wooded Colne valley, five miles west from Huddersfield. The moor capped hills rise on either side of the valley with streams fed by numerous springs running down cloughs into the river Colne in the bottom of the valley. Running parallel to the river is the Huddersfield Narrow Canal which was constructed in 1795, linking Huddersfield and Manchester. Slaithwaite had its own docks as this was the main means of transport until a trunk road was built in 1820/22 on the south side of the valley.

At the top of the north slopes of the valley are the twin masts of the BBC transmitter at Moorside Edge, which have provided a well known landmark for many years.

Most of the hill tops are covered with peat and moorland vegetation, whilst the lower slopes provide grazing for sheep and cattle. The hillsides are pitted with quarries from which stone was cut to build most of the older houses and mills in the valley and also transported by barge to build cotton mills in Lancashire.

Until the entail was broken in 1962, most of the land in Slaithwaite belonged to the Dartmouth estate and could not be sold. Although the Earls of Dartmouth were absentee landlords they had a paternal concern for the welfare of their tenants. In January 1808 Lord Dartmouth agreed to pay the local apothecary ten guineas a year to vaccinate 80 people against smallpox. Records exist that this was still operating in 1855.

The manor house, near to the church, was built in the mid 16th century. The western end is now occupied as a cottage and the eastern end is used for the estate office. In the garden is a dial stone which is almost identical to a Roman milestone in the British Museum. This dial stone was taken to Douglas, Isle of Man by Harry Wood in 1931 and only came back to Slaithwaite after Harry's death. His brother Haydn Wood was born at the Lewisham Hotel and is well known as the composer of *Roses in Picardy*. He is remembered in the valley every year with the Haydn Wood Musical Festival.

In the precincts of the manor house is a small square stone building over the entrance of which is carved 'Lock up erected by Public Subscription'. It contains four small cells, no windows and a stone bench to sit on.

Near to the manor house is the old free school (now used as a funeral parlour). The free school was maintained by Robert Meeke, a curate of Slaithwaite, and endowed in his will.

To the west of the village is the hamlet of Slaithwaite Hall where the oldest structure in Colne valley can be found – built in the 13th century. Excavation in this cruck-framed building has revealed a central hearth, and it is hoped that restoration will be possible. Also in this area evidence has been found at Booth Banks of a Roman road built in AD 79.

Smuggling was once rife in the valley and this has led to the legend of the 'Moon Rakers'. Contraband goods were sometimes hidden from excise officers in the canal and on one occasion men were caught by revenue officers when pulling goods out of the canal, who claimed they were trying to capture the reflection of the moon. This event is now celebrated by the Community Association at a Moon Raking Festival held annually in February.

Cottage industries were developed in the houses of the inhabitants for carding, spinning, weaving and fulling etc and there are still examples of weavers' cottages in the area. Later small mills were erected on many of the small streams running down the hillsides where water power could be harnessed. With the coming of coal and steam power, these were replaced by larger mills which were developed in the bottom of the valley near to the canal and later the A62 trunk road and railway. These larger mills continued until the 1970s when the upsurge of man made fibres and other economic factors forced them to close down or diversify and change to other products.

Slaithwaite is well served with churches, Anglican, Methodist, Baptist and Catholic, although all nonconformist churches had to be built on the perimeter of the village, as in the 19th century the Dartmouth estate would not allow them to be built on estate lands.

In the early 1900s there was a thriving spa with gardens, band-stand, swimming baths and tennis courts. These have since fallen into disrepair and disappeared but there is now a new swimming bath and leisure centre in the village. There is also a thriving Philharmonic Orchestra which celebrated the centenary of its formation in 1991.

Lower Sprotbrough

Sprotbrough 🌿

Sprotbrough is a village clustered on the hillside overlooking the river Don, and has been described as one of the most charming to be found in England. It existed before the Norman invasion, and was listed in the Domesday Book of 1086 as Sprotesburg. Sprotbrough was an estate village and its size was more or less controlled by the Copley family, who were the most influential landowners, having a close association with the village from 1516 to 1925.

In the 1851 census, there were 74 households. Most of the residents worked on the Copley estate, or were employed in domestic service at Sprotbrough Hall. There were farmers, shepherds, labourers, craftsmen, a gamekeeper, watermen, quarrymen, and a miller at the cornmill. Sprotbrough Hall and its estate were sold in 1925, and the following year the Hall was demolished. Houses were built in its park, the village spread and the population increased. The 300 year old wrought iron gates leading to the Hall gardens now stand near to the church, in the original wall of the estate.

The church, dedicated to St Mary the Virgin, celebrated its 800th anniversary in June 1976. No definite date has ever been confirmed for the beginning of construction, but, as the foundations of one of the pillars have been dated 1176, this is presumed to be the date. The west tower has an unusual sundial on its south face. Among interesting objects within the church is a 'Frith Stool', one of only three remaining in

197

England, made of stone in the style of the 14th century. It was the ultimate point of sanctuary for fugitives taking refuge in the church. Also inside the church are two fine brasses, and a memorial chapel to the Copley family.

The only meeting place for the people, other than the church, was the village inn in Lower Sprotbrough, overlooking the canal and river. This was the Ferry Boat inn, which was rebuilt and renamed the Copley Arms. This closed in the 1860s and became a farmhouse. The village was without an inn until the Ivanhoe was built in 1930. In the 1980s the original stone building of the Copley Arms was bought, modernised and refurbished, and became the Boat inn. The arms of the Copley family can be seen carved into the stonework.

The canal, which runs alongside the river Don, has recently been dredged and deepened, and a new electrified lock has been added. The canal was once widely used for transporting coal by barge. Limestone from the local quarry was also transported, but is now conveyed by road. The toll house by the bridge was used by the toll keeper, but payment of tolls was discontinued in 1888. In the 1970s, the then derelict toll house was bought and today is the home of a well known artist. Beneath the bridge is a wooden staging, this was to allow horses towing barges on the canal to reach the towpath. The iron river bridge replaced the old ferry crossing between Sprotbrough and Warmsworth in 1888. The Yorkshire Wild Life Trust has developed a popular nature reserve, 'Sprotbrough Flash', which is well known for its bird life and aquatic habitat. People today enjoy walks around The Flash, and alongside the river.

Personalities associated with Sprotbrough are Sir Walter Scott, who reputedly lived at Boat Farm in Lower Sprotbrough whilst writing *Ivanhoe*, and Sir Douglas Bader, the famous airman of the Second World War, who lived (with his mother and the rector, who was his stepfather) at the Old Rectory.

In January 1973, the threatened demolition of two old cottages was halted by local WI members, supported by the village constable and the Doncaster Rural Council Planning Department. The whole of Main Street was declared a conservation area, so preserving the 17th century cottages which face the grassed triangle (with its lime trees) where the village cross once stood. Nearby is the Estate House, formerly the residence of the Copley estate manager, its notable features being Gothic-style windows and twisted chimneys. The old village pump, which used to stand near the Estate House, was restored in the late 1980s, and resited by the entrance to the former vicarage in Boat Lane.

Modern Sprotbrough is a thriving and growing community, the residents mainly commuting to industrial and commercial centres such as Doncaster, Rotherham and Sheffield. Both St Mary's church and the Methodist chapel, together with the church hall and the converted stable block nearby, are the centre of many village activities.

Stainton 🌿

Stainton was first recorded in the Domesday Book of 1086, under the name of Stantone with Helgebi. Even before this time, remains of a Roman temple indicated a settlement – indeed, according to some historians, there could well have been an encampment of ancient Britons, the Brigantes, who lived in the ancient Kingdom of Elmet.

Spellings in later documents record the village as Steyntone, Stanton and Stenton. The name is a corruption of 'Stone Town', because, from very early times, limestone has been quarried from the area, a practice which continues today. It is thought to have lain alongside an ancient highway from the East coast to Wales. There was once a family line whose name was Stainton, which died out in Edward I's time. A member of this family, Elizabeth de Stainton, was prioress of Kirklees – she is reputed to have bled Robert Hode (Robin Hood) to his death.

The tiny church, which some say has Saxon origins, certainly boasts a lovely Norman arch. It is dedicated to St Winifrid who was a Celtic princess living in Wales around AD 400–600.

The church is still thriving because many from the village, or those with ties, regularly attend the one Sunday service. The church is much loved and is kept spotless and in good repair. An old tradition of Stainton is that when the bride and groom leave the church after their wedding, the village children tie up the gates to the churchyard and demand payment from the bridegroom before letting the couple out. Another tradition still upheld is the Harvest Festival Feast. After the Thanksgiving service, held on a Friday evening, all the congregation is invited to a Feast and it is still free!

The population has not substantially altered since 1851, when it totalled 262. The village is situated in a pleasant small valley, with a stream running through some gardens, and bordering the main village street. There are still some farms in the village, some interesting old houses and, of course, the church and the pub. The latter building is quite impressive for the size of the village. In 1907 the first shaft of the colliery was sunk between Stainton and Maltby. It was then thought to develop Stainton as a mining village, with a railway link complete with small inn, to accommodate visiting mining officials. The existing pub was enlarged and renovated before a change of policy saved Stainton, and the pithead was located in Maltby, which is now a small town.

There is no shop now. There used to be a post office on the main village street, in Rose Cottage (which still exists). In the late 19th century, there was a postman, Bill Saunderson, who was famed for the fact that, though only possessing one arm, he could ring all three church bells by virtue of tying one bellrope to each foot and pulling the other with his one arm! The village has no natural gas or mains sewerage.

Although a small community, Stainton just qualifies as a parish, with a parish council. It is by dint of great effort, mainly on the part of Miss D'Arcy Vera Hogg OBE, that the village was able to retain part of the school building and convert it to a meeting hall. The little school was closed and sold – to the great regret of everyone – and Miss Hogg, a retired HM Schools Inspector, worked tirelessly to acquire the old pinfold for the community.

There are few 'famous names' connected with Stainton, but Fred Trueman OBE, the former Yorkshire and England fast bowler, was born here, the family moving about three years later.

Although there is still a strong tradition of farming here, not many people work in agriculture now, most villagers commuting to local towns to work. However, some people have set up their own businesses and work from home.

The village suffers greatly from industrial deprivation in the form of the huge, expanding quarry, which gobbles up fields and blasts holes into pasture and woodland every day. The stone that the Saxons and Romans found to be so good for roadbuilding is still being used today for motorways. The parish council have to be constantly vigilant to maintain a remotely liveable environment.

Despite these drawbacks the village remains a delightful community, small enough for people to care about each other, and situated in a picturesque valley, with a long and distinguished history. When the industrial giants have departed – as they will one day – it is hoped that Stainton will remain a small South Yorkshire village.

Stanbury

From a distance Stanbury appears a typical Pennine hilltop collection of stone dwellings. The houses sit comfortably together as if to present a solid whole. They are built along a ridge above two steeply sloping valleys making a further extended area, all of which considers itself as part of Stanbury village.

To the north the boundary is the river Worth fed directly by Ponden reservoir. To the south the Sladen beck runs into the Lower Laithe reservoir, then resumes as a stream until it joins with the Worth. This is the furthest eastern point at Long Bridge. The western extremity is the Pennine way at Top Withens. From the time of man's earliest settlement this site must have presented an ideal refuge. It had valleys where he could catch fish and game, grow corn and gather fuel for his fire. An abundance of building materials made for a safe shelter. Most important, there is a good view of approach in all directions. In pre-Saxon times, Stanbury stood upon a busy route for foot travellers between Yorkshire and Lancashire, the border between the two at that time being just a short distance away. Eventually, it was also to become a well trodden track for pack animals.

Although we see a village built of stone, water could also be said to be the key element. Even though small farmers, hand spinners and weavers built the earliest houses, it was the coming of water power to the mills which changed Stanbury from a hamlet to a true village. Not only more houses, but church, chapel, school, shops and three hostelries formed a populous and industrious place. They would be almost self-sufficient with a hard working farming community, for good fields within stone walls surround the houses in all directions.

In 1656 from nearby Hebden Bridge came a small influx of handloom weavers. These were Quakers who were seeking refuge from persecution. They were readily absorbed into the community. As they eventually died a small area was set aside for their own cemetery, for even in death Quakers were still outcasts to consecrated ground. The last burial was in 1718 and this small area has no grave stones, but is marked with a stone cross within the wall opposite the school. An interesting coincidence occurred concerning the old records of the Quakers. During the passage of time official records of their graves were lost. Following the completion of the Lower Laithe reservoir in 1926 one of the workmen moved to Liverpool. There he bought a secondhand chest of drawers in which he found the lost papers. He was just the man to know how much their recovery would please local interests.

The last surviving hand spinner and weaver was Timmy Feather who lived at Buckley Green. His wheel and loom can be seen in the Cliffe Castle Museum at Keighley. The Industrial Revolution eventually brought five mills to the valleys. Firstly, they were powered by water wheels and eventually all were converted to be steam driven. This resulted in coal pits being dug upon the moors. Much stone was also quarried for buildings as the population boomed. This would also be the time that the main street as we know it came into use, for the old street is the quiet, narrow back lane we can still walk peacefully along today.

The church is set at the centre of the street. Within is the Grimshaw pulpit made from the top tier of a three decker used in the old Haworth church until after the times of Patrick Bronte. Of note too is the wooden screen carved by a local craftsman. Soon followed a large local chapel which has now been transformed into pleasing homes. The original school was a dame school and the building is still called school house, although the present school celebrated its centennial in 1983.

There have been various shops and trades within the village, but the main centre for many years was the Co-operative Society shop. Service by this shop included the only telephone for the village for contact with the doctor, etc. This Co-op had an excellent record for dividends and its friendly, helpful staff brought customers from a very wide area. Many could probably have obtained goods more conveniently nearer home, but then, being careful with pennies was a virtue not a fault.

At the top end of the main street will be seen a row of tall trees. These were planted by the householder many years ago who felt that a neighbour who had windows facing his way was always watching him. Local residents have named them the 'trees of spite'.

The character of Stanbury today has completely changed. It is still a busy place although less people live here and many travel quite far to business and work. The small farmsteads which once supported large families are now often homes with paddocks. Where once there were five farms actually within the village proper, there are now only three farms in the whole area. Even so, the same surnames from the earliest records still echo today. The general appearance however, is very little changed. Although dwellings have been extended and improved, and shops, barns and farm buildings have been converted into homes, only new buildings for agriculture have been built, for this is the green belt.

Tourism brings in many visitors and travellers. Haworth church and the Bronte parsonage are only one mile away. Ponden Hall is where the Bronte sisters frequently visited their friends. They often walked along the Sladen valley over the 'Bronte' bridge, by what was then their favourite waterfall and up and over the moorland tracks. As they walked they no doubt discussed much of the surrounding landscape which features within all their novels. Particularly so in *Wuthering Heights*, which so describes the surroundings. This village atop the hill lights up to the first dawn rays of the sun. In the valleys the brown trout swims in tinkling becks, the heron awaits his food to drift by with the current. In spring the lapwings mew and whistle above the bleating lambs and still the curlew calls. The hay meadows are full of wild flowers and the purple heather is a summer time glory. Autumn browns and golds herald winter and we can hear the red grouse chuckle. As the weather hardens the kestrel wind hovers in the golden sunset mirrored in the small lakes. At dusk the silent barn owl is a white ghostly form against the evening star. In the night sky all the constellations are revealed. Whatever the time of day, or season of the year, the changing scene will delight you.

Stanley 🐚

Stanley is today an urban district two miles from Wakefield and eight miles from Leeds. Pictures of its past would include a tree-lined Aberford Road with two bar houses, surrounded by pits and rhubarb fields; a busy canal and river Calder, part of the important Aire and Calder Navigation, with an aqueduct and river basin for the 'tom puddings' waiting to transport the coal brought by train on the nagger lines from the pits; a main railway line from Leeds to London where trains stopped at the small station to collect the forced rhubarb for selling at Covent Garden, at a time when rail fares were only two shillings and sixpence return to Scarborough.

Stanley received a grant from the Waterloo fund to build a church, which was dedicated to St Peter and opened in 1824. The unusual design of the church included two towers at the west front. On 18th February 1911 a terrible fire swept through the church and only the outer walls were left standing. The church authorities wasted no time and the new building, a fine church, was reopened on 5th July 1912.

Various Roman coins were found near Aberford Road in 1812, leading to the belief that there may be a Roman site in that area. Some of these coins are now in the British Museum. In 1869 arrow heads and other flints, relics of prehistoric times, were discovered, showing that people settled here long before the Romans.

The only way to cross the river Calder was by a ford in Ferry Lane, where an old Roman road from Pontefract led to Lingwell Gate, until the introduction of a ferry boat. The boat and rights were eventually sold to the Aire and Calder Navigation Company. In 1835, while foundations for the aqueduct were being dug for this company, a Bronze Age canoe about 18 ft long was found and it is now in York Museum. The suspended cast iron aqueduct, unique in Europe, was completed in 1839. In 1879 a bridge was built to carry the water pipe to Altofts and a toll of a halfpenny for pedestrians and twopence for a horse or pony was charged. The toll bridge was closed each night at 9 pm.

There were three large houses built in the village, namely Clarke Hall, Stanley Hall and Hatfeild Hall. Clarke Hall was surrounded by a moat and in the entrance hall a door behind the fireplace led to a secret passage to Heath Hall. This Hall was later purchased by the last tenant, Mr H. C. Haldane, who restored it completely. After his death it was sold to the West Riding County Council to be used as a Folk Museum. Stanley Hall was also sold to the West Riding County Council and is now a hostel for the nurses at Pinderfields Hospital. Hatfeild Hall, built entirely of stone, had several owners until 1897, when it was bought by a Wakefield solicitor, Herbert Beaumont. He restored a fine oak dining room and Georgian drawing room. Sadly the Hall is now in a derelict state, but it is to be an hotel and leisure complex and the grounds a golf course.

Time passes quickly and Stanley has improved in the last years. Now a suburb of Wakefield and under the Wakefield Metropolitan District Council, most of the mines have been closed down and the men sent to outlying pits. The station has been dismantled and the lines removed and a housing estate (The Chase) built where the station and its yard used to be. Aberford Road is a busy link for the coast to coast M62 and used by heavy goods vehicles en route for Yorkshire and Lancashire. Most of the trees have over a period been taken down to make way for building homes and the village is a thriving place of houses and bungalows. A hospice was built in 1990 close to Aberford Road, and a library and community centre followed.

A new bridge, replacing the unsafe toll bridge, was opened in 1971. In 1981 a new aqueduct superseded the old one, now a scheduled Ancient Monument. Pleasure boats occupy the basin where the tom puddings were moored and an extended building is now known as the Ferry Boat inn.

There are good schools for the children and various forms of entertainment. A very good bus service supplies the village from Wakefield to Leeds and Castleford. The village also has a very modern health centre. The latest project is the Stanley Marsh, opened by the Mayor of Wakefield. The Wakefield Civic Society and the school children have planted many trees and in time it is hoped to attract large numbers of birds.

Steeton 🦜

Steeton is situated in the Aire valley on the Keighley to Kendal turnpike road, being three miles from Keighley and six miles from Skipton.

The village is ancient, dating back to Saxon times and possibly before. When mentioned in the Domesday survey Steeton had 550 acres under cultivation, suggesting there was a township long before this date. In Saxon times a man called Stephen or Stiveton was the manor lord, hence the name for the village, Stephen's town.

The chief old properties in Steeton include High Hall or Elmsley House, occupied by the Garforths until the 16th century. In the 17th century it was owned by the Currer family from Kildwick, and altered by them in 1674 and 1705.

Low Hall, or Steeton Hall Hotel as it is now, is the original site of the manor in earlier days. It was occupied by William Garforth in 1611. The west wall had three plaques, two dated 1611 and 1662, and one with the coat of arms and crest of the Garforths, being a goat's head – hence the name of the public house. The inn is old, originally built by Anthony Garforth and rebuilt by Thomas Pearson in 1827. The house called 'Ingle Nook', built in 1710 by Edmund Garforth, has a magnificent inglenook fireplace. This was the original Goat's Head inn.

At Mill Lane top are some old cottages. One of 1710 by William Currer is reputed to have been the Old Star inn prior to the present inn of 1836 at the top of Steeton.

St Stephen's parish church was built in 1880, being a fine building with Gothic influences. The ceiling is most handsomely painted. Prior to its building, villagers used a wooden church and before that (1869) they joined Kildwick parish church.

The Wesleyan chapel built in 1888 was unfortunately demolished in 1988 owing to increasing costs. The new chapel has been successfully incorporated into the old chapel school building, which was alongside the site of the old chapel. The Primitive chapel was demolished in the 1970s.

There are two school buildings, one built by public subscription in

1851 and enlarged in 1872. The larger school was built in 1909. In 1852 scholars were charged 2d per week for reading and spelling.

There are two recreation grounds, given by local benefactors. One is adjacent to Chapel Lane, and one lies near Keighley Road. Another ground was given a few years ago to the village and is primarily used by the local football club. The cricket club, formed in 1868, has had three other fields, the first one in the Shroggs grounds. The present field in Summerhill was made after the war in 1947. An excellent bowling green provided by generous benefactors in 1936 is well used.

The oldest business in the village would have been the corn mill. Now demolished, the land and dam have been made into a pleasant village green area. There is no longer a blacksmith, after centuries the forge was closed. The old bobbin mill belonging to the Dixon family flourished for over 180 years, employing 500, but has sadly made way for a housing estate. The mill made textile bobbins worldwide, being the premier mill of its kind. An old spinning mill has also finally closed, belonging firstly to the Cloughs and finally to Courtaulds. This is also to be made into flats and houses.

In Station Road, there is a new factory, Ohmeda, manufacturing medical equipment for theatre use in hospitals. Another factory of size is run by Damart, a well known clothiers.

In 1847 the railway came to Steeton, and the original station is still used as a house. The station itself closed in 1965 but reopened in 1990 and is again well used. A hospital built in Steeton in 1969 has 633 beds and provides work for many in the village. There are also two nursing homes, and a clinic with a team of doctors.

There are still many pleasant walks around the village, despite the continuing encroachment of building.

Stocksmoor

'The Village with Three Corners' – that is how children see Stocksmoor, and it takes only ten minutes to walk round the triangle. Most cars race through on the road leading to Thurstonland or turn in at the pub with its large car park, but the village is not on any main route. Even though it is only a quarter of a mile from the A629 and five miles south of Huddersfield, it is usually quiet.

Fifteen years ago the pub was a dark little house, built in the 18th century with a barn and a small field front and back. A goat grazed in the front, joined by a pony from time to time. Now the barn has become part of the pub and the fields are car parks. The pub is said to have been a meeting place for the cloth makers guild and it is still called the Clothiers. Railway travellers could – and still can – slip through a gap in the wall for a quick one.

The station next to it, on the Huddersfield to Sheffield line, is almost hidden in a deep cutting. A few years ago there were moves to close the line as it carried so few passengers. The trains ran only every two hours with none in the evening. Now, re-routed through Barnsley, they run hourly with many more passengers. The journey, with its viaducts and tunnels and much new single track line, is worth taking for its own sake.

Directly opposite the station is the village hall. It stands as an unrepentantly simple building in pebbledash and wood panels. It was opened in 1973 after much fund-raising among the villagers. Now there are about 130 houses in the village but there were fewer then so the hall was quite an achievement.

From this corner with its old buildings runs Station Road, with 20 year old detached brick-built houses with imported Derbyshire limestone features. Many owners are members of the Stocksmoor Allotment Society and all take a pride in their gardens.

At the crossroads at the end of Station Road are two older buildings and at first glance you may think you can see many more up the hill but these, in reclaimed stone and with 'rural barn' features, were actually built in 1988. The old village well also stands at this corner and supplied the older buildings besides passing horses.

Turning right you pass a real mixture of houses, old and new, with a row of ancient weavers' cottages on your right. The large house on the left was known as The Beeches until Sir John Quarmby moved to it in 1927 when he named it The Manor, and that is how it is still known today.

At the third corner, opposite the post box and telephone, is a house that used to be the village shop. It closed about 15 years ago. The terraced houses on the third side of the triangle are mostly without garages but neighbours will always help anyone who is without a car. Also the train and regular bus service make Huddersfield easily accessible. Like the train journey, the bus journey from Huddersfield, over the tops, affords many spectacular views.

Besides the triangle there are two outlying groups of old houses. One, Sun Side, has only three homes, one of which was newly built in 1988 but blends in easily. The other, Whitestones, is an ancient hamlet dating from the 18th century. Older residents call it 'Whistance' and it is surely worth a visit.

The village is surrounded by hilly working farmland, mainly for dairy and beef cattle. One farm actually in Stocksmoor is in Whitestones and the other straddles a road winding up from the well crossroads. A hundred years ago farming was a main occupation of villagers but now they mostly commute to town jobs.

One village business that has survived is the coal yard, still working from beside the railway station even though coal has long ceased to come by rail. One resident, known to generations of children as Uncle Herbert, worked in the yard. The TV crew from *Last of the Summer Wine* was once filming there and spotted Herbert's ancient, coaldust-filled tweed jacket. They said it was impossible to fake such years of grime and bought it off his back for £5. It was for Compo. Herbert was delighted and told them he had another one at home, just the same!

The film crew had come to Stocksmoor because of the beauty of the surrounding hills. Many people walk here for the same reason. You could join them.

Sykehouse

Sykehouse, the longest village in Yorkshire at seven and three quarter miles, simply means 'house on the stream', and is virtually enclosed by river and canal on all sides. The Went and the Aire & Calder New Junction Canal are part of British Waterways. Coal barges ply the canal with tom puddings (a South Yorkshire expression for coal hopper), 17 containers to each barge, holding Hatfield Main coal bound for Goole, for export in the 'old days' and now to supply the power stations. Three locks served the canal and, until about 1980, the bridge was opened and closed by hand each time a craft passed through. The lock keeper's house was built in 1899, and for 47 years a Mrs Meggitt lived there, until she retired a few years ago, the house then passing out of the family. She worked seven days a week – 5 am to 10 pm in summer, and 6 am to 9 pm in winter – for a wage of £5 per year, payable the week before Christmas.

Early in 1991, the 20th century swing bridge was repainted, necessitating the road being closed. This resulted in a two mile detour to visit friends or neighbours who lived only 600 yards or so away. Only 40 years ago you would have been able to row over in a boat!

The Old George public house was kept by the Bulmer family from 1848 to 1965. Once self-sufficient as shop, slaughterhouse, blacksmith's shop, and even for a while a dame school, it has a grandfather clock which shows XIII for eight o'clock (much loved today on that score by treasure hunt compilers). Opposite the school is the Three Horseshoes inn, which indicated to travellers that there was a smithy close by. This is now the village shop run by one of the blacksmith's daughters, Mrs Bullass. The Sykehouse mill, built in 1868 by Mr G. W. Sail and formerly owned by Mr G. Bullass, is now a private residence. The same Mr Bullass helped to found the Agriculture Show, now in its 108th year and still a crowd puller.

When the new school was built, Annie Bulmer wrote an account of life in 1907, which was placed, together with coins and photographs of the staff and pupils at the school, under the foundation stone. This came to light when the stone had to be moved in 1975/6 to facilitate the addition of a new window. When the stone was relaid, with members of the original photographs present at the ceremony, copies of the findings were replaced, together with present day money, a corn dolly and photographs of children attending the school at that time. Also included was a depiction of life in 1975/6, written by one of the girls, a direct descendant of Annie Bulmer.

The village is not without its characters. How many people do you know who made their own teeth from a silver gilt spoon? Such a man was Mr Earl. Another was Mr Tom Greensitt, who lived to 101 – to reach 90 years or more is not unusual here.

The structure of Sykehouse remains remarkably unchanged today. Farming is still the backbone of the village, with ten to twelve working farms and two good dairy herds. There are approximately 500 inhabitants, some of whom are self-employed and others commute to the nearby towns of Thorne and Doncaster. The village has a good community spirit, with charities receiving considerable amounts of money which are raised annually. One of the happiest events is the New Year's Day Party for the senior citizens, arranged by the local WI. Although Sykehouse has all the modern conveniences of today, the villagers remain thoughtful and caring towards one another and the quality of life is as it was 50 years ago.

The Old George Inn, Sykehouse

Tankersley 🎋

The earliest written record of Tankersley may be found in the Domesday survey of 1086. It describes the extent and nature of the Manor – 'there is a church and a priest there. Wood pasture one mile long and one mile broad. The whole manor one mile and a half long and one mile broad. Value in King Edward's time, 20 shillings, value now, 7 shillings.'

William the Conqueror gave the three manors of Tankersley, Pilley and Wortley to his half-brother, Robert, Count of Montain, whose coat of arms may be seen in the church.

The Saville family, who built Tankersley Hall in the middle of the 16th century, held the manor from the reign of Richard II to James I, and there was a close link between them and the great Earl of Shrewsbury. In 1598, the seventh Earl bought Tankersley Hall for £700, and extensive alterations were made. Thomas Wentworth bought the Hall and park, from the Earl of Strafford in 1631, and Tankersley descended with the rest of the Wentworth estates to the Fitzwilliams, eventually passing to its present owners. The Old Hall, as it is known locally, was the location for the film *Kes* by Barry Hines in recent years.

St Peter's church is mostly 14th century with a 15th century tower. Inside are cannonballs, found after a Civil War battle between Royalist and Parliamentary troops in Tankersley Park, and the area was also the site of battles during the earlier Wars of the Roses. During the 19th century there was an annual custom to 'embrace the church'. Young people from the village would join hands, encircle the church, and sing to the accompaniment of buglers sitting on the church roof. A list of rectors in the church gives a link with the priory at Monk Bretton, showing that one of the rectors was 'from Monk Bretton'.

After the decay of the Hall, changes began to take place, when shallow ironstone and coal mining altered the countryside. The Elsecar and Milton furnaces and the Worsbrough Rockley furnace were probably built about 1832, and the Rockley furnace can still be seen. Today, the mature woods at Hood Hill, Bellground, Westwood and Upper Tankersley conceal most of the scars of mining. Reminders of the 'Bell Pits' can still be seen on Tankersley Golf Course. The Wharncliffe Silkstone Colliery Company began working the coal seams in Tankersley Park in 1854.

The first buildings to house the miners were built in the colliery yard, and many residents can still remember living in them as children. A new infant school was built, and opened on 21st November 1887, as the population increased. The rectory was completely rebuilt around 1870, and the garden laid out with many unusual trees and plants. This rectory was sold in 1982.

The colliery closed in 1971. The cottages and huts in the colliery yard have now gone, and much of the area is covered by the Wentworth industrial park. The slag heap has been contoured and planted with trees. The Tankersley Conservation Group, along with the Tankersley Women's Institute and other community groups, keep the interest and concern for the environment strong, and are trying to improve the surrounding area. There is a development and management of a community wood at Broad Ings Plantation, with walks and a picnic area. A 'park and stride' car park for walkers has been developed near the church – a good centre for sight-seeing.

A pond on the Wentworth industrial estate has been protected from the effects of the motorway, and has been marked as a site of the Great Crested Newt. A fishing pond at the New Biggin plantation has been developed for the disabled to enjoy. Tankersley parish took part, along with neighbouring parishes, to form C.A.R.E. (Community Action in the Rural Environment), a scheme that won the Time/Riber Community Enterprise Award presented by Prince Charles. Various large businesses are situated here, including the Midland Bank Computer Centre.

Tankersley, surrounded by beautiful countryside and with its interesting history, is well worth visiting.

Thorne 🌿

Remains found in the area show that Thorne became a settlement in Anglo-Saxon times, and it probably had a population of 100 by the time of William the Conqueror and the Domesday Book. Today, situated some eleven miles north of Doncaster, it has a population of approximately 17,000, with much of the older part now gone. The area is of an agricultural nature, the features being those initiated by the Dutch engineer, Cornelius Vermuyden, who in the period following 1626 introduced drainage to the surrounding wetlands. Up to that time there were thousands of acres of marshes, until he began to drain Hatfield Chase in Charles Stuart's day, beginning a great task which others finished. Thorne Hall was once the home of Makin Durham, one of the drainage engineers working with Vermuyden.

Thorne Moor, where peat is extracted, is a favourite place for naturalists. A Bronze Age timber trackway was discovered there, and well preserved Scots pine, birch and oak are frequently dug out of the peat. These are part of the pre-Roman forests.

Thorne had its first market charter granted in 1658, and to this day has a busy open-air market on Tuesdays, Fridays and Saturdays. The market place is also the site of the White Hart inn, one of the oldest public houses in Thorne, built in 1737 as a post coach house.

Set back from the market place is the parish church of St Nicholas, which has a medieval font. It is a clerestoried building with Norman features, the south chapel and the top of the tower being chiefly 13th and

15th century. It had a gallery, and used a barrel organ for services in the 19th century.

The bailey castle, dating before 1100, served at one time as a prison, before being demolished in the 17th century. The outline of the moat and the motte are visible today at Peel Hill.

The railway arrived in Thorne in 1856, and it now has two stations. Prior to this most of the transportation was waterborne, the town being adjacent to the river Don and the Sheffield Keadby Canal, constructed in the 1970s. Because of the water, there was the industry of ship and boat building, but sadly today the industry has all but faded away. Employment also came from the town's brewery, owned by the Darley family. This was eventually amalgamated with a larger brewery company, Vaux, but this closed in 1987. The only remaining signs are those found on the public houses, and the gateway with the company logo embellished overhead, which is to be preserved.

1909 saw the sinking of the shaft of Thorne colliery at Moorends, a task which took 17 years to complete. At that time it was said to be one of the four deepest coal mines in England, the shaft being 3,000 ft. Moorends was a separate village, built to house the influx of people who came from various parts of Britain. The colliery is no longer active, though from time to time revival plans have been contemplated.

Waterside, a mixture of 18th century cottages and modern bungalows, is a small settlement on the northern edge of the town. It was a port from the earliest recorded times, being particularly prosperous in the early 18th and 19th centuries, but the river bed is now silted, although the quay still exists. It is here that a gentleman by the name of Thomas Crapper was born, the inventor of the flush toilet.

Thorne is today an attractive small town with a lot to offer, including many groups and societies. A regeneration project has been established to make the most of its heritage, and work is to be initiated to improve facilities around the banks of the canal. In the Memorial Park facing Thorne Hall is a Crimean War memorial pump, very few such pumps existing in England today. The park is a pleasant place to spend time, with formal flower beds to please the eye, and seats set at random where the weary can rest their feet.

Thornhill 🦩

The village of Thornhill lies on a triangular-shaped plateau with the valley of Smithy brook and Howroyd beck on the south side and the Calder valley and the town of Dewsbury to the north and east sides.

Many visitors come to Thornhill to see the parish church of St Michael and All Angels, which has been said to be one of the finest in Yorkshire. Parts of stone crosses and a stone coffin dating back to the times of Alfred the Great are to be found in the church. They show that there must have been a religious establishment of some kind in Thornhill for at least 1,100 years. The stones bear inscriptions in runes, an ancient lettering of straight lines. The fragment of the stone coffin has Roman lettering on it and dates from about AD 870. It was made for a man named Osbert and possibly could have held the body of King Osbert, who was killed by the Danes in AD 867 near York.

The Domesday Book entry shows that the township of Thornhill, which in 1910 became part of the newly-extended County Borough of Dewsbury, was made up of three manors in 1086. As Thornhill grew, the lords of the manors assumed the name 'Thornhill'. In 1317, at the request of Sir John de Thornhill, Edward II granted a charter permitting a weekly market and an annual fair. The stump of the market cross still remains but the weekly market disappeared long ago. In 1988, members of Thornhill WI revived this custom with a 'Medieval Market' being held annually, on the first Saturday in July, at the site of the original market. Local groups and churches are invited to take part.

In 1370 the heir to the Thornhill estates was, for the first time, a woman, Elizabeth de Thornhill. She was married into the Savile family, who to the present day own much of the land in this area.

During the Civil War the Saviles supported the Royalist cause and in 1648 a detachment of Parliamentarians, led by Colonel Fairfax, was sent to take possession of Thornhill Hall. Lady Anne Savile was in Pontefract Castle at the time and the Governor of the Hall, Thomas Paulden, resisted bravely whilst awaiting orders from Pontefract. His forces were outnumbered and he had to surrender, but before he and his men were able to leave, some of their powder caught fire and blew up the Hall. A few ruins of the moated Hall still remain in the Rectory Park, across the road from the parish church. After the Civil War the Saviles made Rufford Abbey their main seat until the present Lord Savile returned to the district and now lives about ten miles away from the family's old home.

The Industrial Revolution brought changes to Thornhill. As the manufacture of cloth was taken from the home into the mills, coal mining became important. Combs Pit, the largest mine in Thornhill at the time, was to be the scene of two pit disasters. The first was in 1893, when an explosion killed 139 men and boys, only seven survived out of the whole shift. Most families lost a relative. Money and expressions of sympathy poured in from all over the country and £36,823 was collected for the dependents. The second was in 1947, when eleven men were killed.

Although the pit ceased working in 1972 there are still many miners in the community, who travel further afield to work. The Yorkshire Mining Museum is only three miles away, at Caphouse Colliery, Wakefield.

From 1767 to 1793 the rector of Thornhill was John Michell MA, FRS. He was an outstanding scientist and whilst living at Thornhill rectory he invented the Torsion Balance, by which the earth's density can

212

be measured, and a telescope which, after his death, was bought by Herschel, the astronomer, who used it in preference to his own.

Several influential families, though not nearly as wealthy as the Saviles, lived in Thornhill. Amongst them were the Elmsalls, who were probably yeoman farmers until well into the 17th century. In 1638 William Elmsall married Ann Johnson in Thornhill parish church. A descendant of theirs became the wife of Claude Bowes-Lyon, 13th Earl of Strathmore, and Queen Elizabeth II is their grand-daughter. Her Majesty the Queen, therefore, is a descendant of two people who lived in Thornhill some 300 years ago.

Thorpe Hesley 🐝

Thorpe Hesley is situated four miles north-west of Rotherham, seven miles north of Sheffield and six miles south-east of Barnsley. It is a very old village, mentioned in the Domesday Book, where it was called Torp. By 1595 the village was known as Hesteley, and in 1611 it was known by its present name.

In an isolated rural setting, the village had a friendly inter-related community. The population in 1871 was 1,949 and in 1951 it was 3,136. By 1961, with new building having taken place, it had risen to 10,102.

Monks from Lincolnshire came in 1160 and they mined and smelted iron-ore on a site near Kirkstead Abbey Grange, which later became a farm. Legend has it that a tunnel led from there to Hesley Hall, half a mile away. The present Hesley Hall dates from 1650 and is a listed building. It once had a moat and a drawbridge, and there is evidence that there was a building on the site in the 12th century. Hesley Hall has been a working farm for many years.

The early life of the village saw many cottage industries in progress – nail making, weaving, clay pipe making and lace making, but the most important occupations were coal mining and farming. The last coal mine closed in 1972, but farming is still in evidence today. Over the years, residents also found employment at Wentworth Woodhouse, the stately home of the former Earls Fitzwilliam, which lies two miles from the village.

Keppel's Column is one of Thorpe Hesley's notable landmarks. Built in 1778, it is a memorial to Admiral Keppel, who was appointed by George III to command the Channel Fleet. The column is 155 ft high, and was once a noted viewpoint and beauty spot and a popular gathering place for families, who celebrated Easter there. Sadly the column is now unsafe and in need of repair, and a housing estate has been built where the celebrations once took place.

Methodism came to Thorpe Hesley in 1742. John Wesley preached on more than one occasion at open air meetings in Thorpe Street. His

Thorpe Street at Thorpe Hesley

brother, Charles, also visited the village and they stayed at Barley Hall, which is now demolished. In 1979 the Wesley Steps were erected near the place where the Wesleys preached. The steps commemorate the bicentenary of Wesley's journey from his home in Epworth in Lincolnshire to Paradise Square in Sheffield, via Thorpe Hesley. Methodism has a thriving society in the village. The parish church of Holy Trinity was built between 1837 and 1839. Prior to that, all Anglicans attended the church at Wentworth.

About 1893 the village was nicknamed 'Mutton Town'. Some say that this was because so many sheep were raised in the neighbourhood, and others say it was because the residents had a name for sheep rustling!

Today Thorpe Hesley is growing rapidly. The nearby M1 motorway enables many residents to commute to other towns. However, there is still a thriving community spirit. The village has a brass band and a choir, based at the junior school. The Ladies' Club, formed after the Second World War, raises money for various charities, and all age groups are catered for with Brownies, Guides, Beavers, Cub Scouts and Scouts, and two senior citizens' centres. There is also a division of the St John Ambulance Brigade, and a WI was formed in 1985.

Older 'Thorpers' are getting to know the 'Comers' because of these various village activities, and all are happy to play their part in the ongoing life of Thorpe Hesley.

214

Thurcroft ✍

The village of Thurcroft lies towards the southernmost boundary of the area today known as South Yorkshire.

The village itself can be called a 20th century village, since it did not exist until the local colliery was sunk about 1909. Prior to this time, there were only three farms in the area – New Orchard Farm (now demolished), Green Arbour Farm, and Sawnmoor Farm, both of which still exist. The oldest building in the present village is the farm cottage at Green Arbour Farm, about 16th century, and this is shortly to undergo some form of renovation. Together with Thurcroft Hall and a few steadfolds, these were the only inhabited places at the end of the last century.

At the time the village was built, it was looked upon as a showplace of industrial housing with regard to its layout and general environment. Many European experts visited the village, and in 1913 one leading German visitor was very impressed with the housing scheme. The village was well laid out, all the houses having private front gardens and rear individual yards, and toilets of their own – unusual innovations for an industrial area!

An hotel was built at the end of 'Pit Lane', and many older residents recall 'No 10 Downing Street', where only 'the great unwashed' entered its portals on their way home from working in the mine, in order to 'slake their thirst'.

The Rothervale Colliery Company was the dominant employer of village labour until the 1960s. In 1933, the Company employed 1,550 men, and by the early 1950s, this number had risen to over 1,700, with the village having a total population of around 5,000. The population today stands around the 8,000 mark, with fewer men working at the pit, and many people commuting to work outside the village.

There are a number of light industries on the new trading estate. One of the most modern brickworks in Europe, as well as a large residential hotel, is within its boundaries. The M18 motorway runs nearby, and caused great interest for the local children some years ago when it was being built.

The local parish church began its life in 1914, and expanded with the building of the present stone church in 1937. It is still in regular use, although the Methodist church, the Spiritualist church and the Salvation Army buildings no longer operate as churches. The Spiritualist church was pulled down some years ago, and the Salvation Army hut became the Headquarters of the local army cadet troop. The former Roman Catholic church is now used by members of the house church group.

A number of characters were well known in the village in the past. There was 'Gas Billy', who used to maintain all the gas lamps, and from whose home could be bought the gas mantles for the lights in the houses.

These had to be handled very carefully for fear of breaking them, either whilst being carried home after purchase or when putting them in place on the gas bracket which hung from the ceiling, or projected from the wall. Many a wail would go up if the mantle was broken before it could give off its welcome light on a dark night. Electricity did not come in for lighting up the colliery houses until about 1946, or later.

Then there was old 'Tom Plummer', whose services were called upon when the miners wanted to hold a meeting, and the following poem was written about him: –

Owd Tom – T'and-bell Ringer

When I wor a nipper and t'village won't as big as it is terday we 'ad some grand owd characters ivverybody knowed.

Do yer remember Tom Plummer – Mester 'and-bell ringer 'issen! I' times o' stress fer t'village and usin' loudest cry 'e'd ring 'is bell in ivvery street so's yer's goa ter se wor it wer all about.

'Oyez! Oyez! Oyez! D'ahn at t'Welfare 'All there'll be a meetin' termorrer neet!'

Yeh, yer cud 'ear 'is call up t'street, dahn t'street, shatterin' t'air – nivver know'd 'im loise 'is voice . . . or 'is bell!

Nifty on 'is pins an' all, bah gum, cud 'e shift! We used ter foller 'im up t'road but we 'ad ter run ter keep up wi' 'im. 'E din't tek part i' t'Star Walk fer nowt tha knows! Reet up ter t'end o' 'is days 'e cud allus shift cud Owd Tom.

Ay, we miss 'im, bur ah'll ber 'e's ringin' 'is bell up yonder – p'raps tellin' t'angels as God wants ter see 'em fer a union meetin'.

Thurcroft, once a close-knit village community, like many others is now becoming a busy little township, but 'home' to its inhabitants.

Thurlstone

Thurlstone, a Pennine village in South Yorkshire, is mentioned in the Domesday Book as Turulfeston. The village straddles a steep sided valley of the upper river Don, and its development was largely due to geographical factors. The nearby moors provided extensive grazing areas for sheep, and the soft lime-free water which penetrated the local millstone grit was ideal for the washing of wool. Early weavers settled in this and neighbouring valleys of the river Don, and it is interesting to find that in 1811 the population of Thurlstone was 1,282, and that of nearby Penistone 516. The Industrial Revolution and the coming of the railway brought further industry to Penistone, whilst Thurlstone has remained a rural village.

216

In Thurlstone cloth was manufactured in the tall, many-windowed weavers' cottages that were built around 'folds' and 'yards' or close to the river. Thurlstone is fortunate to have many fine surviving examples of these early industrial cottage homes, and probably the best examples are at Tenter Hill on the main Manchester road. Here the finished cloth would have been dried and stretched on 'tenters', large wooden frames which were sited outside the dwellings. The manufacture of cloth was also carried out by local smallholders, who combined the trade of farming with that of cloth manufacture. Their wool probably came from the Penistone breed of sheep, which produced a white woollen cloth known, as one might expect, as 'Penistones'. Today agriculture in the form of dairy and sheep farming still plays an important part in the economy of the area.

Thurlstone did not only depend upon the wool trade, there were other cottage industries, including rope and rug making, and wax candle manufacture. The road now known as High Bank was previously named Tallow Crap. Here the Greaves family boiled fat and dipped flax to make candles or tapers, the only form of lighting in those days.

In Victorian times, Plumpton mill had a reputation for producing the finest wool cloth on the Don. The mill owners, T. Tomasson and Son, were noted for their 'Livery Drabs' for coachmen, cloth which never wore out! During the depression years of the 1930s, the mill ceased production of cloth, and J. Durrans purchased the buildings for use in the manufacture of industrial blacking. J. Durrans and Co Ltd occupy Plumpton mill to this day, and in 1988 celebrated 125 years of trading in the Thurlstone area.

Despite the decline of Thurlstone's traditional industry, some inhabitants still work locally. Durrans' blacking business thrives, South Yorkshire Home Improvements occupy the old linseed oil mill, manufacturing replacement windows, and Hoylands produce umbrella frames. Many smaller businesses also trade locally, together with the usual shops – butcher, baker, greengrocer, general store and, of course, the post office.

The village church of St Saviour was erected during the early 1900s at the bequest of two sisters, the Misses Bray, who lived in the village. Other local places of worship include a Baptist chapel, a Kingdom Hall and the Methodist chapel in nearby Millhouse. A Sunday school, erected by subscription in 1751, is now incorporated into Thurlstone school, which provides primary education for the village children. It is the meeting place for the world famous Thurlstone Bell Orchestra, formed in 1855 and still going strong, and other active local organisations. Thurlstone also boasts a very successful brass band, which pre-dates the Bell Orchestra by one year, being established in 1854.

Thurlstone's most famous son was born in 1682, just around the corner from the school in Smithy fold (now Towngate). Nicholas Saunderson was blinded by smallpox at the age of two, but it is believed that he taught himself to read by passing his fingers over the carved script on tombstones in Penistone churchyard, 150 years before Braille. He attended Penistone grammar school, and became Professor of Mathematics at Cambridge University. He died in 1739 at the age of 57, and is commemorated by an inscribed stone from the building where he was born, which is set in a wall at the centre of the village.

Many of the present day occupants of Thurlstone commute daily to their work in Barnsley, Sheffield, Leeds and beyond. However, the village still retains its rural charm and sense of identity.

Thurstonland ⚘

Thurstonland is a small village in the Pennines. It is a thriving mixture of old weavers' cottages, the oldest dating from around 1596, and a few modern houses, and is well known to walkers who can enjoy its marvellous views across the Holme valley.

There are several young people's groups such as Beavers, Cubs, Scouts, Rainbow Brownies and Guides meeting either in the church school or the church room. The endowed village junior school was built about 1875.

The former chapel was well attended in years gone by but is now closed and being converted into a house. St Thomas's church was built in 1870 and is now having better attendances than in the last few years. A Mothers' Union group and a Sunday school meet in the new church room. After much fund-raising this was created at the back of the church where several pews were taken out. The original organ has also been overhauled and was rededicated in January 1991 by the Bishop of Wakefield.

An essentially rural village about six miles from Huddersfield, Thurstonland used to be busy with farming but now only three large farms remain. Former clubs have gone and there is now one pub and a shop-cum-post office. The cricket club has its own field and this and the football field are used by other clubs, too. It is altogether a very pleasant village to live in.

Tickhill ⚘

Tickhill is seven miles from Doncaster and within easy reach of railways and motorways.

St Mary's church, built in the 13th century, with its tower and crocketed spires, is one of the most splendid Perpendicular churches in South Yorkshire. Listening to the church bells daily ringing out one of their seven tunes seems to emphasize the pastoral character and charm of Tickhill, but Saturday's 'Home Sweet Home' must reflect the sentiments of many of its inhabitants. The Flower Festival and accompanying Son et Lumiere bring a riot of colour, fragrance and light to the church's majestic interior.

The parish room was St Leonard's Hospital in 1470. Its striking timber and plaster work was refurbished in 1851. It is one of the most used buildings in Tickhill, being the venue for many local groups.

The 13th century friary, now a private house, belonged to the Augustinian order and closed in 1538, but the ghost of a monk is reputedly seen at intervals, probably watching players on the floodlit tennis court.

When storming the castle in 1644, Oliver Cromwell was supposed to have remarked, 'Tickhill, God help them' before the Royalist stronghold was defeated. The castle still retains its gatehouse, moat and curtain wall. The motte has a wonderful view of Tickhill. It is now owned by the Duchy of Lancaster, and several times a year the grounds of the castle are open to the public for special events. Medieval Tickhill provided London with two of its Lord Mayors.

There were many crafts in the 1851 census. There was the mill, the dam supplying the power, the flour being used in local bakeries and bought by residents. The paper mill supplied the Doncaster and Nottingham *Gazettes*. Hops were grown and beer made for the beer houses in Northgate. The candle factory in Tithes Lane made up to 16 candles to the pound from butcher's fat. Tithes Lane, as it suggests, was where tithes were collected from farmers. The gas works, originally situated by the market cross, was moved to Sunderland Street at Toll Bar (where tolls were collected). There was a lamp lighter with a long pole, for the streets were gas-lit. Miss Miles was a famous milliner, who made wonderful bonnets. Twenty-four farms, many quite small, lay inside Tickhill's boundaries, including a pig farm where pigs roamed the fields in Sunderland Street.

The Earls of Scarbrough have been the largest landowners in the area, with their ancestral home, Sandbeck Park, only a few miles from Tickhill. The estate gave employment to both men and women. There were stables for several horses and pheasants were reared for shooting, the gamekeeper usually dealing with poachers, who apparently came in gangs from surrounding villages. The present Earl is a Deputy Lord Lieutenant of Yorkshire.

On into the 1900s old Tickhillers recall how much walking was done, few had bicycles before 1918 and there was no bus service. Tickhill's railway station was open to passengers, but situated more than a mile from the centre of the village. The station was closed to passengers around 1930. Tourism was unheard of in Tickhill, any visitors from more than a few miles away were regarded with interest, if not suspicion. During the First World War, visitors from Durham were questioned by the police. Suspected as German spies, their accents were not recognised!

The old buttercross, built in 1777, stands at the convergence of two major routes, and was the market place of bygone days. The water pump,

219

with its well by the cross steps, would fill the troughs with water for the animals brought to the fairs and markets, also supplying shops and houses in the area. Later a Victorian case was added to the pump at the base of the cross. Today the troughs are filled with flowers, which together with the hanging baskets decorating the buttercross, make an attractive display. Well kept flower beds in and around the village gained Tickhill a place in the Britain in Bloom Competition – a well-earned accolade for the hard working committee of volunteers. The buttercross is still the centre of the market place, surrounded by a variety of shops where anything can be bought, from this week's groceries to a house and furnishings. Whilst browsing, the aroma of freshly baked bread assails the nostrils and tickles the taste buds.

On Christmas Eve one road is closed to heavy traffic, and villagers gather round the buttercross for community carol singing. Steam rises in the cold crisp air from voices raised in joyful praise, after which many return to excited children. Others go to public houses to replenish hoarse throats and enjoy the company of friends, one popular 'watering-hole' being the Red Lion, an old coaching inn which served the London to Glasgow mail coach.

Tickhill is now a small country town, in a traditionally agricultural area, with a rural atmosphere and a lively community spirit. Although development over the last 20 years has provided homes for commuters working in the neighbouring towns, Tickhill still retains some of its medieval grandeur and charm.

Todwick 🐿

Originally a Roman and then a Saxon settlement, Todwick is situated off the A57 adjacent to junction 31 of the M1 motorway. The name has evolved from the Saxon Tatewic, meaning 'village on the hill', and the Domesday survey of 1086 records 'in Tatewic a church is there and three acres of meadow'.

The early 11th century building forms the nave of the present church, dedicated to St Peter and St Paul. Additions were made during the 14th century, with the Perpendicular tower with its eight crocketed pinnacles built in the late 15th century. From the top of the tower, Lincoln Cathedral can be seen on a clear day. Interesting old memorials include brasses of 1609 and 1664, and enclosed behind the altar rails is the Todwick Byble of 1639. Jacobean high box pews from the reign of James I form the seating within the nave.

The Abbots of Roche were at one time joint lords of the manor, and legend tells of a secret passage from the Abbots' House, now a private residence, to Roche Abbey, a distance of some five miles. Most of the parish fell within an estate owned by the Osborne family, the most famous of whom was Danby, who was active in the Revolution and a signatory to the invitation to William of Orange to assume the throne. His reward was to be made Duke of Leeds, interestingly of Kent not Yorkshire. In 1699 a mansion was built by the family abutting the village border, known as Kiveton Hall. Nothing of this now remains, as it was demolished in 1812. Popular myth for the demolition was that the sixth Duke had 'rendered himself liable by a game of chance' to pay a large sum annually to the Prince of Wales as long as the Hall stood!

In 1840 George Colton Fox purchased the manorial rights and patronage of Todwick church from the Duke of Leeds at public auction. For the next 100 years, life in the village continued under the family's benevolent eye, and the grounds of their family home at Todwick Grange were regularly used for garden parties and fetes. The most recent use of the Grange has been as a children's home run by Sheffield Council.

Myths and legends abound about the Old Manor House, demolished in 1945 and of which only the moat remains, reputed to be 'Torquilstone Castle' of Sir Walter Scott's novel *Ivanhoe*. The site of Robin Hood's Trysting Tree, immortalised within the same novel, is attended every May Day at sunrise by the local Morris men performing in traditional celebration of the coming of Spring. The White Lady, said to be the ghost of Catherine Lox who died in 1787, is reputed to regularly walk the village.

The first village school, now used as the village hall, was incorporated in 1868, and built on land gifted by the Duke of Leeds. In the early 1960s new premises were built on adjacent land and, with 130 pupils, the school continues to thrive and forms a focal point of the village. The local hostelry, the Red Lion, is still affectionately known as 'Mary Ellen's' after a landlady at the turn of the century. Originally a coaching inn, it was rebuilt in 1920 and recently converted into a luxury hotel.

For centuries Todwick was a small remote community with a stable population of 200, and memories are still held of Stacey the Carrier, who would collect local produce with his horse and wagon, twice a week, for sale in Sheffield. Expansion followed the break up and sale of the Duke of Leeds' estate in 1921. However, it was not until the 1960s that significant development took place, with the population now increased to 2,800. This expansion has resulted in the loss of many items of historical interest, such as the toll bar situated at the crossroads at Todwick Bar on the A57.

With little opportunity for employment, Todwick has become a dormitory village, with most residents commuting to Worksop, Rotherham or Sheffield.

Treeton 🦢

The 12th century sandstone church of St Helen with its extended limestone tower stands proudly on the hill, with the homes of some 2,000 villagers scattered about its base.

The church has a peal of six bells, which although in good working order are only rung occasionally in these modern times. However, it was not always so. The ancient practice of ringing number three bell three times a day (6 am, 12 noon and 8 pm) was first recorded in 1777, when the duty of ringing the bell was reimbursed to Mr Richard Peel of Glebe House by allowing him the use of the 'Bell Field'. Though this practice was known to have been suspended during the two World Wars (as bells were to be rung at this time only in the case of invasion), the custom was resumed after the Second World War by the then verger, Mr F. Frost, who was given special permission to 'clock-in' at the colliery a few minutes late – a rare privilege, to enable him to ring the 6 am bell exactly on time. His duties included the winding of the church clock each day, climbing the narrow winding staircase to ensure accuracy. The clock and the bell did much to keep the village people on time, and bus drivers were known to check their timetables by them. Children were told to come home for bed as soon as they heard the 8 pm bell.

Taking a step further back into the church's history, Rev Sherland Adams became involved with the Royalist cause during the Civil War, which he preached from the pulpit. He informed a troop of Royalist horsemen where his neighbour had hidden horses, which they stole, and a barn was burnt down. His parishioners, angry at this latest incident, met on Rotherham Moor and drew up a petition known as 'the Ploughman's Vindication' (original copy now in the British Museum), and as a result Rev Adams spent some time in Sheffield Castle.

Approximately a hundred yards from St Helen's church is the modern Methodist church. The old chapel had to be demolished in 1985 due to subsidence from the colliery, and some of the stone was moved down the road to build a new vestry onto the church. The foundations for this were dug out by miners who were on strike at the time. Digging is all the same whether it be coal or earth! The Baptists held their first meetings in a cowshed rented from a local farmer for one shilling per week, the present building being built in 1884.

The great change came to this farming community in 1875 when the first shaft of Treeton pit was sunk, which dramatically increased the population. Terraced houses were built on each side of the three roads leading from the village and prosperity came to the community, but also tragedy and sadness as men were killed and maimed in accidents. A local farmworker clearly remembers driving the horse-drawn hearse from the pit to Sheffield with its sad load. The pit closed in 1990. A service was held in the parish church for miners and their families, and the Miners'

222

Union banner was fixed onto a wall in the church by wrought iron supports, made by the pit blacksmith. It is good to remember that Treeton is thought to be the first village in England to have electric street lighting. This was generated from the colliery and lit by arc lamps, which had to be maintained thrice weekly. The original generator became a feature in the entrance of St George's Hall, near Sheffield University.

The village has a post office, two general stores, a newsagent and a doctor's surgery. Woodlands Farm, a riding stable, has large stone barns in good order. The three roads leading out of Treeton wind past fields, woods, meadows, streams and a pond, and become Long Lane, Treeton Lane and Wood Lane. With this variety of habitats, and one good sized lake, used by the Water Ski-ing Club, it is not surprising that there is wildlife and plant life in abundance. Though the heavily polluted river Rother winds wearily through our boundary, the adjoining streams provide food for herons and kingfishers. In 1988 a list of 98 flowering plants was recorded in the area of 'Towd Dyke', and interesting marsh plants and wild orchids can be found within the parish boundary.

Education of the children has played an important part in village life. Today's children have an excellent new church aided junior and infants school with an enthusiastic and competent staff. They are more fortunate than the little ones of 1879, where it is recorded in the school log on 13th June that 'Many children have been absent because of their parents' inability to pay school fees'.

An attractive feature of the village is its lovely sandstone walls, best seen on Church Lane and Station Road. The red sandstone was quarried from Bole Hill, and the yellow from the Hilly Fields. Some handsome listed buildings were built from the local stone. The old rectory is one, now re-named The Georgian House. Treeton Grange, once the home of Sir Walter Benton Jones, is now owned by British Steel, and Treeton Hall, formerly occupied by Lady Fothergill Cook, has been demolished to make way for a warden centre and bungalows for the elderly. There is one pub, the Station, which stands squarely beside the railway bridge overlooking the site of the once very busy station, now non-existent.

Upperthong ⚜

Upperthong is a former agricultural and weaving settlement situated in an elevated position in the foothills of the Pennines, 925 ft above sea level and one mile west of Holmfirth.

The hamlet dates back to Saxon times and to the time Danish invaders swept up the Humber and affected many Saxon settlements in the area, either by force or agreement. One of these was Thong, from the Danish 'thing', meaning a place of military gathering. The prefix Upper was not used until much later and the village is still referred to as Thong by many of the older residents.

Thick forestation bordering the village is long gone and new development over the last 20 years has greatly changed the face of the area, but the heart of the village remains with the weathered stone dwellings nestling snugly together along both sides of Towngate, the main street of the village.

This small region covering five and a half acres is now a conservation area and includes the charming village pub, the Royal Oak, the manor house, the various homes that have been converted from farms and barns and the three-storey dwellings with stone mullioned windows and steeply pitched roofs which originally housed the weaving families.

Stone was available in abundance and used for the building of the boundary dry stone walls which also give shelter to the sheep on the moors, as the centuries old solid stone houses of the village give warmth and protection to the villagers from the harsh elements often experienced in this exposed area. The quarrying of stone has played an important part in the economic and social history of the district and has caused the land to be pock-marked with old quarries and spoil heaps, many of which can be seen on the outskirts of the village.

All the requirements for early textiles were to be found here – the sheep in plenty on the surrounding moors, the soft water for washing the wool and the skilled labour. The women and children would sort and wash the wool, then comb and spin it. The weaving was generally done by the men of the family in the upper chambers of the house, working their faithful handlooms unceasingly throughout the day and needing the aid of the dim, yellow glow of tallow candles during the winter.

The Sunday school, built in 1837 from voluntary subscription, was constructed in local stone and opened originally as a school house to teach the scholars in 'reading, writing and accounts'. Nineteen local trustees were appointed, ten of whom were described as clothiers. It remained a day school for 40 years and a Sunday school until 1965. It was recorded as having 201 scholars in 1858. The children were instructed to have clean hands, faces and pinafores. Four consecutive absences led to expulsion. Today the school is known as the village hall and run by a committee who organise many varied events for the enjoyment of the villagers.

The Holme Valley Beagles have been kept at Upperthong since 1928, thereby carrying on a valley tradition of over a thousand years. Hare hunting with a foot pack takes place twice weekly during the season September to March.

Wadsley 🦡

Wadsley lies to the north of Sheffield, on one of seven hills on which the city, like Rome, is built. Sprawling housing estates have replaced the fields and lanes. The church, the mental hospital and some fine old residences – Wadsley Grove, The Hall, Wadsley House and The Manor House to mention a few, are still there, though not all as residences.

A stretch of moorland and pasture, Wadsley Common and Loxley Chase, provide bridle paths for horse riding, scenic walks and sports grounds, including one of Sheffield's most testing golf courses. Loxley Chase is said to be so called because the Earl of Loxley, otherwise known as the legendary Robin Hood, roamed these parts, possibly hunting deer. Wadsley Common is covered with bilberries, which have provided generations with fruit for jam and pie-making, while heathers make a glorious splash of colour. The view over Bradfield Dale and Derwent Moor is breathtaking. The common stands in the path of the prevailing winds; as the old folks said, 'Tha gets t'Blackpool breezes theer, thas nowt twixt t'Common and t'Irish Sea to stop 'em.'

The infamous Frank Fearn was the son of a Bradfield farmer. In 1778, Fearn was apprenticed to a filesmith. In the hope of easy money, he lured a respectable jeweller from Sheffield to bring watches to a watch club at Bradfield. On the road at Loxley Edge, Fearn brutally murdered him. He was arrested the following night, later being condemned and executed. An Act of Parliament of 1752 decreed that the body should be hung in chains on a gibbet; this gruesome spectacle was to deter other wrong-doers. He was gibbeted at Loxley in 1783, but it was not until Christmas 1797 that his body fell from the chains. The gibbet is believed to have been used later as a footbridge across either the river Loxley or Rivelin, afterwards being washed down the river to Sheffield and being used by a builder in the construction of some cottages. One villager claimed that his great grandfather had the doubtful privilege of driving a nail into the gibbet!

Ghosts have been seen on the Common. One in particular was reported by several people. It was a woman, her identity never known, who, dressed in white, glided silently about the old coal pits and ganister workings, waving her arms in despair.

There were several stone quarries and pitshafts on Wadsley Common – Coal Pit Lane having a pitshaft at the roadside. It was poor quality coal, but it warmed the little cottages and cooked food for the villagers, most of whom were very poor.

Ganister beds, used to make bricks for lining furnaces, were found under the coal. In 1856, Sir Henry Bessimer brought ganister into prominence as a material capable of withstanding great heat. With the sinking of ganister pits, many of the Wadsley men found jobs as miners and even to this day Wadsley Common is honeycombed with tunnels.

Another means of livelihood were the little cutlers. There were about a hundred of them in Wadsley. In the 19th century they mainly produced pocket knives, the blades being known as Wadsley flatbacks. Early in the 19th century, the cutlers produced a complete knife themselves, forging, grinding and hafting from material in the rough. Later on the factors provided the necessary blades and springs etc, and they bought back the finished goods. The cutler earned about one pound a week. They worked by candlelight in the winter and saved their candle ends for Christmas. When the last knife was finished before Christmas, the ends were placed in a row in the windows and lit. Each of the three weeks before Christmas were designated calf week, cow week and bull week. If all the work was done the cutlers had 'got the bull down', but if delayed they were 'kicked by the bull'. As the candles glowed in the windows, villagers knew who had 'got the bull down'.

Wadsley church was built in 1834 through the generosity of the Misses Harrison. In 1884 it was partly destroyed by fire, and reopened in 1885. There is a fine old vicarage and school house nearby. The little Wesleyan chapel at the other end of the village was famous for its open air sermons. Every year, about two weeks after Whitsun, was Wadsley feast time. Hundreds of people came to the fair, and also to the chapel sermons. A platform was erected in a field on Fair Sunday, and the Sunday school scholars sang their hearts out.

Where the feast was held and where the children sang, and fished in the village pond, there is now a school, a supermarket and a new chapel. The old school house dates from 1838, and was known as the Wadsley National school. It existed as a school until 1963.

Wadsworth 🐚

Wadsworth Township covers a large area of hillside and moorside on the eastern side of the Pennines above the Calder valley. The villages of Old Town and Pecket Well now contain the greatest concentrations of people but a view from the moors shows farms and houses spread out along the hillside from the old boundary at Foster Clough through Old Town and Pecket Well to the Crimsworth valley. The houses we see today are often built on the site of earlier dwellings, the position having been well chosen for protection from attack by water and man and for adequate provision of fresh spring water.

Wadsworth and Crimsworth are both mentioned in the Domesday Book and Old Town derives its name from 'Old Ton', which dates the site to before the 13th century. In these times, the middle and upper hillside would be the only habitable places, the moorland being too harsh and barren above and the valley heavily wooded and marshy below.

The early timber dwellings have been replaced or simply encased in stone. Frequently a small quarry would be opened near the building site.

The stone is millstone grit, and in its natural colour is a pale golden colour. Natural weathering changes this to pleasing browns and greys while industrial smoke and fumes have produced the black stone buildings typical of the industrial valleys.

One of the oldest buildings is the Old Town Hall dated 1590, which is a handsome stone built dwelling standing behind a fine Tudor archway. The present building stands on a site of an earlier timber house from which it derives its design, although one wing has partially gone now and the other is divided into separate cottages. As one dwelling it must have been exceptional in size and design for the district and gives some indication of the wealth of the clothiers at the end of the 16th century and beginning of the 17th century. At the back of the hall a wing extends to the west. The upper room was originally a ballroom. This room has the longest run of mullioned windows in the county and has been restored by its owners.

The building of two mills in a short space of time caused changes in the village, where the cottage industry of spinning and weaving was the main livelihood and where most people were related. People now had to come to the mill to work and did so from a great distance. Children were brought from a York workhouse and whole new families brought in from other areas. Houses were built to accommodate these people.

Acre Mill was built in 1859 by James Hoyle. The mill was used for spinning and weaving cotton. It was John Hoyle, a son of James Hoyle, who made it prosperous and had greatest success with the manufacture of very strong cloth used to line Dunlop tyres. Special looms were needed and new sheds were built in 1910 and extended in 1920.

In 1939 Cape Asbestos took over Acre Mill and began to manufacture asbestos products. It provided work for people in the village at a time when there was little else, but a number of deaths from Asbestosis caused an investigation into the circumstances under which they worked. The mill was closed down and demolished in 1987. In March 1990, the workers who died were remembered with a poignant ceremony when a commemorative plaque was unveiled and a tree planted at the site.

The other mill, called Mitchell's Mill, was owned by the Cousin Mitchell family and was built in 1857. They held most of the water rights of the hillside above Acre Mill. Rather than pay the Cousin Mitchells for the water that he needed, John Hoyle established new wells and cisterns to supply Acre Mill, two rows of cottages which housed his workers, the Wesleyan chapel, and his own home Summerfield.

Although the Wesleyan chapel, Walker Lane was built by independent men who would take no support from John Hoyle for the building of it, yet it was the chapel he attended and was known to some as Hoyle's Chapel. The carving around each of the six windows was the work of six different stonemasons who gave their services free of charge.

In 1750 a small group of Baptists in Wadsworth gathered around a Baptist minister and a church was built in Wainsgate. The land was given by one supporter and the others must have worked hard and given generously to build a small church. It was rebuilt in 1815, again solely by the efforts of the faithful, but had proved inadequate for the needs of the congregation by 1860 when the present church and schoolroom was built.

The village today has a museum of vintage cars, a cricket club, bowling green and golf course nearby. An annual village fair is organised by the Community Association on the green in late summer, with events such as a tug of war, a local Rose Queen, and a Fell race with competitors coming from all over Yorkshire to take part.

Walton ✺

A visit to Walton is a visit to the home area of Squire Waterton of Walton Hall, a great English eccentric who established the first real nature reserve and bird sanctuary in Britain.

Walton is a village in West Yorkshire about three and a half miles south-east of the city of Wakefield. It has two churches, one Anglican and one Methodist, two schools, one public house, a post office and a few shops. It has an active parish council, which owns the village hall, and the population is approximately 3,000. The village has a long history – it is mentioned in the Domesday Book where it is recorded that 'the king holds land at Waleton'. It became Walton in medieval times.

The history of the village is closely linked with the history of the Waterton family. In 1435 Constance and Richard Waterton had a Hall built for them at Walton, of which the ruined gateway still stands and is the oldest remaining structure in the village. The Waterton family continued to live in Walton for over 400 years, in unbroken succession from father to son from 1435 to 1876, when Edmund Waterton sold the Hall and moved to Leicestershire.

In the 17th century the Waterton family developed coal mines in the village and owned two corn mills powered by water from the sluices in the lake. This lake was an artificial dam covering 30 acres. In 1767 the old Hall was pulled down and a square Georgian mansion was built on an island in the lake, linked to the mainland by an elegant arched iron bridge. This mansion still stands today and is now an hotel.

The most famous member of the Waterton family was Charles Waterton, who was born at Walton Hall in June 1782. He was educated at Stonyhurst College where his interest in natural history was encouraged by his tutors. In 1804 Charles was living in South America and was unable to return home because of the Napoleonic Wars. He went to British Guiana where his family owned sugar plantations, which he helped to manage. Later he decided to explore the tropical forests, travelling with a few Amerindian guides and sharing their food, including monkey, armadillo and toucan. Throughout the journey Waterton went bare foot!

On one of his journeys he captured an alligator over three metres long and rode it to the shore, increasing his reputation for eccentric behaviour. In later years he made more South American journeys of exploration and acquired a vast collection of birds, mammals, reptiles and insects. He developed his own system of taxidermy and preservation which no-one has been able to equal. His natural history collection is on permanent display in the Wakefield City museum.

Perhaps Charles Waterton's greatest achievement was the setting up of a nature reserve at Walton Hall. This was possibly the first in the world and he dedicated the last 40 years of his life to this work. When he died in 1865 aged 82 he was buried in a simple grave among the trees by the lake. He will be remembered through his most famous book *Wanderings in South America*, published in 1825, and through the many books written about his life and his travels.

From Saxon times Walton was a quiet agricultural community and in spite of the opening of the Barnsley Canal in 1799, which went right through the village, it continued to be so. The late 19th century saw the development of coal mining and Walton colliery worked from 1890 to 1979.

In recent years Walton has grown considerably with a great deal of modern housing but, although on the outskirts of Wakefield, it retains its rural village life and character.

Warmsworth ஜ௸

Warmsworth, situated three miles west of Doncaster on the A630 to Sheffield, is an ancient village recorded in the Domesday Book.

The old village has a certain charm about it. The Hall, built by John Battie sometime in the 17th century (possibly 1668), and also lived in by Lady Charlotte Fitzwilliam in 1882, is now part of the splendid and modern Moat House Hotel. Another feature of the village is the Belfry in Glebe Street, which is unique in that it was situated half a mile away from the old church, which is now demolished. It is claimed the Belfry is the oldest building in the parish.

At one time the village was mainly populated by a farming community, but in 1750 John Battie saw the great potential in quarrying the high quality magnesium limestone, and in consequence of this many new and old residents were involved in this work.

The celebrated Quaker George Fox had connections with Warmsworth, having preached at the Quaker meeting house, which is still situated in Quaker Lane. The old church school still exists in the old village, but is now a community centre.

Warmsworth is adequately served with two excellent schools, a very good library, a park, the Cecil Hotel, and a popular playing field, cricket field and sports club. Conisbrough Castle is within easy reach, and there is a first rate bus service to Doncaster, Barnsley, Rotherham and Sheffield. What was once a small village is now a dormitory for Doncaster, Sheffield and Rotherham, and the population has increased to many thousands.

Wath-upon-Dearne 🐝

Wath-upon-Dearne is situated five miles from Rotherham and three miles from Wentworth Woodhouse, the home of the late Earl Fitzwilliam. As its name implies it is on a river, but this is not immediately apparent to visitors.

The church of All Saints is Norman, and some of its windows are over 600 years old. The May Day celebrations include the throwing of bread buns from the top of the church tower, which was originally started by Thomas Tuke, a local benefactor, to feed the poor and needy. Close to the church is a very old gaol, which is now in a state of disrepair. It comprises two windowless stone cells for drunks and troublemakers, and a police constable's room above the cells.

There are a few dairy and arable farms, many old inns and a wide variety of shops. Wednesday is market day, when a few stalls are erected in the local car park. Until recently, Wath was a mining village, with Manvers Main and Wath Main collieries, but this land is now being used to build new factories, shops and leisure facilities. The schools are well situated, with large playing fields for sporting activities, and there are also swimming baths. A small hospital has been built on the edge of the bluebell wood, which was originally for treating fever and TB patients but now cares wonderfully well for geriatrics.

Before soft water was brought to the area, Whitworth's brewery produced very good beer due to the hard borehole water. The old navigation canal, with its famous 'Bay of Biscay', has been drained to make the new bypass road for heavy traffic between Barnsley and Doncaster. Mention must be made of Wath's famous Rockingham Pottery, the kiln of which still stands today.

William Addy, a pioneer of shorthand, was born in the village, and was the author of a shorthand bible published about 1687. Another personality was Henry Partington, who preached in Wath for a total of 64 years during the 19th century.

Today village life is good, with many activities associated with the church, particularly for children. The Rockingham College of Further Education provides varied courses for young and old. Legend says that when Queen Victoria rode through the village, she declared it was 'the queen of villages'.

The Round House, Wentworth

Wentworth

Wentworth is a small village in South Yorkshire four miles from Rotherham. The area is recorded in the Domesday survey as Winteworth and the stately home Wentworth Woodhouse lies in 157 acres of parkland to the east of the village. This is a very large house once owned by the Fitzwilliam family. There is a good view of the Palladian east front from the footpath. The park is a beautiful area in which to walk. There are follies to see, mature trees, a herd of red deer, and four lakes let for fishing purposes. The kitchen gardens are now a thriving garden centre.

The oldest building in Wentworth is the ruined church first recorded in 1235, now administered by the Redundant Churches Fund. The most prominent person buried there was Thomas Wentworth, Earl of Strafford (1593–1641). He was Chief Minister to Charles I, Lord President of the North, Deputy of Ireland and he was beheaded in the Tower of London mainly for his services to his king. His body was secretly removed from the Tower and probably brought to his home in Wentworth. It is fascinating to sit in the church, look at the monuments, and think of Wentworth during the Civil War.

There is an 18th century map by Fairbank showing cottages in the churchyard where there is a well, and it is interesting to note the clock on the tower faces away from the present village. Looking across Main Street from the churchyard you will see a 16th century cruck built cottage, now the house of the woodturner.

231

Another old building is the charity school and almshouses at the Barrow, built by Thomas Watson-Wentworth in 1716. The former school is now a house but the almshouses have been renovated and again fulfil their original purpose. The George and Dragon on Main Street was built in the 17th century and the market was held in their car park. The stocks were on the site of the telephone box and the remains of the buttercross is at the junction of Main Street and Clayfields Lane. The tollbar cottage on Main Street and the windmill on Clayfields Lane are 18th century buildings.

Wentworth was a thriving agricultural village with an army of servants needed for the house, gardens and sporting activities. The road was moved away from Wentworth Woodhouse to its present position in 1743; it is still known locally as the new road and joins Main Street to run through the centre of the village.

The village of today developed mainly in the times of the fifth and sixth Earls. They built the Victorian church in 1877, the school and the Mechanics Institute in 1835. Wentworth with its grey stone buildings is not pretty but it is interesting to look at, especially at the position of the houses and cottages and their roof lines. Many would have been small farms. Paradise Square is a pretty example with the farmhouse at the top, its buildings at the sides now cottages, and the well kept gardens once the farmyard.

Great changes came in 1949 with the accidental death of the eighth Earl. There were death duties to pay and many treasures of Wentworth Woodhouse were sold. The villagers lost their main source of occupation and way of life. A large part of the house became a college of physical education.

The village continued in a quieter manner. The estate was controlled by the agent on behalf of the Fitzwilliam family, who still owned most of the property in the village. Many people worked outside the village in Sheffield, Rotherham or Barnsley.

The tenth Earl died in 1979 leaving no issue and the title became extinct, but before his death he organised the Fitzwilliam Wentworth Amenity Trust to safeguard the future of the village, which is in a conservation area. The rents from the houses, cottages, farms and rural industries maintain the village. He gave land to Rotherham Corporation to build bungalows for the elderly and the Corporation is now responsible for the Mechanics' Institute, which is still the centre of village activities. The Victorian vicarage is now a rest home for the elderly and there are private houses in the vicarage gardens.

Wentworth continues to function as a self-contained community; some people work for the Trust or for the estate, the school continues to thrive, house property is rented from the Trust and much has been renovated. The church is active spiritually and socially. There are two public houses, a cafe, a general store, a butcher's, a post office and a hairdressing shop. It is well served for the population of 250. The Sports and Community

Association is active with social functions for young and old, and there are regular cricket and football matches.

With many tourists visiting the village and the park, Wentworth is a fitting memorial to the Fitzwilliam family who have owned it for so long.

Wetherby 🐑

In 1990 Wetherby celebrated the 750th anniversary of the granting of a market charter by King Henry III, on 15th November 1240, and still continues to hold a weekly market each Thursday.

Local legend suggests that the town derived its name from its even climate – it seems to miss the worst excesses of the weather, but equally the local shepherds used to drive wethers (male sheep, often castrated) past here on their way to market.

Situated at a bend in the river Wharfe, the town has a fine road bridge carrying the old Great North Road, but sadly the last of the coaching inns, the Angel, is now awaiting redevelopment. The weir was restored in 1982 by an enthusiastic band of volunteers who have just completed the project with a picnic area on the banks of the river.

Spiritually the needs of the community are served by four churches. The parish church of St James has been on the site in the middle of the town since 1842. A thriving community supports a silver band, choral society, dramatic society and numerous local organisations. Sports enthusiasts can enjoy National Hunt racing at a picturesque racecourse on the edge of town, go swimming at the indoor pool, play tennis or squash. Cricket and rugby pitches and a new bowling club are to be found in the attractive setting of Grange Park which is also the venue for the annual Wetherby Show, supported by farmers from surrounding areas.

Formerly a junction for trains going to Harrogate, Leeds and York, the railway became a victim of the Beeching cuts and now the derelict permanent way has become a very pleasant walkway and recreational area.

Wetherby has been highly placed in the Britain in Bloom competition, the hanging baskets and window boxes making a very colourful show in the summer. At Christmas the town is equally attractive with every trader sporting a small Christmas tree decked with coloured lights above each shop and silver stars cascading down the larger buildings.

The annual church summer fete is a focus of community activity in June. Church Street is decked with flags and the fete queen makes her procession to be crowned through stalls manned by local organisations, with half the proceeds going to the church. There are various activities for the children and the day concludes with a barbecue.

Recent years have seen great changes in Wetherby, from its humble

233

beginnings as a small market town and coaching stop on the Great North Road to a modern pleasant centre for people who work in the nearby large towns – keeping up to date but retaining its village spirit and many traditions and links with the past.

Wharncliffe Side 🐉

Wharncliffe Side is a small village, six miles north of Sheffield near the edge of the Yorkshire moors, nestling in the valley below Wharncliffe Crags. It is part of the Wharncliffe estate, hence the name, Wharncliffe Side. It is a community of around 2,000 people and growing slowly year by year, as new houses are being built on the south side of the village. Most people commute to the nearby towns of Stocksbridge and Sheffield, but a few still work at the Dixel paper works.

The stone built cottages house most of the workforce for Dixon's paper mill, now renamed Dixel Tissues. The mill was built and managed by Peter Dixon's family, who for many years resided in the nearby mansion, known as Spring Grove. This was the venue for many fetes and carnivals over the years, one very successful pageant being based on the 'Dragon of Wantly'. This dragon was reputed to have come down from the crags and terrorized the local people, until a knight by the name of More, from More Hall situated half a mile north of the village, did battle with the creature and finally killed it. A cave up on the crags is still known as the 'Dragon's Den', and local children peer into its depths with fear and trembling.

In the old village were small file cutters' shops attached to the ends of cottages, where files were made. These were packed into bundles and strapped to the backs of donkeys, and taken to the distant town of Sheffield for their final finish. The old school stands in the centre of the village, a fine building of local stone. It was quarried and erected by voluntary labour but over the years, as one by one the trustees died, became the property of the church and is now used for adult education and youth clubs. There are two public houses and a Methodist chapel in the village, the latter being the centre of social life for many years. The only remaining shop is the post office, nearby supermarkets being responsible for the general dealer closing his doors.

There seem to be a lot of bygone characters, including Old Harry Firth, with his corduroys tied up with a six inch nail, who sat on the wall from morning until night having a word with everyone who passed by. Also old 'Cheesy' Wood, a stern upholder of Methodism, who put fear and trembling into the Sunday school scholars, but nevertheless was a good man. Mr and Mrs 'Chinny' Burley were a pair of 90 year olds. She was all hunched up and used to trot to the pub every day for a pint of beer with her little pink jug.

The milkman delivered twice a day, by horse and cart with two large churns of milk strapped on the back. He would ladle out 'gills' (half pints) of milk, then whistle to the horse who trotted on to the next row of houses.

At Whitsuntide the Sunday school children walk around the village, stopping at various points to sing hymns. Sadly the ranks are depleted, but it is an old custom that has long been part of village life. An old custom at Christmas time is the singing of local carols. These have been handed down through the generations, often by word of mouth only, and are sung in half a dozen or so of the nearby villages. People come into the local pubs from the towns to hear the 'sings', when all the locals gather to keep up the tradition. The chapel choir also visits the outlying farms on Christmas Eve to sing the carols.

Wharncliffe Side, set amid fields and woodlands and only minutes away from the heather moors, is situated on the main Sheffield to Manchester road, with a frequent bus service. The villagers are fortunate to live in such lovely surroundings – the air is clean, and each season the woods and fields are decked out in their various colours, bringing joy to the eye of the beholder.

Whiston

Whiston is a pretty village nestling in a valley three miles from the centre of Rotherham in South Yorkshire. There was a settlement here in the Stone Age, as a fort and flint tools have been found. A Roman road passed through the village, and a large collection of Roman Constantine coins has been found. In AD 937 the battle of Brunanburgh was fought in the area.

The present inhabitants have diverse occupations, the older ones being miners and steelworkers, but with the building of new estates there are also now professional people.

The old village lies snugly in the hollow around the brook, where old men will tell you that trout could be caught by the handful and you were not a true Whistonian until you had fallen in.

The most imposing building is the church situated at the top of a steep hill. It is a combination of medieval, Early English and Victorian Gothic architecture and was founded 800 years ago. It boasts a priest's stone and a knight's stone which indicates that two local people went to the Crusades. The Methodist church in the High Street was built in 1866, although Methodism is known to have been celebrated here since 1771.

There have been several schools in the village, the first when Joseph Hammond left money for the education of children and a board school was established near the church. The church school was built at the bottom of School Hill just below the church but this is now demolished and houses built in the playground. In 1961 a school was built on Saville Road in a modern estate and in 1968/69 a second school at Worry Goose Lane.

At one time Whiston had three farms: Whiston Hall built in 1500 and now an old people's home, Abdy Farm built in 1738, and Manor Farm on Moorhouse Lane, now demolished to make way for houses.

Morthen Hall just outside the village was built prior to 1738 for Rev Obadiah Brown, rector from 1689–1738. Howarth Hall on Whiston Meadows was demolished to make way for the M1 motorway. This was the site upon which Sir Walter Scott placed Rotherwood, home of Cedric the Saxon in *Ivanhoe*. It was said to be haunted by Elaine Howarth, murdered by Sir Hubert Vayne of Tickhill Grange.

The post office, one of only a handful of shops around the brook in the centre of the old village, was originally just around the corner in Turner Lane in 1846. There were many old cottages in the village, mostly now demolished, but Melrose Cottages built in 1842 remain. A corn mill stood on the corner of Mill Hill and High Street and opposite the present Sitwell Arms was a blacking mill producing shoe polish, wrecked by an explosion in 1871.

The main source of water during the 19th and early 20th centuries was the Waterloo Well, known locally as the Spout Well. In 1988 members of Whiston Women's Institute created the first well dressing.

The manorial barn on Chaff Lane, which dates back to 1350, is believed to be the oldest secular building in Yorkshire and the only remaining example of its type in the country. At present it is being restored and when completed will house a wall hanging depicting the village made by the Women's Institute.

Whiston has had its share of characters, such as Nick Nevison, a highwayman who is reputed to have made the ride to York, and not Dick Turpin as popularly believed. Spence Broughton, a well known robber operating from Whiston crossroads, was eventually hanged in Sheffield. Walter 'Tubby' Jarvis was the last man to be placed in the stocks, still to be seen in the churchyard near the lychgate which houses the war memorial. The present oldest inhabitant is Harry Armitage in his nineties who has lived in the village all his life.

In Victorian times skating was possible in winter on the frozen ponds of Whiston Meadows. At the beginning of this century a football match was held on Easter Tuesday between the Millers and the Sweeps, the Sweeps being blacked up. At the end of July, to celebrate the dedication of the church under the patronage of St James, a feast day was held with stalls in the centre of the village. Each year the Sunday school held a tea in the school, afterwards going to the church fields where there were swing boats and other attractions. There were also sports days, galas and May Queens.

Wibsey ✤

Wibetese, the island among marshes where withs and willows grow, was listed in the Domesday Book as one of five berewicks attached to the manor of Bolton. Ancient Britons lit the Beltone fires on top of the highest point, Beldon Hill; local place names such as Carr and Bank indicate there were once Saxon and Scandinavian inhabitants.

By the middle of the 16th century, poor quality surface coal was being extracted and later ironstone mines were being worked. The living was hard and precarious and the village consisted of squat, thick-walled colliers' and mineworkers' cottages, often single storey but sturdily built to withstand the buffeting of the Pennine weather – many had only one room. What farming there was, was poor and run on the open field system. To eke out their living, many cottages had hand looms, with the entire family employed in carding, combing and spinning wool – all under one roof. Later, some houses had 'mule 'oils' built on to accommodate the new spinning mules. The miners were rough, uneducated and their social status was very low.

By the 1800s the land was barren and desolate, crossed with 'iron roads', the railway lines that ran to and from the mines, a drab and dismal place 'full of white heathens'. In 1791 the ironworks were extended and in 1835 the first of several mills was erected and, slowly, life began to improve.

There was no shortage of public houses, where a parched miner could slake his thirst – there were ten such establishments in Wibsey. Traditionally, mines were named after their managers; the Upper George was named after an adjacent mine. One of the oldest surviving buildings, the White Swan, supplied the whole village with water from its well. It accommodated the Magistrates' Court; the lock-ups in the cellars are now used as changing rooms for the local Rugby Union club. When the Wesleyan reformers found themselves temporarily without a place of worship, they gathered in the stable-room of the White Swan. On the slack or moor, geese wandered freely – one renowned old gander reputedly lived to the grand old age of 90. The Gaping Goose on Slack Bottom was probably named in his honour!

Provision was also made for spiritual refreshment. Although several non-conformist chapels and an Anglican church were built, these were entirely products of the 19th century. John Wesley preached in the village, but meetings would most certainly have been held in houses before this. The Wesleyans pioneered social improvements by establishing a Sunday school in a hired room in 1816. Later permission was granted to let the building for a day school. The Methodists required the children to attend Sunday school regularly with hands and faces washed, hair combed and never to use bad words or call ill names. Sometimes the schools were built before the chapels; they were centres for social activities and must have had a most civilizing effect upon the white heathens of Wibsey!

And there was always the Horse Fair to look forward to. Then, the village was invaded by dealers who camped on the hillsides. Before the Reformation, Wibsey was owned by the monks of Kirkstall Abbey, who established the annual fair, arguably the oldest in the country. From 5th October to 25th November the village bustled with excitement as coupers, driving their horses, converged from every corner of the country. Horses lined the street from end to end, striking sparks off the cobbles as they were put through their paces. Gaudy banners waved above their heads, or hot potatoes clamped beneath their tails startled the horses into a brisk high-stepping canter! But perhaps these ploys were only practised at the Ketty Fair on the last day, when old, broken-winded nags were up for sale. Cows were driven in too, and women ran out of their houses for a jug of free milk.

There were stalls on the fairground, and side-shows, wax-works and donkey rides, fat ladies, boxing booths and sword swallowers. The dolly man came with his puppets and travelling players performed heart rending tragedies. One late inhabitant recalled the time when the menagerie was set up alongside her low cottage. 'There were t'lions,' she said, 'gapin' at me through t'bars while I were doffin' missen (getting undressed)'.

The fair still comes to Wibsey, all pop music and space rides now, but the only horses likely to be seen are the odd one or two on the kiddies' roundabout. But, Wibsey Horse Fair lives on in the music of Delius. His sister Clare believed he gained inspiration for *Briggs Fair – An English Rhapsody* whilst staying with her at Folly Hall when she lived in the village.

Wibsey was incorporated into Bradford in 1899. Councillor Enoch Priestley, a local provision merchant, fought against the enclosure of common land and as a result Wibsey Park was established for the residents in perpetuity. He also recognised Wibsey's isolation and campaigned for a road, with electric trams to connect it more directly to the city. Built like a spur, with a gradient of 1 in 14 and over 1,710 lineal yards, it was a mammoth task. Enoch was unofficially canonised by the grateful locals and the road named St Enoch's.

There is little evidence left of Wibsey's mining past, except that now and again a long forgotten shaft is discovered during building work. Recently one was found underneath a huge slab of stone which for over a hundred years had formed the front step of St Paul's first school. Sometimes, too, a piece of the shiny blue-green dross from the iron works is found embedded in an old road.

Wibsey has grown over the years and is overflowing down its hillside. Although its architecture spans almost four centuries there is a definite Victorian West Riding aura about it. Nearby are fields and woods and from St Enoch's Top there is a splendid view of the city.

Wickersley 🐏

For a village of nearly 1,000 years old, there is very little recorded history of Whychersley, as it was then known. It is mentioned in the Domesday Book and the records give the impression it was a very small, poor community.

It is thought that there has been a church in the village since before 1150, but the first known rector, Guydo, was recorded in 1240. The oldest of the three bells has an inscription bearing the name of John Elcock, rector from 1438 to 1491. The present church was rebuilt by the rector of the time, John Foster, who came to the village in 1804. He demolished everything except the tower and built the present nave in 1836. The later rector, Frederick Freeman, a wealthy man, spent a lot of his own money on the church and persuaded his friends to spend some of theirs. In his time in the parish from 1880 to 1908, the east wall was broken by the chancel arch, the chancel and sanctuary added and every window filled with stained glass, which in itself is worth a visit. The stone reredos was brought from Oberammergau, where Rev Freeman and his wife had seen the Passion Play.

The Grange, a two storey Georgian house, was once only one storey with a thatched roof. It is said that the owner left the property to his two sons with instructions never to disturb the fabric of the homestead. With complete disregard of his wishes, they promptly demolished the house and found a fortune in bags of gold hidden in the thatched roof. However, the ghost of Mr Moult was thereafter said to haunt the place, headless and riding a white horse.

The Wickersley Club, next to the Grange, used to be an old coaching inn named 'The Needless Inn'. It was licensed to perform Methodist marriages until John Wesley's followers built a chapel of their own in 1824, followed by another some years later, which were subsequently known as 'top' and 'bottom' chapels.

Moat Farm once belonged to the Abbey of Worksop and was used as a house of rest and convalescence by the monks. The moat is still there, but not the fish!

The Institute was built by an eccentric man, Dr Holt Yates, who hoped to have it consecrated as a church, following a difference of opinion with the rector. The Archbishop of York refused, so the building was subsequently used as a museum, savings bank, library, concert hall for socials, dances etc, and is still in use well over 100 years since it was built.

In the past people of Wickersley worked mainly on the land or in the stone quarries, which were worked from the 17th century until just after the First World War, when the introduction of the corundum wheel under anti-silicosis legislation brought it to an end. During the time of the quarrying industry, grindstones were provided for the Sheffield cutlery trade and were also exported to Scandinavia and Germany. All the older houses and cottages in the village were built of local stone, evidence of a flourishing industry.

From a small, rural village of a few hundred people, the population has increased since the mid 1930s, starting with the Listerdale estates built by the well-loved character Joe Lister, to its present population of several thousands, making it a very busy suburb supporting many shops, schools and three churches. The village has retained its rural links by staging an annual Agricultural Show, which is well attended and stands as one of the social events of village life.

The village has nearly changed out of all recognition, and yet over all the modern buildings and the busy dual carriageway stands St Alban's church with its fine tower – a lasting memorial to the lives and dedication of the villagers of yesteryear.

Wike ∂🍃

Wike is a tiny hamlet of 25 scattered dwellings situated midway between Leeds and Harrogate, with no shops, no street lighting, not even a village inn. In the 1950s one could buy any amount of oxyacetylene welding but not a loaf of bread.

In earlier days to offset lack of shops there was a noble tradesman, Mr Bell, who came from York twice a week, braving all weathers, bringing bread and all kinds of vital groceries. A hardware van and a chemist made unscheduled visits through Forge Lane (then Town Street). Several villagers relied on travelling salesmen chiefly arriving to order, but the Smith family from Spofforth have steadfastly brought fresh fish weekly to Wike for well over 30 years. Similarly the West Riding and now Leeds City Council have sent a mobile library fortnightly. Obviously one needs a car to live in Wike comfortably today, or a pair of good cycling legs. The delivery men diminish as petrol costs increase.

However, free range eggs were always available over 30 years ago, from School Lane Farm (mixed farming) and from a retired farmer's wife at Throstle Nest. Milk was delivered daily by the farmer's daughter at Manor Farm, which was also a stud farm.

Water on tap did not reach Wike until the 1940s. Prisoners of war helped residents to dig the necessary trenches and effect the alteration. Until then pumps were in constant use, with water also supplied from Burble Well at the south of Wike – still flowing strongly, and Gin Well at the north. Here there is a recent sign to preserve the name for posterity but the spring has been directed through pipes and is no longer visible. An elderly resident well remembered fetching precious water quite a distance to her cottage. She still washed clothes with the aid of a peggy tub and posser and turned them through an iron mangle, with wooden rollers, until her death in 1968.

Down School Lane is a unique church built in 1726, through the generosity of Lady Betty Hastings. She lived at Ledston Hall, near Leeds, and was renowned for charitable works. Originally built for religious and scholastic purposes, it provided schooling for local children. In a row of stone cupboards built inside the north wall the children kept their books. On Fridays children put their desks in the out-house and turned their benches around to form pews for Sunday church. On Mondays lessons could not begin until the system was reversed. At this time there was a useful church choir. Harvest Sunday is beautiful here, with flower baskets hanging from brackets, window sills lined with rosy apples, scrubbed potatoes and giant onions, evergreens everywhere and home baked bread on the altar. Reward for attendance – apple pies and wine for the congregation! The church is the only building where villagers can gather; its loss would be disastrous and end the memorable village parties which do much towards preserving the fabric of happy village life.

Life is already changing. Horse shoes are no longer made and the wheelwright's forge was sold at auction. One transformed cottage, Prospect View, still has a bee bole built into the garden wall, but the owner does not keep bees, although a thriving apiary existed next door for over 30 years. Further down Forge Lane is Elm Tree Cottage where the interest is in breeding race horses. Goats are also tended. School Lane Farm chiefly produces milk. Low Green Farm is mainly arable and sheep farming. At The Beeches, a comparatively new residence looking down Forge Lane, the owner has fields given over to cattle and sheep. Manor Farm is now a private residence.

Forge Lane was originally Town Street, meaning the way to the town, and was changed to preserve for posterity the existence of the forge. At that time its closure could not be foreseen, but Town Street did not in any case conjure up the beauty of Wike; its hawthorn hedges, holly trees, willows or hazels, or its roadside verges overrun with creamy flowers of beaked parsley, bluebells in the woods, marsh marigolds by the marsh and swallows on the wing, swooping and diving on their many forays to secure their mealtime snacks.

Wilshaw

Once upon a time a farmer named Hirst lived on the bare eastern side of the Pennines, some miles from Huddersfield. He married well; she brought him a tidy little dowry and they were blessed with a large family. A family of 14 children, however, can be a mixed blessing if you are only a small farmer, so two of the sons decided to try the woollen trade.

They farmed out the wool to local spinners, collected the yarn for the cottage hand-loom weavers and toted the bales of cloth to the market. (Until a magnificent Cloth Hall was built in Huddersfield, the cloth was sold from the flat top of a churchyard wall.) Joseph and his brother worked hard; Joseph also had a good head on his shoulders and this was noticed by his mother's brother, who gave him a lot of land close to the old homestead. He built himself a house, Wilshaw Villa, and a mill. A mill needs workers and workers need homes. So Joseph built houses. Families tend to have children, so a school was built. What else? There was a good water supply tapped from the moor on the west. However, there was one thing lacking, so in 1863 Joseph built a church, St Mary's, a memorial to Mary Hirst.

All this was in the middle of the 19th century when nobody had heard of planning permission, so the mill and the chimney appeared in the heart of the moorland. The work prospered and, like his father, Joseph Hirst married well. But they only had one child who died young. Towards the end of the century Joseph died and the business did not last much longer. The village, however, was almost self-sufficient: houses, school, church, almshouses, and two farms – Wilshaw.

Between the wars the village had a thriving tennis club, a football team for a short time, an annual garden party in the vicarage garden and concerts and socials in the winter. A working men's club had its premises in the ground floor of the old mill; a billiard room and two reading rooms. There was a village library and to meet all other needs an enterprising woman opened a shop in her cottage. The moor on the west came to the edge of the village, smelling in autumn of heather honey, offering blissful hours of bilberrying.

Up to the beginning of the Second World War this was a fairly satisfied inward-looking community, but the war changed the whole concept of village life. The amenities disappeared because the young people were not there any more; the farms were sold; the houses were sold one by one and strangers came who worked away and travelled by car. Some were attracted by the golf course on the western side of Wilshaw and the popular golf house at Thick Hollins. Incidentally, it was John de Thick Holyns who was empowered by a 14th century document to cut wood in Willow Shae or Shaw, now Wilshaw.

In the valley beyond the golf course is the reservoir, made to supply water to Brook's cotton mill at Meltham Mills. The mill later became the foundation of the David Brown Tractor Works. The tree-lined reservoir, the wooded hillside rising behind it and the extensive views over the hills to the north and west are much admired by visitors. Castle Hill, Huddersfield's favourite landmark, is prominent on the skyline to the north-east.

Public footpaths through the woods and fields are appreciated by many visitors and because it is surrounded by green belt, Wilshaw is still a pleasant little dormitory village. The mill has gone, the chimney has gone. The school is now the village hall. The church and almshouses centre a scattering of some 50 houses, a dozen of which are new. We are blown by high winds and there is plenty of spade work when it snows. In the daytime there is the cawing of birds from the rookery and at night the occasional bark of a fox.

Woodsetts 🐑

The village of Woodsetts lies 16 miles east of Sheffield, and two miles from the border of North Nottinghamshire. The four main approach roads to the village pass through pleasant farmland, hamlets and the broad expanse of common land leading from the famous Lindrick golf course, scene of the Ryder Cup tournament in 1957. The first recorded mention of Woodsetts, spelled Wodocestes, was in 1378, and suggests a settlement or farmsteads close to a wood.

Mains water was brought to the village in 1936. Prior to this, water for everyday use was drawn from the village trough, the latter sporting long queues on a Sunday evening in readiness for Monday wash-day. Electricity was installed in the village following the Second World War, to replace the use of oil lamps. The first doctor's surgery was opened in 1988 and, in addition to the three shops within the village, weekly calls are made by a butcher, fishman, library and greengrocer. There is an hourly bus service to the towns of Worksop and Sheffield.

One of the oldest cottages still occupied in the village is over 300 years old and the post office, in spite of being modernised, still retains some of its charm of a century ago. When there are more than two customers at any one time, it is 'full up'.

It is a delight to walk round Woodsetts on a summer evening, and see the colourful displays of flowers in carefully tended gardens and well kept lawns. It is around the crossroads that the original character of much of the village can be seen. On one corner is the parish church of St George, built in 1841, and records show that as early as 1378 worship was held in this particular area. On the opposite corner is the local hostelry, known as the Butcher's Arms, recently modernised and bearing little resemblance to its original 'cottage' state.

For a variety of reasons many of the former customs of the village have ceased, partly due to many of the present inhabitants travelling back to the cities or towns for entertainment. The annual garden parties for the local church and chapel are still held, as is the processional walk to neighbouring villages on Rogation Sunday. A wide variety of organisations within the village are very well supported.

In spite of development, Woodsetts has a strong tendency to look backward, particularly by its older inhabitants, or 'original Woodsetters' as they are known. They love nothing more than relating tales of the many colourful characters the village has known. The local chimney sweep had an amazing ability to cycle carrying his brushes on his back, as he went around the area sweeping the chimneys for two shillings. His garden was allegedly the best in the village due to the 'soot spreading' it received. The village grave digger was a very popular person, who seemed to know the history of everyone and everything in the village. He could be seen propping up the corner of the bar at the local pub in between his duties as church bell ringer, clock winder and 'caller-up', for those needing to get up early for work. One villager recalls with great affection that doors could be left open whilst visiting Worksop, there being no need to lock anything up – not so these days!

The whole function of the village has changed over the past 30 years. It is no longer an isolated family community, depending mainly on agriculture for its livelihood, but a dormitory for a commuting population. However, Woodsetts has not lost its identity completely, and remains alive in so many ways.

Worrall 🌿

A traditional Christmas Sing is held every year at the Blue Ball pub, from 12.00 until 2.00 pm every Sunday from Armistice Day until Christmas, including Christmas Eve, Christmas Day and Boxing Day. The sing is increasing in popularity, and folk singers are even known to travel from the south coast. The carols sung in this area go back to the rise of the non-conformist movement, when chapels were set up. Most of the tunes are local to this area, although some are sung in different parts of the country, one even being an Easter hymn *How Beautiful Upon the Mountains*. Many of the carols were written by locals from Bradfield, Malin Bridge, Stannington, Worrall, etc. *While Shepherds watched their flocks by night* has at least twelve different tunes, and it is sung in the Blue Ball to the tunes of 'Liverpool', 'Lloyd', 'Pentonville', 'Sweet Chiming Bells' and 'Old Foster'. *Mistletoe Bough* and *Christmas Tree* are sung as solos. Years ago women were not expected to take part, but if they did they were labelled 'pudding burners' – a woman's place was supposed to be at home cooking 'Yorkshire Pudding'!

The stone-built Worrall Hall has been listed by the Secretary of the Environment as being of special architectural and historical importance. The large circular plaque over the main doorway bears the coat of arms of the original owner and the date when the Hall was built – 1720.

Low Ash Farm, a boarding school for gentlemen, was established in 1850 by a Mr. Linley. It ceased to exist when he died. The original two buildings, joined by an added cottage, is now a riding school.

Built in 1826 of local stone, Worrall Independent Chapel is a Georgian building. On the ground floor is a school room, now used by the local community groups. The chapel is on the first floor, access being from outside or inside steps.

Standing on a gentle wooded slope overlooking Coumes Vale is a long, low, whitewashed cottage, known as the Old School House, Onesacre. Now a private residence, it has a stone slate roof, and long and short quoins where the south and east walls join. The earliest parts of the house date back to 1100, and a cottage on the site is mentioned in the Domesday Book. The original 'one-up and one-down' structure had a ladder for access to the upper room, and the original ceiling beams remain in this part of the house. At a later date two additional rooms and a school room were added. High on the south-east wall is a space where the original bell, used for the school, was hung. At some time the bell space was closed, but it has since been restored and a bell hangs there once again.

The convent between Worrall and Bradfield, built in 1871 as an industrial school for girls, was later a boys' reformatory. The Duke of Norfolk gave the buildings and eighteen acres of land in 1910 to the Carmelite Order (which is an enclosed Order). When it opened on the 16th July, 1911, there were a Mother Prioress and 15 Sisters. In 1958, however, it became a Monastery. The present Mother Prioress was 22 years of age when she entered the convent, and has been there for nearly 40 years, never setting foot outside the grounds.

The O'Neill family, industrialists from Sheffield, are the major benefactors, the chapel being built by them, together with the high enclosing wall around the grounds. In these grounds are the graves of the O'Neill family and the nuns. Alderman Dan O'Neill JP was Lord Mayor of Sheffield in May, 1969, and died the following year. He had been a Magistrate since 1942, and was the first Roman Catholic Lord Mayor since the Duke of Norfolk in 1897. The chapel is open to the public on Sundays. The nuns always stay out of sight, speaking through a grill to outsiders, where they cannot be seen. They have a small shop, selling items which have been made or grown by them, eg beads, cards, cuttings.

The Worrall Male Voice Choir was formed in 1971, and originally had twelve members. Over the years this has increased to 60, and, during that time, they have won many major competitions. In 1987, they were the winners of the Cornish Open Championship, which was the first time the Trophy had left Cornwall. They contribute several thousands of pounds to numerous charities, including the World Student Games, and have recently recorded music for this event.

Worrall is an agricultural area, with two working farms, although the majority of the residents commute to Sheffield, Barnsley and the surrounding area.

Worsbrough

Worsbrough village has changed little over the years, and stands at the head of the parkland which rises from the A61 road to Barnsley.

'Surely this must be the garden of England', exclaimed Princess Victoria, when changing horses at one of the old coaching inns overlooking the Worsbrough Valley in the year 1835. Today the scene is still breathtaking, with its beautiful reservoir, and land studded with well-kept farms. This area is known as Worsbrough Country Park, and the recently restored Saxon water mill is open to the public, where flour is still ground by water power in the traditional way, using millstones. The mill attracts many visitors, who find it fascinating to see such skills as wood turning, sheep shearing, weaving, pottery, straw-work and spinning.

Central to the village is the 13th century church of St Mary's. It is built of crumbling old sandstone, and parts of the chancel date back to Norman times. It was originally a 'Chapel of Ease' to Darfield Church. The east window is 14th century, and the tower is over 400 years old. The font is 1662. There is a splendid oak monument, looking very like a double-decker bed, the base of which is enriched with heraldry. A knight lies on the upper ledge, and below a skeleton, both carved in wood and painted. Roger Rockley (1534) is the knight, in armour, with his feet on a cushion, and his hands in prayer. In 1977, Medieval Mystery Plays were performed in the churchyard, and, as they proved very successful, have been repeated every three years or so.

Worsbrough Hall is an example of Elizabethan style of architecture with its centre and two wings. It once housed a valuable collection of paintings and rare books. Unfortunately, it is now only a shadow of its former glory, and needs much renovation.

The canal, built in the valley during the Industrial Revolution, is now a recreation area, but along its banks used to stand an iron and brass foundry, a glass and chemical works, and also a colliery, the canal being the main source of transportation for all these industries. Many of the local inn-keepers had several trades. For example, the landlord of the old Red Lion inn produced hand-made brass buttons, which were sold in Barnsley market.

Rockley Old Hall, on the outskirts of the village, is basically Elizabethan, but built at different times. Until quite recently it was a farm, but now it has been modernised and turned into private dwellings.

At the edge of the Country Park is a house that means much to the people of Worsbrough. Called 'Houndhill', it is the home of Mr and Mrs A. O. Elmhirst. It is built on a medieval site, and the earliest part of the timber-framed east wing dates back to 1566. On the south gable are the initials 'R.E.', which stands for Roger Elmhirst. During the Civil War, the house was fortified, but, nevertheless, it was robbed of its books and papers. However, some of these items have been returned to the family following a petition to the Houses of Parliament. The Elmhirsts have always been mentioned in the history of this corner of South Yorkshire, right back to 1300. In the church is a plaque in memory of Leonard and Dorothy Elmhirst, the husband and wife who founded the famous Dartington Educational Establishment, and the Dartington Estates, which include the Glass Factory. They are a family who have always stood up for their rights, and the rights of their neighbours, and regarded themselves as caretakers of the land.

Wortley 🐚

Wortley lies ten miles north-west of Sheffield, bordering the southern Pennines. In this area of rolling hills, criss-crossed by drystone walls, the land has been farmed for centuries. Throughout recorded history, until 1929, Wortley men also forged iron.

The name is Anglo-Saxon – 'a clearing for growing vegetables'. There is evidence of an early British settlement and of Roman occupation. In the Domesday survey of 1086 Wortley is recorded as 'waste' – ravaged by the Normans, when 'Wharncliffe dead and Wortley dead were left to rot for many a day'.

This is a compact village, where old and new blend happily. The heart of Wortley is the Square. Sit beneath the old chestnut tree and all is to hand – the church, the post office-cum-village shop, the bistro, the Countess Tearooms and the village school. Around the corner are the Wortley Arms and the old reading room (now the club). Wortley was largely rebuilt around 1830/50 by the first Lord Wharncliffe so there are some attractive houses of this period. In the surrounding area there are many very interesting houses and farms.

The Wortley family (Earls of Wharncliffe) have been here since the 12th century but on the death of the fourth Earl the title was inherited through the male line by an American cousin, who lives in Maine.

Lady Mary Wortley Montagu, wife of Sir Edward, was a renowned 18th century beauty, wit and letter-writer. She accompanied her husband to Constantinople on his appointment as Ambassador and there witnessed a Turkish method of inoculation against the dreaded smallpox. She determined to introduce her discovery into England and, in spite of much opposition, succeeded. A group of cottages in the Wortley woods is still known as The Chemistry because of an association with Lady Mary and work on smallpox inoculation.

The family home of the Wortleys was, until about 1950, Wortley Hall. This was rebuilt in the 18th century on the site of a 16th century building. Today the Hall is used as a holiday home and conference centre.

Adjoining Wortley is an extensive area of ancient woodland from which the Earls of Wharncliffe take their name. Wharncliffe, once a King's hunting ground, rises to 1,000 ft and is crowned by a millstone grit escarpment known as Wharncliffe Crags.

In 1639 John Taylor recorded how Sir Francis Wortley entertained him to dinner in a cave with 'a good deer pie, cold roast mutton and an excellent horn of Martinmas beef' not to mention three barrels of liquor! The splendid view from Wharncliffe Crags across the deep river valley to the Yorkshire/Derbyshire moors is largely unchanged apart from the Ewden reservoirs and the now defunct railway line.

The Wortley forges were situated by the upper river Don. The Romans tramped down Finkle Street but the iron making was probably begun by Cistercian monks. During the Civil War Sir Francis Wortley mustered 900 men for Charles I. Returning triumphant from the battle of Tankersley they later had to defend Wortley Hall against the Roundheads, no doubt ably assisted by the locally produced cannon balls! Wortley forges became noted for the high quality of their railway-axles. There were two forges – the Top Forge and the Low. Little remains of the Low Forge apart from cottages, but the Top Forge has been lovingly restored and is in the care of the Sheffield Trades Historical Society. There are frequent open days and many enthusiasts visit the 17th century ironworks by the river in the woods.

The church is dedicated to St Leonard. There was probably a chapel of ease here in the 13th century. The present church was built about 1753 by Edward Wortley Montagu. This square-towered church with its

The Square, Wortley

round-faced clock is a well-known landmark. A peal of eight bells was given in memory of the Marquis of Drogheda by his widow '. . . for the continual joy and comfort of the people of Wortley.' The church contains three hatchments and several interesting memorials including a seated figure by John Flaxman RA, and possesses some fine plate. The modern doors were made by Thompson of Kilburn with mouse carvings to prove it! There are two lychgates, the later one being a memorial to the village dead of the two World Wars.

Wortley has a thriving golf club, cricket club and the usual village activities. On church festivals and gala days St George's flag flies from the tower.

Together with the attractive adjoining hamlets of Hermit Hill, Bromley and Howbrook, Wortley remains a true country parish.

Wrenthorpe 🐦

The centre of Wrenthorpe, about half a mile from the old A650 Bradford/Wakefield road, is formed by the confluence of two streams and five roads. The bridge was built by Alverthorpe's Surveyor of Highways in 1825. The name of the village at that time was Potovens, as between 1450 and 1750 there were many sites, particularly near the ford, where one of the earliest potteries in the north of England became established.

A variety of pot sherds, sagger and small pipes are often revealed during excavations. Potovens was the centre of the township and Bunkers Hill, now reduced to a footpath in part, was in 1805, Potoven's Town Street.

In those days it was virtually surrounded by market gardening areas and smallholdings set out under the Wakefield Enclosure Act, but later became a market gardening area producing principally forced rhubarb in long low sheds, fired with cheap gas coke, for distant markets, or fruit and vegetables for local consumption.

A great change has taken place since 1945 and Wrenthorpe is now virtually a town, with over 2,000 dwellings.

Rope and twine was manufactured here by Calverts and Wilds until shortly after the Second World War but the old woollen mill, once established near the streams, did not survive after 1923. Railway shunting and marshalling yards with more than 20 sets of buffers, daily provided for the assembly of many goods trains carrying coal from nearby collieries, now closed, and Wrenthorpe Junction. Electrification schemes have ensured that Inter-city trains pass through the village almost every hour.

With the demise of Stanley UDC in 1974, unused capital funds were shared, from which Wrenthorpe received a handsome park, tennis courts, bowling green and two additional welfare halls and rooms.

There are two primary and junior schools. Also in the village is the famous Silcoates public school, which in recent years has extended its facilities to include a swimming pool and a nine hole golf course. One of the larger houses, the Haugh, is now Sunny Hill House pre-prep school, working in association with Silcoates school.

Some years ago, Wrenthorpe Mission gained notoriety when one resident, who had received a spinal injury during a pit accident, was, after much prayer, visited by two pastors who anointed him with sewing machine oil, whereupon he was able to walk from his long basket chair; a miracle which induced locals to leave their pubs and join the queue of observers which ended at 2 am.

Today, Wrenthorpe is a thriving community of overspill housing for Wakefield and Leeds. There is a Community Association and an Environment Society. The latter in recent years has campaigned to rid the village of unpleasant stench from a nearby animal by-products factory, now in liquidation and hopefully in future more effectively controlled.

Nearby Lindle Hill, rising 325 ft above sea level, is a vantage point with excellent views of the Pennine foothills and Selby cooling towers. The hill contains a quarry which was formerly used for obtaining stone to repair roads, but since the construction of the M1, within a mile, it has been delightfully wooded in part, enhancing its use for picnics and gathering of blackberries.

The Stanley Main seam of coal is near the surface in Wrenthorpe and the deeper seams, Gawthorpe, Warren House, Haigh Moor, Flockton and Silkstone were extensively mined in former days.

Roads through the village, which once were graced by an occasional pony and trap or horses with carts, now throng with cars, lorries and buses, but local pony trekkers and the West Yorks mounted police serve to preserve the rural memory and supplement the village scene retained by open spaces such as the park and Silcoates playing fields.

St Anne's church carries the memorial to 47 war dead in the First World War and 25 in the Second World War. It also records the deliverance of the area when on the night of 14th March 1941 large enemy bombs found a soft landing in cultivated fields, causing only broken windows in schools and churches. The foundation stone at the church carries the long inscription 'Let no man despise our poverty. For we have done what we could, but rather let him amend our work and always pray for us.'

This reflects that the church, built in 1873, did not have the benefit of the million pound Waterloo fund as did Alverthorpe St Paul's, St John's and Stanley St Peter's, so a more austere sanctuary resulted. It does however serve to indicate that in former times, Potovens had a struggle to survive. Wrenthorpe now enjoys more affluent experiences and much free travel for the older folk, but is still prepared to achieve its aims by its own endeavours.

Harden Village

Index